EX LIBRIS

Pace
University
New York · Westchester

PACE PLAZA
NEW YORK

D0204018

Language and Desire
in Seneca's *Phaedra*

Language and Desire in Seneca's *Phaedra*

Charles Segal

PRINCETON UNIVERSITY PRESS

PRINCETON, NEW JERSEY

Copyright © 1986 by Princeton University Press

Published by Princeton University Press, 41 William Street, Princeton, New Jersey 08540
In the United Kingdom: Princeton University Press, Guildford, Surrey

All Rights Reserved

Library of Congress Cataloging in Publication Data will be found on the last printed page of this book

ISBN 0-691-05472-X

Publication of this book has been aided by a grant from the Whitney Darrow Fund of Princeton University Press

This book has been composed in Linotron Galliard type

Clothbound editions of Princeton University Press books are printed on acid-free paper, and binding materials are chosen for strength and durability

Printed in the United States of America by Princeton University Press, Princeton, New Jersey

PA
6664
.P53
S44
1986

To the Memory of Alison Goddard Elliott
(September 7, 1937 – September 18, 1984)

Near the snow, near the sun, in the highest fields,
See how these names are fêted by the waving grass
And by the streamers of white cloud
And whispers of wind in the listening sky.
The names of those who in their lives fought for life,
Who wore at their hearts the fire's centre.
Born of the sun, they travelled a short while toward the sun,
And left the vivid air signed with their honour.
   —Stephen Spender

Contents

Preface

This work attempts a close, largely (though not exclusively) psychoanalytic reading of Seneca's most influential work. No one is more aware than I of the problems and perils involved in the psychoanalytic study of a literary work. I expect the results to be controversial, but I also hope that they may promote more serious inquiry into a body of dramatic texts that all too frequently receives only superficial generalizations about rhetoric, imitation, and irrationality.

Although I draw heavily on traditional Freudian concepts (the unconscious, repression, displacement, etc.), as well as on traditional critical methodologies, my approach is much influenced by the thinking of Jacques Lacan. I am concerned not so much with getting at the repressed contents of the unconscious *per se* (to the extent that such an endeavor is possible in literary analysis anyway) as with examining the processes by which these contents are displaced into language and particularly into the deliberately distorted, artificial language of Senecan rhetoric. Instead of dismissing this rhetoric as a mere literary exercise, therefore, I subject it to close scrutiny. Properly approached, I believe, it can sustain and reward such scrutiny. So too rather than regarding the derivative quality of Seneca's play as a fault, I accept that secondary status at face value and try to work out some of its critical implications and possibly positive literary values. I have been encouraged and aided in this direction by the recent surge of new interest in Senecan tragedy and by a critical spirit that is more inclined to accept the textuality of the work, that is, to regard the work not merely as a transparent message about life but as a complex signifying system that calls attention to its own signifiers (as well as its signifieds) and their mode of producing meaning.

Despite the psychoanalytic orientation, I have tried to avoid jargon and conceptual straightjackets and to remain close and faithful to the text. My reading, I hope, will prove useful to students of Seneca even if they do not share my psychological approach. Nevertheless, I believe that this approach enables us to view in a new light many of the linguistic and structural features of the play. While I have not neglected Seneca's relation to the previous literary tradition, I have not restated points well established in the traditional scholarship on the play. For these the reader is referred to the notes and bibliography. As this study was written essentially in the period 1981-83, I was unable to take as full account as I should have liked of the work of Boyle, Davis, Petrone, or of the essays in the *Ramus* volume on Senecan drama. I have tried, however, to incorporate as much of this material as was feasible; and I am grateful to A. J. Boyle for allowing me to see his forthcoming study of the play in advance of publication.

I drafted a first version of this work during a sabbatical leave from Brown University in 1981-82. During this period I also had the honor of holding a fellowship from the John Simon Guggenheim Memorial Foundation. I am grateful to both institutions for encouragement and support, both material and other. I am particularly grateful to the Guggenheim Foundation for continued interest in a project that grew into a form rather different from that which the Foundation originally sponsored. Much of the initial research for this work was carried out at the American Academy in Rome; and I would like to extend my warm thanks to the then Director, and now President, of the Academy, Mrs. Sophie Consagra, for the opportunity to work in that congenial setting. The staff of the Academy Library, as always, was unfailingly helpful and courteous. I profited from the opportunity to present portions of my work in lectures at the American Academy, the Istituto di Filologia Latina of the University of Pisa, the Ecole Normale Supérieure J. F. in Paris, the Centro Romano di Semiotica, Princeton University, the University of California at San Diego, and the Program in Semiotic Studies of Boston University. I am grateful to the colleagues who helped organize these talks and to the audiences for helpful comments and critical interest.

I owe particular thanks to Froma Zeitlin of Princeton University, Marylin Arthur of Wesleyan University, and Karen Bassi of Brown University, who read the manuscript in whole or in part and offered numerous suggestions and improvements. Frances Eisenhauer and Ruthann Whitten typed successive drafts with exemplary patience and accuracy. The anonymous readers of the Princeton University Press performed their task with a thoroughness and commitment to scholarship for which I am deeply grateful. Working with the staff of the Press has again helped to humanize the trivial and to make the tedious reasonably tolerable. In particular I am indebted to Elizabeth Powers for perspicacious editing. And, once more, I warmly thank Joanna Hitchcock, Assistant Director of the Press, for the friendly concern, positive suggestions, and tactful patience that encouraged fruitful rethinking and rewriting.

I cannot list all those whose support lightened my task, especially during a time of sorrow and loss. I owe very special thanks to my colleagues and students in the Department of Classics at Brown, whose ever-ready assistance and sympathetic concern meant much more than they could have known. I cannot leave unmentioned the kindness and considerateness of Katherine and David Goddard, Robert and Rosemary Goddard, Martha Schaffer and Charles McKinley, Frances Bené, Robert and Elva Mathiesen, Charles and Nancy Fornara, Ross and Nancy Holloway, Karen Newman, Michael Putnam, Kurt and Deborah Raaflaub, Adele Scafuro, William and Sandra Wyatt, Craig Manning, Gian Biagio Conte, my brother and sister-in-law Richard and Susan Segal, and my sons, Joshua and Thaddeus.

My deepest, and saddest, thanks are addressed to the memory of the beloved companion to whom this book is dedicated. Alison shared with me the excitement and the effort of this book's early stages. Her sound judgment, sharp critical intelligence, deep commitment to scholarship, keen judgment of literature,

and her enthusiasm, intensity, and joy in life and in work con-
tributed far more to this study than a mere verbal acknowledg-
ment can express. That this work is not worthier of her high
standards and of the efforts and advice of the many friends and
colleagues who have offered help is due solely to my own limi-
tations.

Providence, Rhode Island
August 5, 1985

Abbreviations Used in the Notes

CW	*Classical World*
D-K, Diels-Kranz	Diels, Hermann, and Walter Kranz, eds., *Die Fragmente der Vorsokratiker*, ed. 6 (Berlin 1952), 3 vols.
G & R	*Greece and Rome*
HSCP	*Harvard Studies in Classical Philology*
ICS	*Illinois Classical Studies*
N, Nauck	Nauck, Augustus, ed., *Tragicorum Graecorum Fragmenta*, ed. 2 (Leipzig 1889), with Supplement, ed. B. Snell (Hildesheim 1964)
P. Oxy.	*Oxyrhynchus Papyri*, eds. B. P. Grenfell and A. S. Hunt et al. (London 1898ff.)
RhM	*Rheinisches Museum für Philologie*
TAPA	*Transactions of the American Philological Association*

Translations, unless otherwise noted, are by the author.

For the Latin text of *Phaedra* I have used Grimal (1965) and Giardina (1966), with deviations as noted

Language and Desire
in Seneca's *Phaedra*

Satis enim magnum alter alteri theatrum sumus.
For we are a sufficiently great theater to one another.
   —Seneca, *Letters to Lucilius*, 7.11 (quoting Epicurus)

The poets and philosophers before me discovered
the unconscious.
   —Sigmund Freud

It is only through the confining act of writing that the
immensity of the nonwritten becomes legible.
   —Italo Calvino

Senecan Tragedy and the Drama of the Self

I

From August Wilhelm von Schlegel down to comparatively recent times Senecan tragedy has suffered from comparison with its Greek models.[1] To view Seneca in the shadow of the Greeks, however inevitable, is also to miss the unique qualities of these plays. Instead of the theological concerns and intellectual questioning of Greek drama, Seneca develops the moral conflicts which he took over from the Greek dramatists in ways that owe at least as much to Virgil and Ovid as to Sophocles and Euripides. From his Roman predecessors he inherited a rich vocabulary for exploring morbid states of mind, the dark world of family hatred and jealousy, the corrosive effects of anger, fear, resentment, the lust for power. These passions appear not so much in open conflicts with the gods or with social or religious norms as in the isolation of the individual soul, trapped in the hell of its own torments.

Greek tragedy, properly Athenian tragedy, was created for a homogeneous, tightly knit city-state and performed at a religious festival before the entire citizen populace, or at least the male citizen populace. Every play was in some sense a political drama, usually reflecting more or less directly on the decisions and attitudes that were still under the control of the citizen body of an autonomous republic. Its issues were the openly debated questions of a vigorous democracy: think of the *Oresteia*, *Antigone*, or *Trojan Women*. The issues of Senecan tragedy have

---

[1] See A. W. von Schlegel's notorious condemnation of Seneca's tragedies in his *Vorlesungen über dramatische Kunst und Litteratur* (1809), Kohlhammer ed. (Stuttgart 1966) 1.233-35, repr. in Lefèvre (1972) 13f. Eliot, "Seneca in Elizabethan Translation" (1927, 1961) 54-57 indirectly echoes Schlegel's notion of a "cruder" sensibility.

political implications, to be sure (the exercise of power, the corruption of a monarch like Atreus);[2] but the atmosphere of suspicion in the imperial household made any overt discussion of current events highly dangerous. Even proximity to the imperial power could be fatal, as Seneca's own end showed.

Like the architecture of the theater itself, cut into the hillside and open to the sky, Greek tragedy is a public, outward-facing form. Seneca's tragedies were produced for a relatively small coterie in a vast autocratic empire where the majority is far removed from the center of power. Whether intended to be acted or recited, his plays are realized in more or less private circumstances, and they face inward.[3] Even allowing for the frequent appeals to celestial or chthonic divinities or to quasi-divinized forces like Nature or Fortune, their world is less the Greeks' universe of warring deities and cosmic or social conflicts than the world of the soul. The antithesis suggested by some interpreters between Seneca's "aesthetic" tragedy and the "ethical" or "metaphysical" tragedy of the Greeks is an oversimplification;[4] but it is probably true to say that the meaning of Seneca's plays unfolds in the immediate foreground of an emotional present, whereas most Greek tragedies more directly and integrally implicate the world-order, something that includes but transcends the personal lives of the characters. Questions about the divine governance of the universe, for example, appear in the choral odes of *Phaedra*, as of other Senecan dramas; but they do not

[2] For suggestions about these political implications, emphasizing the corruption of power, see Petrone (1984) 74ff. and 121ff.

[3] The question of the performability of Seneca's plays has been much discussed. For a useful summary of earlier views, see Zwierlein (1966) 9-11, who has been the strongest opponent of stage performance; see *contra* Fortey and Glucker (1975) 699-715; Lefèvre's review of Zwierlein in *Gnomon* 40 (1968) 782-89; Herrmann (1924) 153ff.; Enk (1957) 306f.; Herington (1982) 520; Fantham (1982) 34-49, who concludes in favor of recitation or a text intended for reading. The latest study I have seen is Albrecht Dihle, "Seneca und die Aufführungspraxis der römischen Tragödie," *Antike und Abendland* 29 (1983) 162-71, who argues in favor of recitation on the basis of the Roman fondness for presenting set pieces from plays, either recitatives or arias, in the theater.

[4] For these terms see Liebermann (1974) 154f., who speaks of Seneca's "Allgegenwart des Schauerlichen" (154).

enter into the action as fully as analogous themes in Euripides' *Hippolytus*.

The poetry of Seneca's tragedies conduces less to the objective description of realistic detail than to suggestion and fantasy. Words are used more for their associative than for their denotative power. Liebermann's study of the messenger speeches has fully documented this point.[5] But studies of Seneca's language and dramaturgy, even the excellent recent studies of Seidensticker and Liebermann, have tended to be negative, stressing what Senecan tragedy is not.[6] The present work attempts a more positive approach, namely to show that this lack of precision about objective reality has another side, namely the rich depiction of an inner world, a psychological landscape.

Rhetoric is the dimension in which Seneca's characters move and in which they have their psychological reality. They are not so much fully developed three-dimensional personalities as emblematic, emotionalized focal points for ethical conflicts that are crystallized into highly elaborate, imagistic language. Rather than treating the rhetoric as an obstacle between us and realistically conceived characters, we need to accept it as the substance of the characters themselves.

Seneca goes far beyond Euripides in the demythologizing of drama.[7] He adds relatively little to the basic plots of the Greek plays, and his action is often starker than the original outlines. Instead he lavishes his attention on the thickly enfolding fabric of rhetorical figures and on the emotional atmosphere around characters shown in limited perspectives. He surrounds his figures with an almost tangible envelope of feeling, what Bruno

[5] Liebermann (1974) passim, especially 14-84, 119ff., 235ff.; also Leeman (1976) 210.

[6] For surveys of Seneca's reputation from antiquity to the nineteenth century see Regenbogen (1930) 167ff.; Enk (1957) 288ff.; Liebermann (1974) 1-13; Calder (1976/77) 1-11; Opelt in Lefèvre (1972) 93f. with the notes; Mette (1964); Boyle (1985); Herington (1982) 519-22. As this volume went to press, the survey articles on Senecan drama announced for *Aufstieg und Niedergang der römischen Welt*, 2.32.2, had not yet appeared.

[7] See Tschiedel (1969) 56 on Seneca's "Entmythisierung der Tragödie."

Snell calls "the cloud of their milieu."[8] His much-maligned rhetoric enables him to find a verbal equivalent for the life of the emotions as something set apart from the world of public action or the interaction of family life. Even plays based on domestic conflicts, like the *Agamemnon* or *Medea*, convey little of the emotional reality of family life in the Greek originals. Seneca's stage serves as the setting for a more private, static, and inward reality. The distortions and exaggerations of his language, the insistent grimness of his imagery, the deliberate vagueness of locale all create a realm that seems to float free of time and space, something closer to the nightmarish atmosphere of parts of Ovid's *Metamorphoses* than to the relatively objective, externalized world of Greek tragedy.[9]

The *Phaedra*, like Senecan tragedy in general, develops the element of what the ancient critics term "the terrible"—*to phoberon* or *to deinon*—or what Euripides, in describing the bull of his *Hippolytus*, calls *to phrikōdes*, "the shudderingly fearful."[10] Seneca's terror-arousing spectacle is not the Euripidean event of rival gods destroying mortals but rather mortals destroying themselves through their own hidden monstrosity. His psychological reinterpretation of Euripidean myth thus makes possible Racine's rediscovery, centuries later, of "myth as a metaphor for psychodrama."[11] The house of Phaedra's origins belongs to a dark past where the authority of King Minos and the imported artistry and technology of the celebrated Daedalus keep hidden from the eyes of the people a monstrous secret that has to do with the mother's unrepressed sexuality.[12] Unlike Racine, how-

[8] Snell (1964) 27. See also Mugellesi (1973) 43ff., 53ff.; Pratt (1963) 218-24; Owen (1968) 296ff.

[9] See Tarrant (1978) 258ff., especially 261.

[10] Eur., *Hipp.* 1202, 1216. For the "terrible" as a feature of literary style, see Ps.-Longinus, *On the Sublime* 9.5; cf. Aristotle, *Poetics* c. 14.

[11] See Mueller (1980) 46. Mueller has only a brief discussion of the Senecan play (47f.), but it would be interesting to read his study of *Phèdre* (which I found only after the completion of my manuscript) in the light of mine of *Phaedra*.

[12] See Orlando (1978) 30. The *Thyestes* also exploits the associations between artistry and monstrosity: Atreus is an artificer of monstrous vengeance: see Segal (1983b) 242-44.

ever, Seneca did not have to be embarrassed or defensive about the Greek myths.[13] Thanks to predecessors like Virgil and Ovid (and also to the fact that his milieu was still pagan), he could still draw freely on their ancient symbolism to enrich his diction and imagery.

The aura of antiquity that the Greek myths already have for the cosmopolitan Roman intellectual of the Empire makes them an ideal vehicle for exploring the kind of regressive behavior acted out in the plays. If theater provides the place, literal and figurative, for staging the unconscious, then mythical theater, in a post-mythical age, has the added advantage of combining suggestive archaism with the symbolic condensation contained in myth.

When the Athenian audience of 428 B.C. watched Euripides' *Hippolytus*, they knew that they were viewing very remote events; but they also knew, however faintly, that these events formed part of the continuous history of their city, founded by Theseus. For the audience of Seneca's *Phaedra* that thread of continuity is broken. To enter a world coterminous with a Minotaur or a descent to Hades is to experience a far greater pull between a rationalistic description of experience (such as Seneca's prose works exemplify) and a description of another kind.[14] In reinterpreting the Greek myths in psychological terms, Seneca is modern in the sense suggested by André Gide in his own version of the Oedipus myth: "In the advanced state of civilization where we are and since the death of the last sphinx at our father's hands," his Eteocles says, "neither the monsters nor the gods any longer inhabit the skies or the fields, but are within us."[15]

---

[13] See Orlando (1978) 23-28.

[14] This pull is even stronger and harsher in Racine. Mueller (1980), 46, speaks of Racine's Phèdre's surrender to her passions as "the regression from a world governed by the moral and aesthetic criteria of bienséance and vraisemblance to a world of monsters and mythical terrors."

[15] A. Gide, *Oedipe*, Acte II: "Dans l'état de civilisation avancée où nous sommes, et depuis que le dernier sphinx a été tué par notre père, les monstres ni les dieux ne sont plus parmi les airs ou les campagnes; mais en nous."

The Minotaur locked in the bowels of the Minos' palace, Hercules battling monsters in Hades, Thyestes made to eat his children's flesh introduce us to a split-level reality. They make us feel the division between our conscious, waking world and a world of another sort. Because that other world is also presented as temporally far anterior to the present, these plays also create the sensation of taking us back to something archaic in ourselves. The myths of monstrosity in the *Phaedra*, then, serve as metaphors for the uncovering of the monstrous in ourselves. Senecan tragedy, however, goes beyond even the Greek and Elizabethan in projecting cosmic monstrosity as an image of immersion in self-destructive evil.

Consider for a moment the great climactic scene of the Senecan and Euripidean *Medea*. Both heroines, on the verge of killing their children, have their moment of surrender to the maternal sweetness of the children's embrace. The Euripidean heroine, however, about to send her sons to carry the poisoned gifts to Jason's new bride, reflects on the conflict between her vengeful anger and her rational counsels (1074-80):

> ὦ γλυκεῖα προσβολή,
> ὦ μαλθακὸς χρὼς πνεῦμά θ' ἥδιστον τέκνων.
> χωρεῖτε χωρεῖτ'· οὐκέτ' εἰμὶ προσβλέπειν
> οἵα τε †πρὸς ὑμᾶς†, ἀλλὰ νικῶμαι κακοῖς.
> καὶ μανθάνω μὲν οἷα δρᾶν μέλλω κακά,
> θυμὸς δὲ κρείσσων τῶν ἐμῶν βουλευμάτων,
> ὅσπερ μεγίστων αἴτιος κακῶν βροτοῖς.

O sweet embrace, the soft skin and sweetest breath of children! Come to me, come. I am no longer able to look at you, but I am defeated by my evils. And I understand what evils I intend to do; but stronger than my reasoning counsels is my angry passion, the greatest cause to mortals of their evils.

Euripides attains his powerful depiction of Medea's terrible conflict through the emotional situation alone, expressed in the almost unadorned simplicity of her language, with its triple repetition of the general but important word *kaka* ("woes," "evils," "sufferings") in emphatic line-end positions. With superb restraint Euripides breaks the scene off at once, and then has his chorus sing a low-keyed, straightforward ode on the tribulations of having children (1081-1115). Everything remains on the level of universal human experience. Even allowing for the elevation of the poetic vocabulary, there is scarcely a word beyond the familiar vocabulary of the emotions.

Seneca's Medea has already destroyed her enemies and received her children back after they have delivered the fatal robe. She now meditates on the next stage of her revenge, murdering the boys. Like the Euripidean Medea, she begins with a mother's tenderness in embracing her children (*Medea* 945-47):

> huc cara proles, unicum afflictae domus
> solamen, huc vos ferte et infusos mihi
> coniungite artus.

> Hither, dear children, sole consolation of a ruined house;
> come hither, and join your limbs entwined with mine.

The basic situation is the same as that of Euripides' play; but Seneca's more general, depersonalized, and abstract vocabulary (*proles*, "offspring," *solamen*, "consolation") checks the emotional immediacy. Whereas Euripides stresses the sensations of the children's physical proximity (1074f., cited above), the periphrasis of Seneca's "limbs poured over me" (*infusos mihi artus*) is both more self-consciously artificial and in the context somewhat sinister.

Medea's next lines take up the division within the house (the conflict between mother and father immediately afterwards, 947f., 950f.). Her destructive emotions become the subjects of the active verbs as she renews her seething pain and festering hatred (*rursus increscit dolor / et fervet odium*, 951f.). The emotional climax is conveyed in the progression from the emotional

words, *grief* and *hatred*, to the chthonic imagery of the "ancient
Erinys" (951-53):

> rursus increscit dolor
> et fervet odium, repetit invitam manum
> antiqua Erinys.

> Grief again grows and hatred seethes; the ancient Fury
> claims back my hand, unwilling though it be.

This gradual personification and mythicization of her rage cul-
minate in her second-person address, at once, to her *ira*
("wrath") as her guide: *ira, qua ducis sequor* ("Wrath, wherever
you lead I follow," 953). Now, far from being the loving
mother of *cara proles* in 945, she rhetorically transforms maternity into a monstrous fertility of hatred as she compares herself
regretfully to the prolific Niobe: "For vengeful retribution I
have been barren (*sterilis in poenas fui*); and yet—what suffices
for my brother and my father—I have given birth to two sons"
(956f.). In her next lines she resumes the chthonic motifs of the
Furies and Megaera, motifs that accompany the play's recurrent
fusion of Medea's maternity with her monstrosity (*Medea, mater, monstrum*).[16] Her description of the hellish Furies, with
their fiery weapons (958ff.), and of her murdered brother's
shade (963ff.) continues to depict her inner violence as subterranean monstrosity. This movement has been prepared for by
the choral odes, and especially by the first two stasima, which
project upon the large screen of space and time Medea's emotional plunge from the innocence of children to the evil locked
in Hades.

In contrast to the relatively direct, first-person description of
emotion in the Euripidean scene cited above, Seneca's rhetorical buildup escalates the emotional level and steadily pushes
Medea toward the supernatural equivalents of murderous
hatred: the Furies and their underworld paraphernalia of flaming torches, snakes, blood, whips, and darkness (958ff.). The

---

[16] See Traina (1979) 273-75; Segal (1982b) 241-43.

self-consciousness of the passage as an elaboration of material stylistically marked as "literary" shifts the focus of attention from the emotions *per se* to the resources in the language for depicting emotions.

II

The psychological dimension of Senecan drama has ultimately been more influential than its moralistic meaning as a warning against the danger and destructiveness of the passions.[17] Indeed Seneca's portrayal of powerful emotions to shock or horrify his audience seems increasingly refractory to a philosophical interpretation that would view him as combating these emotions. Reuben Brower, for example, attributes the success of *Medea* to its "splendidly consistent non-morality" and its "Stoic consistency for non-Stoic ends."[18] Going even farther (and probably too far), Joachim Dingel has recently argued for a total separation between Seneca's tragedies and the philosophical writings and for a more pessimistic, more questioning, and less moralizing use of Stoic ideas, rather like the poetry of Lucan at times.[19]

In a deservedly influential study Otto Regenbogen has stressed the plays' new vision of tragedy through their charac-

[17] See for example Herrmann (1924) 469f., 488-92; Regenbogen (1930) 189ff.; Marti (1945) passim; Paratore (1957) 56ff.; Ruch (1964) 362f.; Croisille (1964) 292ff., especially 299-301; Shelton (1977) 34f.

[18] Brower (1971) 164; for a recent discussion and bibliography, see Motto and Clark (1982) passim; Herington (1982) 523f.; Henry (1982) 809-13; Pratt (1983) chap. 4, especially 76-81. The older view, emphasizing the Stoic element, may be found in the essays of Egermann (1940), Knoche (1941), and Von Fritz (1955) in Lefèvre (1972) 33ff., 58ff., 67ff., respectively; also Marti (1945) passim and Pratt (1948).

[19] See Dingel (1974) 94-100 and 116f., citing Lucan, *Phars.* 7.445ff. Henry (1982), 829f., suggests, "Should one perhaps see Seneca's tragedies as a means of expressing what his philosophy could not find room for, this element of the monstrous in human nature?" On the other hand, Seneca's philosophical works are often emphatic about the monstrous violence of passion: cf. *De Ira* 1.2 on the vast destructiveness wrought by anger. For a balanced view, see Pratt (preceding note), who stresses the importance of the emotional violence in the plays as warning exempla, the careful analysis and implicit typology of extreme emotional states, and the engagement of the reader as a therapeutic aid to mastering emotions.

teristically Roman combination of pictorial vividness and the representation of intense, pathos-laden emotional states, what he calls "das Bildhafte und Emotionale."[20] Seneca's language, like that of Tacitus, reflects a world in which the experience of suffering and death is pushed to exaggerated extremes. In this world of the Julio-Claudian emperors, the world of Tacitus' *Annals* as well as Seneca's tragedies, the individual appears hemmed in on all sides by the suffering and horror of life, and only the free choice of death by the Stoic hero-sage offers a way out.[21]

In the oppressive atmosphere of Neronian Rome the truths that this poetry has to convey cannot be spoken openly but only through the intricate elaboration of an aesthetic surface. Such texts suggest secrets and secret meanings—philosophical, political, psychological. The last area is our particular concern. The royal houses of Senecan drama conceal ineradicable corruptions which appear stylistically in the strident hyperboles of the rhetoric on the one hand and in a muting or blurring of sharp, overt meaning on the other.

Even more than Tacitean history, Senecan tragedy responds to this atmosphere of corruption by studying the soul's forced exploration of its innermost dark places. The violence done to language by Seneca's rhetoric corresponds to a sense of life lived in extreme conditions, life pushed to the edge of horrors. Whatever the relation of this psychological dimension of the tragedies to their alleged purpose as Stoic moralizing, their vision of the darker regions of the soul is undoubtedly what makes them most interesting to the modern reader.

The rhetoric of horror in modern literature, from Kafka to Solzhenitsyn, the surrealist movement in the visual arts, and the blurring of the line between the real and the unreal in contem-

[20] Regenbogen (1930) 209.

[21] Regenbogen (1930) 213f. cites *Consol. ad Marc.* 20.1-3 as a good example of this mood. For this atmosphere of suffering, violence, and death in the early Empire and the affinities of Seneca and Tacitus, see Regenbogen's suggestive analysis, 211-18, especially 216f. Pratt (1983), chap. 7, offers a balanced appraisal: see especially 164, 193f., 197.

porary nightmares that have become realities all help make Seneca's vision of the world recognizable, alas, as our own. If we abandon Schlegel's standard of the idealized serenity of "those highest creations of the poetic genius of the Greeks,"[22] Seneca's tragedies display their grim power and their psychological intensity. The contemporary critic can no longer accept the view of fifty years ago, that "the principal interest of the work [*Phaedra*] is to allow us to glimpse in two or three scenes the design of [Euripides'] first *Hippolytus*."[23]

The careful reexamination of the language and structure of the plays over the last thirty years and our increased appreciation of the non-realistic conventions through which Seneca presents emotional reality have adequately established the subtlety and complexity of Seneca's characterization of Phaedra. She is involved in a genuine tragic conflict, which includes her struggle against a love that finally overwhelms her, her yielding in confusion and desperation to the Nurse's clever plot to throw the blame on Hippolytus, her remorse, and the spiritual and moral energy of her suicide.[24] An article published just over fifty years ago labelled Phaedra (as character) "a study in baseness."[25] More recent scrutiny of the play—I need mention only the work of Paratore, Grimal, Lefèvre, Seidensticker, and now Boyle—makes that simplistic view no longer tenable. I am also happy to note that the entry for Seneca in the second edition of the *Oxford Classical Dictionary* does not repeat the first edition's judgment that the play has "debased" the myth "to a not very subtle story of minx and misogynist."[26]

In the largely "verbal" action of the play the points of emotional crisis do not stand out in the high relief that they do in Euripides; and it is not always easy to distinguish a momentary

---

[22] Schlegel in Lefèvre (1972) 14; see Segal (1983a) 186f.
[23] Méridier (1931) 326.
[24] See in general Paratore (1952) 222ff.; Seidensticker (1969) 144ff. Jacobson (1974), 157, on the other hand, contrasts Seneca's characterization of Phaedra unfavorably with Ovid's in *Heroides* 4.
[25] Flygt (1933/34) 513.
[26] E. P. Barker, s.v. "Seneca," *Oxford Classical Dictionary*, 1st ed. (1949) 827.

impulse in the language from a point of real psychological tension and resolution. But it is now widely accepted, for example, that Phaedra is sincere in choosing death as the only solution to her conflicted love for Hippolytus in 258ff.,[27] that her idea of "concealing her crime by the torch of marriage" in 596f. rests on the belief, half delusion and half wish, that she actually is a widow,[28] and that in general she is, as H. J. Mette sums it up, "conceived not as a monster but as a woman of deepest feeling."[29]

III

A major concern of this study—in addition to further elucidation of Seneca's text—is the question of how the language of tragedy creates the impression of a full human personality, how poetic discourse constitutes selves that we accept as more or less real persons. As characters in a play are not, of course, real people with real life histories, they cannot be psychoanalyzed; but they can serve as symbolic condensations of the author's insights into the human condition, as the congruent parts of an imaginative sketch into which he distills the most essential details.

Seneca's artificial style makes the problem of the credibility and intelligibility of his characters particularly acute: "gigantic marionettes," Schlegel called them.[30] In directness of appeal and in range and depth of humanity Seneca's characters do not compete well against those of Sophocles, Euripides, or Shakespeare: see the comparison of the two Medeas above. But di-

[27] Seidensticker (1969), p. 100 with note 58; also 101-4 (apropos of *Pha.* 880); Croisille (1964) 288f.; Heldmann (1974) 152-61, with references to previous literature; Davis (1983) 121f.

[28] See Herter (1971), p. 68 with note 66; Croisille (1964) 294.

[29] Mette (1964) 181: "nicht als Unholdin konzipiert, sondern als eine Frau tiefsten Empfindens." See also Herrmann (1924) 413f.; Grimal (1963) 314.

[30] Schlegel in Lefèvre (1972) 14: "Ihre Persönlichkeiten sind weder Ideale noch wirkliche Menschen, sondern riesenhafte unförmliche Marionetten, die bald am Draht eines unnatürlichen Heroismus, bald an dem einer ebenso unnatürlichen, vor keinem Greuel sich entsetzenden Leidenschaft in Bewegung gesetzt werden."

rectness and naturalness are not Seneca's aim. The power and suggestiveness of his characterization work in large part through the figurative language into which he recasts the mythical and literary material of his predecessors.

There is also, as I shall try to show, a close correlation between the formal structure of the *Phaedra* and the emotional and psychological realities that it represents. Stasis, circularity, repetition in the form mirror the entrapment, enclosure, and helplessness before the interior violence of overwhelming passions in the content. Phaedra's only way out is the desperate expedient of leaving life itself. Her palace, with the attendant images of fire, cavern, volcano, and oppressive heaviness, focuses her tragic situation. Her world has an ominous counterpart, a shadow side, in the Minoan palace and the Cretan labyrinth in the background. At the two moments when she emerges from the palace (384, 1159), she addresses a wider realm of external nature, the woods of Hippolytus' hunting and the deep sea of the monster called forth by Theseus (394ff. and 1159ff.). But in both cases that movement outside only sets into relief her imprisonment in the interior fires of her *furor* or love-madness.

Phaedra's tragedy is inextricably bound up with that of Hippolytus, whose conflicts and emotional inadequacies are also projected upon a psychological landscape, a forest realm that he idealizes as a place of Golden-Age innocence. Beneath its veneer of sylvan freshness, however, the diction and imagery reveal the violence and sterility in himself that he justifies in terms of his worship of Diana and his loss of the pure Amazon mother of his infancy. The third figure in the triangular interaction, Theseus, belongs to a landscape of underworld darkness and submarine monstrosity. In all three cases the landscape becomes the screen on which each character projects wishful fantasies and nightmarish terrors. The heavy metaphorical overlays of Seneca's poetic diction make us view the events through the filters of a character's distorting fears and desires.

Chapter 1 addresses the general question of how rhetorical drama of this nature enables the repressed contents of the unconscious to appear in images, metaphors, and other figures of speech. The gradual crystallization and dissolution of the principal characters' fantasies and fears are discussed in chapters 2 through 4. Chapters 5 through 9 examine the symbolic representation of character and the expression and concealment of desire in language, with particular attention to the role of the father and the function of the sword. Another aspect of the rhetorical artificiality of the play is the subject of chapters 10 and 11, namely the self-consciousness about writing and rewriting that develops when an author in a later, more complex society elaborates and transforms an earlier work (in this case Euripides' *Hippolytus*) that is closer to the primary material of myth and ritual. This theme too, as we hope to show, is also related to the problem of authority that centers on the father-figure in the play.

My study draws heavily on traditional Freudian psychology as well as on literary theorists like Barthes, Derrida, Genette, Orlando, Poulet, and others. The justification for applying to an ancient text contemporary theory that is far removed from its historical context is the belief that the ancient poet and the modern psychologist have in common a universal area of human experience that they describe in different but complementary ways.

In exploring the relation between language and desire and the various figures of absence in the play, I am obviously indebted to the work of Jacques Lacan and those who have applied his work to literary analysis. A Lacanian approach, I suggest, is especially illuminating in studying the relations between the signifying processes of language and the emotional and mental processes enacted by the characters. It helps us trace the ways in which the hidden movements of the unconscious are filtered into language and appear in the verbal material of the literary discourse.

For the role of the father in the linguistic texture of the play, for example, Lacan's recasting of Freudian theory is particularly helpful. Lacan reconstructs Freud's primal father not as a living, real father but in language and as an absence, as the Symbolical Father, whose signifier is the Name of the Father, the locus of the Law and of the demands of the social and moral order. The paradox that the very act of naming the Symbolical Father re-presses that for which the name stands suggests a way of getting at the *Phaedra's* mixture of strident invocation of father-figures on the one hand and the elusiveness and ambiguity of the patriarchal authority on the other.

In bringing Lacanian psychology to bear upon an ancient text, however, I have made my own selection and synthesis of what was useful for literary study. I have confined myself to pointing out possible points of contact with Lacan's system in the notes, and I have tried to avoid jargon and as much as possible of Lacan's technical terminology. My approach is an eclectic blend of Lacan, Freud, and other currents of psychological thought. As a friendly reader suggested, it is better described as "Lacanistic" rather than Lacanian. My aim has been to develop a method that could interpret a literary text rather than to support a particular system or dogma.

One of the residual functions of poetry and myth in post-industrial societies is to expose a view of the hidden contents of the unconscious and thereby to tell us something about the self that cannot be spoken in ordinary language. Far more self-consciously for Seneca than for Sophocles or Euripides, the knowledge of the self is a function of what can be expressed in language. Freud's (and more emphatically Lacan's) conception of language as a translucent barrier between the unconscious and consciousness will, I hope, prove fruitful for reading a psychologically oriented author who delights in elaborating the purely expressive features of language and will illuminate for the contemporary reader something of that ability to convey the secrets of the soul that Shakespeare, Webster, and Racine found in Senecan tragedy.

ONE

Language and the Unconscious: Towards a Rhetorical View of Character

I

Consciousness does not cover the entire field of our mental life. There is another area of mental activity that we glimpse in what we recall of dreams, in slips of the tongue, and more dramatically in behavior under hypnosis. This area, the unconscious, resists being known or spoken; and to bring it to consciousness we encounter resistance or repugnance and feel a sense of exertion.[1] Because of its resistance to becoming conscious knowledge, the unconscious has a paradoxical nature. It is both there and not there, both known and not known. "The unconscious, Lacan says, is knowledge; but it is a knowledge one cannot know one knows, a knowledge which cannot tolerate knowing it knows."[2]

As the unconscious (by definition) eludes direct verbal description, the question of the relation between language and the unconscious becomes one of the most difficult and controversial of psychoanalytic theory. Does the unconscious have the structure of language, as the Lacanians believe? Or, with some Freudian critics, is the language of the unconscious a special kind of discourse, an "intransitive" language like the symbolic language of dreams?[3] Or does language merely give us a frame in which to restructure otherwise hidden experience in new forms, more acceptable to the censors that block the unconscious from becoming conscious, allowing us to relive personal transactions in less painful ways or to achieve a therapeutic replay in words of events and emotions that have caused some

---

[1] See S. Freud, "A Note on the Unconscious in Psychoanalysis" (1912).
[2] Cited from the unpublished 1974 seminar of Lacan in Felman (1977) 166.
[3] See Orlando (1977) chap. 1; also 60ff.

trauma? All of these formulations are useful ways of conceptualizing something that by its very nature resists the rational organization by which we are accustomed to isolate and master the various facets of "reality."

We know the unconscious only through mental processes that seem marginal to our rational organization of experience or through forms of discourse that elude the censorship of our conscious mind: the figurative language of metaphor, imagery, or symbolic narrative. In such modes of symbolic transformations we operate within a chain of signifiers which convey the repressed contents of the unconscious through metaphorical and metonymic substitutions.[4] Repression is itself a species of metaphor formulation.[5] Even to describe the unconscious, as the work of Freud and Lacan shows, we have to have recourse to metaphors like Freud's photographic negative or Lacan's elaborate analogies with physical and mathematical procedures or, at a somewhat different level, vicariously through the anecdotes that Freud relates in works like *The Interpretation of Dreams* or *The Psychopathology of Everyday Life*. So too speculation about the unconscious takes the form of paradoxes, tales and myths.[6]

In fictional literature, and particularly in drama, the unconscious, with its repressed contents of unspeakable desires, fears, and anxieties, can find expression in the imaginary events enacted before us on the stage or in our mental reconstruction of the events in which we participate as we read. The metaphorical and symbolic language of drama (as of other fictions) provides the kind of indirect speech through which these contents can be represented, even if the process remains, ultimately, mysterious to us. In drama particularly, the stage is set off as a place where "reality" is made physically visible but where the cause-and-effect consequences of action can also be suspended. Certain

---

[4] See Felman (1977) 110f.
[5] Turkle (1978) 56; see Lacan / Sheridan (1977) 200, 258.
[6] E.g. Freud's *Totem and Taboo*. For the element of "mythical supposition" in reconstituting the genesis of the unconscious, see Lacan / Wilden (1968) 272.

forms of drama (Seneca's among them), therefore, can use the stage as a privileged region of mental experience, analogous to that of dreams and fantasies. This is the realm of what Freud, in a phrase frequently cited by Lacan, calls "ein anderer Schauplatz," another viewplace or "other scene," the place of the Other.[7] This is a place from which and in which we may catch a fleeting glimpse of a reality that we usually do not see or speak. The theater then becomes "the best incarnation of this 'other scene' that is the unconscious."[8]

Drama and fiction enable us to project upon the characters in the story hidden alter egos that reflect back to us what we do not recognize, or refuse to recognize, in ourselves. In the *Bacchae* of Euripides, for example, the responses that the Lydian Stranger (the god Dionysus in disguise) elicits from Pentheus constitute a language that reveals a self hidden from Pentheus. This hidden side of what he is saying, its latent contents as the speech of the unconscious, is mirrored only in the enigmatic *double-entendre* of his interchange with the alluring and mysterious youth who embodies the part of himself that Pentheus has repressed.[9]

For Freud and for his recent interpreter, Lacan, there is a close relation between the rhetorical figures of language—metaphor, ellipsis, pleonasm, periphrasis, hyperbaton, negation, irony, and so on—and the processes of symbolization, condensation, and displacement through which the contents of the unconscious take on visible form. Such displacements or distortions of speech are important as much for what they conceal about their subject as for what they reveal. In such cases, then, language functions as a hidden discourse about the self and becomes the field where the masking and the revealing of the unconscious take place.[10]

    [7] For Lacan's interpretation of Freud's "other scene" (from the *Interpretations of Dreams*), see Lacan / Sheridan (1977) 193, 264, 285.
    [8] André Green, *Un oeil en trop* (Paris 1969) 11.
    [9] On this aspect of the *Bacchae*, see Segal (1982) 287f. and (198–). This language of the unconscious, spoken by a figure who is a projection of your own concealed desires, is, in Lacan's terminology, "the Discourse of the Other": see Lacan / Wilden (1968) 27, with discussion, 106-8.
    [10] Where Freud discusses the "dreamwork" of condensation, displacement,

II

Telling stories about ourselves, transforming life experience into more or less coherently organized narratives, is one of the primary ways in which we know what we are.[11] Knowing the self involves a discourse different from that of knowing Euclidean theorems or knowing the history of the French Revolution. Knowing a self which exists entirely as a fictional creation is a precarious procedure, for we deal here with distillations of events (real and imagined), experiences, fragments of personality, and recollections that are not only composed by the author into a new, imaginary narrative or dramatic structure but are further refracted through a literary language, with its own traditions, conventions, and demands. Approaching the psychology of literary characters requires not only the Freudian attention to the latent content of what is told about the character but also concern for the linguistic processes by which the sense of self is constructed.[12]

---

and the coexistence of opposites in relation to language, his context is historical linguistics, that is the diachronic study of language in the late nineteenth century form of the discipline. In chapter 11 of *The Introductory Lectures on Psychoanalysis* (1916-17) he suggests a relation between these symbolical processes of the dream-work and certain archaic features of language visible still in Latin (e.g. *altus* means both "high" and "deep"; *sacer* means both "holy" and "accursed"). Freud elaborated on this point in his 1910 paper, "The Antithetical Sense of Primal Words," repr. in S. Freud, *Character and Culture*, ed. P. Rieff (New York 1963) 44-50. He is less interested in parallels with the synchronic features of language studied by Lacan, nor does the term "rhetoric" occur in the (German) Index to his Collected Works. For Lacan's rhetorical reading of Freud, see especially the essay, "The Agency of the Letter in the Unconscious," in Lacan / Sheridan (1977) 147-78, particularly 168-75. He remarks (169), "Can one really see these as mere figures of speech when it is the figures themselves that are the active principle of the rhetoric of the discourse that the analysand in fact utters?" Jameson, in Felman (1977) 386, speaks of Lacan's "disengagement of a linguistic theory which was implicit in Freud's practice but for which he (Freud) did not yet have the appropriate conceptual instruments." See also Orlando (1973) 56ff. = (1978) 161ff.

[11] See for example Roy Schafer, "Narration in the Psychoanalytic Dialogue," *Critical Inquiry* 7 (1980) 29-53, especially 35ff.

[12] I am not concerned here with the biographical approach which would see in the character a reflection of the author's (re)writing of his unconscious life. Seneca certainly offers material for this kind of analysis, which has been attempted by Rozelaar (1976) in his psycho-biography, especially 48-52 on Seneca's Oedipus complex. But the personal psychoanalysis of the author lies out-

Psychoanalytic theorists are aware that the various accounts of the origins of the self—Freud's primordial horde or Lacan's mirror stage or Jung's house with its stratified layers from attic to buried ruins in the basement—are to be seen no less as "positivistic sets of factual findings about mental development" than as "hermeneutically filled-in narrative structures,"[13] or even as aetiological myths of a very special kind. What we have available for scrutiny in the stories told us about the self, then, is not just the solid, crystalline factuality of a life history, but also the processes of language by which the subject creates the "I" that expresses himself (herself) and relates himself to others and to himself. As psycholinguists have observed, the personal pronouns that create the relational categories of self and other are among the infant's first verbal acquisitions and among the first losses in aphasia and certain psychoses.[14]

In life as in art the unity of the person is a form of abstraction, the result of weaving many items together into a complicated fabric of relations, in which verbal relations play an important part. The identity of an individual personality is not a given, objective reality, but a unifying extrapolation from an almost infinite series of possibilities—gestures, words, acts, relationships—that are themselves in constant change and flux.[15] In literature too, as Gérard Genette has emphasized, the notion of what makes a given personality "probable" or "realistic" differs for every society and for every epoch of Western society. A literary personage is always a construction in language of a net-

---

side the scope and methodology of my study. For the dangers, see Pratt (1983) 190ff. and Miriam T. Griffin, *Seneca: A Philosopher in Politics* (Oxford 1976) 10ff. Jameson, in Felman (1977) 381f., remarks that "the most crucial need of literary theory today is for the development of conceptual instruments capable of doing justice to a post-individualistic experience of the subject in contemporary life itself as well as in the texts" (382). For the shift in the psychological interpretation of literature from an allegorizing of Freudian "forces" to the problem of representing the self, see the review article of Karen Newman, "Writing the 'Talking Cure,' " *Poetics Today* 3 (1982) 173-82.

[13] Schafer (above, note 11) 53.
[14] On pronouns and other "shifters," see Lacan / Wilden (1968) 161, 182-85.
[15] See Holland in Tompkins (1980) 120f.

work of relations and associations. It is an element in a text, or in other words a signifier analogous functionally to other signifying elements in the text.[16]

On the other hand, a literary character is not only a signifier, not only an abstract narrative function; he is also a signified, the "reality" that the work creates and describes.[17] We inevitably endow a character with a three-dimensional life of thoughts and feelings like our own, through our sympathetic identification with another human being. If this process of identification does not take place, the work leaves us cold, uninvolved, uninterested. Yet the process whereby it takes place depends upon our ability to accept the conventions of "life-likeness," *vraisemblance*, the particular forms of mimesis, of the work in question. If we accept those conventions, that is, decode the system of signifiers that the author uses, we are able to reconstruct the characters for ourselves and enter into their human "reality." If we do not do this and insist on mimetic conventions that are not those of the work in question, we will find the characters unconvincing, in some sense "unreal," and therefore irrelevant to our concerns.[18]

III

When we speak of Theseus' (or Phaedra's or Hippolytus') unconscious, we are using a shorthand expression for a far more complex phenomenon: the engagement of the reader in the action at the level of his or her unconscious fears and desires as he identifies, in succession or even simultaneously, with the var-

---

[16] See Gérard Genette, "Frontières du récit," *Figures* II (Paris 1969) 49-69.

[17] See Philippe Hamon, "Pour un statut sémiologique du personnage," in R. Barthes, W. Kayser, W. C. Booth, Ph. Hamon, *Poétique du récit* (Paris 1977) 115-80 (originally published in *Littérature* 6, 1972), especially 118ff., 124ff., 142ff. Hamon suggests a term like "signifié discontinu" or "morphème migratoire" (124f.) for the ambiguous status of the dramatic personage between signified and signifier.

[18] So Méridier (1931), 326, could regard the *Phaedra* as "a series of exercises where the author, with no concern for psychological lifelikeness (*vraisemblance psychologique*) nor for dramatic movement, has wished to show off his erudition, his descriptive or oratorical virtuosity."

ious protagonists and the relations enacted among them.[19] Thus, to refocus our discussion on the audience rather than the poet, Seneca's symbolic language and action engage the reader or spectator at the level of his unconscious so that he can identify imaginatively with something in the situation of Theseus, Phaedra, and Hippolytus.

The process of identification with the work, of "reconstructing" ourselves in the work is a process of familiarization, of adapting the work to our own "psychic economy."[20] We fill in the suggestions offered by the text with themes, patterns, associations, memories, and resonances that we draw from our own experience, from our own sense of self, our needs, wishes, embarrassments, sufferings, hopes, and beliefs.[21] We perform it, as it were, in our own personal way.

In counterpoint to this familiarizing, adaptive process, however, runs an opposite, alienating process: the work also in its otherness makes us, the reader, appreciate an alien self as our own and our familiar self as strange and unknown. The great works of literature open us to selves beyond our own experience; they enlarge, refine, and complicate our personalities by enabling us to experience men and women totally different from ourselves. They also at times show us ourselves in the estranging mirror of their otherness.

This "other" that emerges as the reader enters into the dialectical process of self-recognition and self-estrangement may be compared to the Freudian or Lacanian unconscious. It is a self that we both know and don't know. In this subtly alienated state of our consciousness we let ourselves be flooded by the "otherness" of the author's thoughts and "surrender" or let ourselves be "carried away" by the "magic" of his language. We thus par-

---

[19] In Lacanian terminology, the entire play functions, at every major stage, as a Discourse of the Other for the reader, or as a series of such Discourses.

[20] Holland in Tompkins (1980) 124.

[21] Holland in Tompkins (1980) 126. See also Walker Gibson, "Authors, Speakers, Readers and Mock Readers" in Tompkins (1980) 1-6, especially 5, on literary experience as a relation between a fictitious speaker and "a projection, a fictitious modification" of ourselves.

ticipate in the re-construction of ourselves in realizing the characters and the action of the literary work.

Sophocles' *Oedipus Tyrannus* is classical antiquity's strongest dramatic instance of showing the alien as familiar and the familiar as the unknown, as "other." Beneath the surface of his secure, stable, competent identity the hero harbors a total stranger, an Oedipus unknown to himself and to others and visible only to the negative sight of the blind prophet Teiresias. Closer to our own time, Nietzsche reverses Socrates' endorsement of the Delphic injunction, "Know Thyself," and makes our fundamental ignorance of ourselves the beginning of the search for wisdom:

> We knowers are unknown to ourselves, and for a good reason: how can we ever hope to find what we have never looked for? . . . The sad truth is that we remain necessarily strangers to ourselves, we don't understand our substance, we *must* mistake ourselves; the axiom, "Each man is farthest from himself," will hold for all eternity. Of ourselves we are not "knowers."[22]

This complex interchange between familiarization and alienation is perhaps more powerful in the dense, rhetorical texts of a reading public (such as Senecan tragedy) than in texts intended primarily for public oral performance (such as Greek tragedy). Whether or not intended for performance (a question that does not arise in the case of Greek tragedy), Senecan tragedy is eminently suitable for reading. In the act of reading, as George Poulet has argued, our unconscious participates in this alienation from itself as it amalgamates with the consciousness of another. In what Poulet calls "the remarkable transformation wrought in me through the act of reading" there is a "strange invasion of my person by the thoughts of another," wherein "I am a self who is granted the experience of thinking thoughts foreign to him. I am the subject of thoughts other than my own.

[22] F. Nietzsche, *Genealogy of Morals*, Preface, Golffing translation.

My consciousness behaves as though it were the consciousness of another." Poulet quotes the famous statement of Rimbaud, "Je est un autre."[23]

Seneca inherits the surface coherence of his plots from Greek tragedy, but his rhetorical language parts company with the Greek tragedians' verbal mimesis of character. He reveals the personal interrelations and psychological conflicts among the characters not so much in scenes of direct confrontation as in the heavily encrusted, self-consciously verbal dramatizing of rhetoric. It would not be too far afield to apply (mutatis mutandis) to the rhetorical structuring of character in a Senecan play a phrase that Lacan uses of one of Freud's case-histories, namely developing, "around the signifying crystal" of an individual's anxieties, "all the permutations possible on a limited number of signifiers."[24] Cut off from lucid reasoning about the proper aims of life, the tragic figure is as much entrapped in the rhetoric generated by his passions as in the passions themselves. Phaedra "follows the worse" instead of the better that she "knows to be true" partly because her language cannot speak or show this objective truth (177ff.).

Seneca's Oedipus, for example, the most guilt-ridden of all heroes, has a psychological interiority without parallel in Greek tragedy except perhaps for a few scenes in late Euripides. In the Senecan *Phoenissae* this hero suffers from a depressive guilt and an unshakable despondency. In the *Oedipus* he is tormented by the harsh and vengeful ghost of Laius. This paternal figure, surrounded by all the ghoulish paraphernalia of his return from Hell, has a subjective, apparition-like quality that is closer to the dreams of the *Aeneid* or to the ghost of *Hamlet* than to anything in the Greek dramatists (Aeschylus' Erinyes are perhaps the closest parallel). This shade of a murdered father is virtually a projection of Oedipus' unconscious guilt: he is an unsparing superego figure who has not a word of forgiveness, understand-

[23] Georges Poulet, "Criticism and the Experience of Interiority" in Tompkins (1980) 43-45.
[24] Lacan / Sheridan (1977) 168.

ing, or compassion. In his eyes the son is as detestable as if he had committed the patricide and incest in full knowledge and with deliberate intent (*Oed.* 622-58).

To an even greater extent in the *Phoenissae*, where Oedipus looks back on events now long past, Laius has become a mental image of the insatiably punitive father, inescapable because introjected as the son's own guilt (*Phoen.* 216-18):

> me fugio, fugio conscium scelerum omnium
> pectus, manumque hanc fugio et hoc caelum et deos;
> et dira fugio scelera quae feci innocens.

> It is myself I flee; I flee a breast guilty of every crime, and I flee this hand of mine and this sky and the gods; I flee too the dreadful crimes that in my innocence I did.

In order for Oedipus to escape the internalized accusers or indices of guilt that belong to the emanations of the Father, that is, to the sky and their gods, he has virtually to perform the self-violating rhetorical figure. He has to act out a kind of reverse synecdoche, fleeing from his own breast (*pectus*) and hand (*manum*).[25] Subordinating literal acts to his own rhetorical reading of the Greek plays, Seneca, one could say, views the old myths "with the very eyes of the unconscious—through the fabric of a dream."[26]

Psychoanalysis, Harold Bloom suggests, might be viewed as the "science of tropes."[27] Just as dream-language leaves its signified concealed or masked by the rhetoric of its language (displacement, condensation, indirect or metaphorical representation), so the rhetoric of Seneca's language can represent the contents of the unconscious (its signified) by calling attention to the signifier. Such an elaborated, rhetorical language reveals its unconscious signified by refusing to become transparent to it. The ornamental, "figural" quality disguises the presence of

[25] See Segal (1983a) 182; also 176f.
[26] Felman (1977) 137.
[27] H. Bloom, *Agon* (Oxford and New York 1982) 93; the whole essay, "Freud and the Sublime," is relevant to this topic.

the unconscious so that it can become visible in its displaced, metaphorical form, as a signifier.[28] Instead of the "transitive" discourse (to use Francesco Orlando's term) of the usual signified / signifier relation, this rhetorical language resembles the intransitive, non-communicating language of the unconscious as it occurs in dreams and fantasies.[29]

[28] On this relation of the signifier and signified to the representation of the unconscious, see Orlando (1973) 60ff. (= 1978, 164ff.), especially 66 (= 1978, 179), "Figure is the perpetual tribute rendered to the unconscious (and how willingly!) by the language of the conscious ego" (my translation). See also Starobinski (1970) 190f., who cites E. Benveniste, *Problèmes de linguistique générale* (Paris 1966) 86f.: "Car c'est dans le style, plutôt que dans la langue, que nous verrions un terme de comparaison avec les propriétés que Freud a décelées comme signalétiques du 'language' onirique. On est frappé des analogies qui s'esquissent ici. L'inconscient use d'une véritable 'rhétorique' qui, comme le style, a ses 'figures,' et le vieux catalogue des tropes fournirait un inventaire approprié aux deux registres de l'expression," etc. See also above, note 10.

[29] Here, one might compare Lacan's conception of the linguistic interchange in psychoanalysis: the analysand speaks to an audience that hears but does not engage in dialogue, an audience that knows both everything and nothing and maintains that knowledge or ignorance in silence. By retaining the distance, and often the silence, of the analytic situation, the psychoanalyst moves the analysand's language out of the familiar signifier-signified relation of the "normal" communicative interchange to a different, less familiar track, wherein the intransitive, non-communicating language of the unconscious comes into play. See Jameson in Felman (1977) 358ff., especially 368f.: "In the Lacanian scheme of things, the uniqueness of the analytical situation . . . derives from the fact that it is the one communicational situation in which the Other is addressed without being functionally involved. . . . So the subject's gradual experience of his or her own subordination to an alienating signifier is at one with the theorist's denunciation of philosophies of the subject and his Copernican attempt to assign to the subject an ec-centric position with respect to language as a whole."

TWO

Imagery and the Landscape of Desire

In all of Seneca's plays the psychological atmosphere depends heavily on imagery. In the *Phaedra* images of fire, enclosure, and heaviness and the contrasting imagery of interior and exterior space depict the stifling emotional world in which the characters seem entrapped. Against this mood of constriction, however, Seneca sets elaborate rhetorical descriptions of sky, forest, or sea. The concentrated energy of such descriptions sets into sharp relief the protagonists' ineffectiveness or helplessness in the face of the emotional violence within and around them.

I

INTERIORITY AND CORPOREALITY

Hippolytus ends his opening song with a call from the nearby forests and the expectation of a shortcut through a long journey (*longum iter*), his last words (82-84). Phaedra enters speaking of far-off places that stretch from great Crete to distant Assyria and from earth to underworld (85-99). When Hippolytus mentions enclosure, he refers to trapping animals (45-47, 74-76). But it is Phaedra, as we soon see, who is trapped in her passions, unable to mobilize the moral energy that could liberate her from her obsession. Hippolytus, outdoors, is surrounded by vigorous huntsmen and eager dogs; Phaedra, inside, converses only with an old domestic servant.[1]

The contrasts between house and forest are important in Euripides' play,[2] but Seneca uses them to explore the psychological implications of Phaedra's interior space. Compare the two descriptions of Phaedra's love sickness:

---

[1] Heldmann (1974) 85 notes how the opening scene concentrates everything on Hippolytus and Phaedra.

[2] E.g. Eur., *Hipp.* 131f., 180f., 208ff.

ἄρατέ μου δέμας, ὀρθοῦτε κάρα·
λέλυμαι μελέων σύνδεσμα φίλων.
λάβετ' εὐπήχεις χεῖρας, πρόπολοι.
βαρύ μοι κεφαλᾶς ἐπίκρανον ἔχειν.
ἄφελ', ἀμπέτασον βόστρυχον ὤμοις.   (*Hippolytus* 198-202)

Raise my body, lift my head. I am loosened in the bonds of
my own limbs. Take my graceful hands, servants. Heavy is
the coiffure of my head for me to carry. Take it away; spread
out my hair on my shoulders.

Removete, famulae, purpura atque auro inlitas
vestes, procul sit muricis Tyrii rubor,
quae fila ramis ultimi Seres legunt;
brevis expeditos zona constringat sinus,
cervix monili vacua, nec niveus lapis
deducat auris, Indici donum maris;
odore crinis sparsus Assyrio vacet.
Sic temere iactae colla perfundant comae
umerosque summos, cursibus motae citis
ventos sequantur. Laeva se pharetrae dabit,
hastile vibret dextra Thessalicum manus.   (*Phaedra* 387-98)

Servants, take away the robes dyed with purple, crusted
with gold. Far from me be the redness of Tyrian dye, the
threads that the remotest Chinese gather from the trees. Let
a small belt contain the folds (of my garment), thus kept out
of the way; let my neck be free of its necklace and let no
snow-white stone, the gift of India's sea, weigh down my
ears, and let my scattered hair be free of Assyrian perfume.
Let my locks, thrown thus in disorder, flow over my neck
and the top of my shoulders; moving in the swift running,
let them follow the winds. Let my left hand give itself to the
quiver, my right brandish a Thessalian javelin.

Euripides' description is almost bare of adjectives. The impression of constriction and heaviness is there in *meleōn sundesma*,
"the bonds of my limbs," and *baru*, "heavy." Seneca's descrip-

tion, however, creates the very different impression of a textured mass. Phaedra's garments are imbued or encrusted, literally smeared (*inlitae*) with purple and gold. She wants her hair, fragrant with Assyrian perfume, to be "poured" over her neck (393f.). In her adverb *temere*, "randomly," the disorder of her hair corresponds to an unruliness of spirit that seeks to throw off restraints.

Euripides' phraseology is also less visual and more general. The physiological vagueness of a verse like *lelumai meleōn sundesma philōn*, "I am loosed in the ties of my own limbs," results partly from the echo of Homeric diction, for in the epic formula limbs are often "loosened" in response to the elemental forces of sleep, death, or love. The rich robes, perfumes, jewels, and silks of Seneca's heroine, with their evocation of the luxurious East in the geographical epithets, owe not a little to the far more developed depiction of feminine sensuality in the literary tradition, from Virgil's Dido to Ovid's Phaedra of the *Heroides*.[3]

In her desire to imitate and pursue Hippolytus, Phaedra needs greater freedom. One physical expression of this desire is a rearrangement of her personal appearance. She wants to contain the *sinus* of her dress, the ample folds that might hinder her movements: *brevis expeditos zona constringat sinus* ("Let a small belt contain my folds, thus kept out of the way," 390). As *sinus* may have sexual connotations, her desire for a more masculine mode of dress and movement is also paradoxically the desire for the freedom from sexual constraints that is more characteristic of the male than the female in Roman society and in classical myth. Later, however, she reverses this yearning for masculine independence as she confesses her desire for enclosure in Hippolytus' embrace.

---

[3] See in general Paratore (1952) and Fantham (1975). Seneca has doubtless utilized the erotic atmosphere of Dido's banquet, *Aeneid* 1.697ff. He also imitates Euripides' "loosing of the limbs" (*Hipp.* 198f.) in 367f., *nunc ut soluto labitur moriens gradu / et vix labante sustinet collo caput* (see Grimal 1965, ad loc.); but again the differences are significant: Euripides' lines are spoken by Phaedra in the first person, and the "loosing" of the "bonds of the limbs" is far more general than the "loosened step," *soluto gradu*, of *Phaedra* 367.

Seneca characteristically conveys the emotional intensity of her desire through tactile, corporeal associations: the jewels and dress, the hair over her shoulders, the ornaments, the perfume. This immediacy of the physical, however, stands in a contrapuntal relation to the self-conscious literariness of the remote geography: Tyre, China, Assyria, India, Thessaly. Indeed this very tension between the intimately physical and the distancing rhetoric of the conventional poetic epithets sets the stage for the paradoxical combination of the need for self-gratification and alienation from self that is the condition of her illicit desire.

What in Euripides is part of the intellectualist theme of deceptive appearances (cf. *Hipp*. 925-31) becomes in Seneca a depiction of emotional intensity conveyed through more overtly physical, tactile sensations and focused on concrete objects. This difference can be illustrated by comparing the Nurse's description of Phaedra's love-sickness in the two plays. Euripides' Nurse says of Phaedra (*Hipp*. 279f.), "She hides her illness and denies that she is sick," to which the chorus replies, "But does not Theseus, looking at her face, infer anything?" (κρύπτει γὰρ ἥδε πῆμα κοὐ φησιν νοσεῖν. / ὁ δ᾿ ἐς πρόσωπον οὐ τεκμαίρεται βλέπων;). The corresponding passage in Seneca is 362f.: *torretur aestu tacito et inclusus quoque, / quamvis tegatur, proditur vultu furor* ("She is parched by a silent seething; and the madness too, although it is concealed, is betrayed by her face").[4] Euripides' words— *kruptei, blepei, prosōpon, tekmairetai* ("hides," "looks," "face," "infers")—belong to the play's intellectual vocabulary of discovery and knowledge.[5] The second half of the Nurse's state-

[4] Zintzen (1960), 42, juxtaposes the two passages only to prove Seneca's indebtedness to Euripides, without observing how radically Seneca has transformed the mood and spirit of the Greek. Barrett (1964), 36, notes the difference in tone, but sees only deterioriation: "after the dialogue, most ineptly, a scene (358-403) based on the sickbed scene of the second *Hipp*. (170ff.), with the determined Phaedra of the earlier scene lapsed suddenly into a neurotic."

[5] Throughout the play the countenance (*vultus*) is also the real or imagined cover for hidden desires. It betrayed Phaedra's love-madness (362f. and cf. 433). In Theseus' view it concealed Hippolytus' lechery ("That countenance, that feigned austerity," 913f.). Cf. also Theseus' remark on "concealing shamelessness with modesty," 918-22. The "regal beauty in the countenance" of Theseus at his return (*regium in vultu decus*, 829) also contrasts with his destruction

ment, *ou phēsin nosein*, "and she denies her illness," focuses the issue of hidden passion on the deceptiveness of language. Seneca's "enclosed love-madness," *inclusus furor*, however, gives the sickness an independent, concrete, and imagistic existence, for *furor*, rather than Phaedra, becomes the subject of two of the three present passive verbs—*torretur, tegatur, proditur* ("is parched," "is concealed," "is betrayed"). The imagery of fire in *torretur* and of spatial and emotional interiority in *inclusus* portrays Phaedra's erotic desperation, while *tegatur* and *proditur* carry connotations of guilt and anxiety. The *prosōpon* ("face") of *Hipp*. 280, on the other hand, places the emphasis far more on the inferential process of discovery (cf. also *tekmairetai*, "infers") than on the guilt itself.

Phaedra's first sentence in the play is a microcosm of her literal and figurative imprisonment (85-91):

O magna vasti Creta dominatrix freti,
cuius per omne litus innumerae rates
tenuere pontum, quicquid Assyria tenus
tellure Nereus pervius rostris secat,
cur me in penates obsidem invisos datam
hostique nuptam degere aetatem in malis
lacrimisque cogis?

O great Crete, ruler of the vast sea, over whose whole shoreline numberless ships have held the sea—whatever (of it) Nereus, where he affords passage to the prows, opens as far as the Assyrian earth—why do you compel me to pass

---

of the son's *decus* in 1110. In this theme of the "feigned countenance" and the contrast of surface appearance and hidden truth Seneca owes much to the motif of the *prosōpon* in Euripides' extant *Hippolytus*: see Segal (1970) 282f., 289f., and Seidensticker (1969) 150. Snell (1964), 43, argues that the motif of the *vultus* derives from Euripides' lost *Hippolytus*; see also R. Merkelbach, *RhM* 100 (1957) 99f.; contra Fantham (1975), p. 7 with note 1. For other aspects of the pathos and psychological depiction of Phaedra through the motif of the *vultus*, see Paratore (1952) 219-21 and Friedrich (1953) 131. Cf. also the chorus's song on the power of love to make even the gods disguise themselves with metamorphoses.

my time of life in woes and tears, given as hostage to hated
penates (household gods) and married to an enemy?

The greatness of Crete and Nereus' opening the sea to ships
contrast present constriction with the lost expansiveness of her
past. This contrast, as we have just seen, is intensified by the pull
between corporeal detail and remote geography in the overt
love-sickness of 387-98. When Phaedra says that she is "a hostage given to hated penates" (89f.), she views herself as a passive
object of exchange ("given"), at the mercy of forces beyond her
control. The words *hated* and *enemy* imply both a repugnance
toward her husband and her alienation from the physical and
emotional space in which she lives.[6]

Phaedra's language presents a world pervaded by sexuality.
Ships cut through the seas as far as Assyria, a place associated
with arousing perfumes (85-88; cf. 393). Here Theseus de-
scends boldly, for sexual motives, through the deep, dark lakes
of Tartarus, uninhibited by the fear and shame that hold Phaedra back (92-98). She, weighed down by the heaviness of unsatisfied desire, spends sleepless nights, bearing a suffering that
"grows and increases and burns within, as smoke billows forth
in Aetna's cavern" (100-103):

non me quies nocturna, non altus sopor
solvere curis: alitur et crescit malum
et ardet intus qualis Aetnaeo vapor
exundat antro.

The imagery of love as a wound nurtured within or as an inner
fire owes much to Virgil's description of Dido and Ovid's of
Phaedra in *Heroides* 4.[7] But the combination of fire, cavern, in-

[6] Gallardo (1973), 72-74, suggests that *hostique nuptam*, etc., may refer to the
historical events in the myth, the war between Athens and Crete; but the dramatic significance is far more personal.
[7] See Ovid, *Her.* 4.15, 19f., 33, 52, 70, etc.; also *Aen.* 4.1-4, 66-69; Ovid,
Met. 9.465 and 13.867ff. See in general Fantham (1975) 5-7, Campos (1972),
p. 205 with note 75 and p. 222 with note 154; Ruch (1964) 358-60; Liebermann (1974) 94f.

teriority (*intus*), and liquidity (*exundat*) is new and powerful.[8] The realistically defined space of a woman's chambers (cf. 89) opens into a remote mythical world of elemental forces.[9] Feeling herself excluded from the torches of holy fires at the altars of the chaste Eleusinian goddesses (105-9), Phaedra suffers the inner flames of an impure and secret passion.

The closed interior of Phaedra's nocturnal inquietude is soon coupled with another image of interior space imbued with illicit sexuality: the dark Cretan labyrinth where Daedalus enclosed "our monster in the dark house" (*qui nostra caeca monstra conclusit domo*, 122). Minos' palace, with its monster and sinister labyrinth, is the recurrent symbol of lust.[10] Against this mythical background Phaedra views herself as a seething hollow space of liquid fire (cf. 101-3). Although her passion leads her to thoughts of meadows and forests, also eroticized (112-17), she comes back to fire and the labyrinth: "What Daedalus could help my flames?" (120).

In the background too is Daedalus' other enclosure for the monstrosity of female lust, the wooden cow that enabled Pasiphae, Phaedra's mother, to satisfy her passion for the bull and thereby give birth to the Minotaur. The Nurse, reacting to

[8] Virgil, for example, brings sea and fire together to depict the passion of Dido, first as remote elements (*Aen.* 4.566f.) and then as a more terrifying threat in her anger and *furor* (600-606). In Seneca these motifs become almost totally internalized.

[9] One is reminded also of Seneca's *Medea*, with its contrast between the heroine's apparent enclosure and helplessness as she pleads for a "narrow corner" (248ff.) and the themes of exploration, the sea, the conquest of nature (301-79): see Lawall (1979) passim and Segal (1983b) 240f.

[10] Seneca could draw on Ovid, *Her.* 4.55-66 and 163f. The imagery of the monstrous creature enclosed in the labyrinth of Phaedra's sinful past may also owe something to Euripides' *Cretans*: see frags. 996 and 997 N (both cited by Plutarch, *Thes.* 15) and now *P. Oxy.* 2461, e.g. line 12, ταύρου μέμεικται καὶ βροτοῦ διπλῆ φύσει ("It is mingled with the double nature of both bull and mortal"). The Minotaur and Phaedra's heredity have been much discussed: see Fauth (1958) 549; Snell (1964) 32; Runchina (1966), p. 32 with note 68; Seidensticker (1969) 103; Vretska (1968) 164; Garton (1972) 200f.; Heldmann (1974) 95-98; Davis (1983) 117f.; Pratt (1983) 91; Petrone (1984) 109ff. The collocation of *caecā* and *monstra* and the rhyme *nostra . . . monstra* in 122 also help associate the monster with darkness and with the family of Phaedra ("our").

Phaedra's account of her passion, associates her criminal desire
with some hidden evil within herself that Phaedra must drive
out (*expelle*, 168). This is an evil that resembles her mother's
passion (168-72):

> expelle facinus mente castifica horridum
> memorque matris metue concubitus novos.
> miscere thalamos patris et gnati apparas
> uteroque prolem capere confusam impio?

> With purifying mind drive forth the fearful crime, and
> mindful of your mother take fear of strange new unions. Are
> you making ready to mingle the bedchambers of the father
> and the son and receive in unholy womb a brood confused?

In its multiple associations with Aetnean cavern, wooden
cow, accursed womb of Pasiphae, and dark Cretan labyrinth, interior space becomes a metaphorical representation of the inner
darkness of Phaedra's empty, incestuous desire. The absence of
her husband, "the father of Hippolytus" (48), in another dark,
hollow, liquid space intensifies in her previous lines (92-98) her
mood of sexual deprivation and allows for the release of the inhibiting fear and shame (*timor pudorque*, 96f.) that sets the action into motion.[11] But between desire and satisfaction stands
the obstacle of Hippolytus' antaphroditic landscape sketched in
his preceding monody: an open, external, virginal world of
fresh rivers, snowy mountains, and murderous weapons.

When Phaedra describes the inner fire of her passion, she uses
images of nurture and growth (*alitur et crescit malum*, "the evil
is nourished and grows," 101) that are absent from Hippolytus'
diction. At the same time this imagery also conveys her alienation from herself: something is growing inside her over which
she has no control. Here, as elsewhere, Senecan tragedy presents this self-estrangement or non-recognition of self through
a physical sensation of alienation from one's own body.[12] In the

---

[11] On the absent father, see Fauth (1958) 550 and Friedrich (1933) 41.

[12] The most powerful example is the end of *Thyestes*, where Thyestes' despair
takes the form of being trapped in himself, crammed full of the flesh of his own
sons: cf. *Thy.* 999ff.; also *Phoen.* 216ff.; in general Segal (1983a).

Phaedra each character's respective setting symbolizes this self-alienation. For Phaedra there is the loss of a rational center of control and decision; for Hippolytus a displacement of erotic into destructive energy; for Phaedra the sexual imagery of the house; for Hippolytus the desexualized violence of the forest world.

This distance between the respective psychological landscapes of the two characters contains the underlying structure of the work. It is a version of "Freud's Masterplot," to use Peter Brooks' convenient term:[13] an urgent sexual desire (vividly represented in the imagery of Phaedra's first twenty lines) comes up against the delaying factors that block satisfaction until finally love and death join together in the climactic thrust of a symbolic *Liebestod*. Penetration by Hippolytus' weapon would be the climax of the drive for both Eros and Thanatos. But the tragic plot must postpone this denouement; otherwise the play would end prematurely. By delaying the climactic penetration until a later point, Seneca creates the crucial retardation and tense excitement, enhanced by an underlying sexual component.

The fact that Phaedra replaces love with death, Hippolytus with the sword of Hippolytus, stamps her life with the tragic character of civilization itself, the ultimate victory of society's demands over individual desire and erotic freedom.[14] This is the theme that Racine, following Seneca, developed to an even great degree. Euripides' emphasis (at least in the extant play) falls on the catastrophic results of that disinhibition of female sexuality rather than on the reassertion of an oppressive patriarchal order. At the end, father and son are joined as victims in a strong male bonding that leads into the closing lamentation, on behalf of the city, for the lost son (*Hipp*. 1445-66). Seneca, however, is more concerned with the status of paternal authority than with the dangers of unrepressed female sexuality. In his play the Father can reach out to the woman, dead though she is, to punish her for her crime.

[13] Brooks (1977).
[14] I have in mind Freud's analysis of the human condition in works like *Civilization and Its Discontents*.

II
IMAGERY OF THE SEA

Phaedra's apparently objective mention of the sea as part of the geography of her homeland is quickly absorbed into the emotional subjectivity of her passion. The broad marine geography of her splendid opening line, *O magna vasti Creta dominatrix freti* (85), soon contracts to the inner waves of hidden passion (99-102: *exundat*, 103). Throughout Acts I and II liquid imagery conveys the force of her desire (204f., 392; cf. 450f.). The Nurse, by contrast, sums up Hippolytus' resistance with the image of the harsh reef (*dura cautes*) that stands unsoftened in the midst of the waves (*undique intractabilis . . . undis*, 580f.).[15] A few lines later, however, Phaedra is still caught in the "heavy tides" of her passion (*aestus graves*, 589; cf. 103).[16]

For Hippolytus the virgin sea, as it was before "the (too) trusting ships cut through the deep," belongs to a lost Golden Age of innocence (530f.), whereas the violence of historical time has left the ocean red with blood (551f.).[17] This nostalgia for an idealized epoch prior to sailing contrasts with Phaedra's pride in the wide outreach of the Minoan maritime power in her first lines of the play (85-88). After Phaedra's declaration of love, however, Hippolytus' sea is again a place of lost purity: not even the farthest seas or their god could wash off the stain of crime with which he feels polluted (715-18). The outcome, however, ironically recasts these invocations of the sea to affirm sexual purity: his sexual unattainability will be fixed irremediably by death from the sea. Theseus' curse brings forth from the sea a monster compared to a gigantic whale (*pistrix*) that "in the furthest sea sucks in or shatters swift-moving ships" (*talis extremo mari / pistrix citatas sorbet aut frangit rates*, 1048f.). Later,

---

[15] The simile recalls Aeneas before Dido (*Aen.* 4.439): see Fantham (1975) 8-10.

[16] Note too the Nurse's *fluxitque luxu* in her warning against love in 205, a reminder, perhaps, of the imagery of sea and passion in Phaedra's first speech (103).

[17] See below, chap. 4.

in the marine setting of his destruction, the sea reverts to a primordial violence far from the unrealistic harmlessness of his Golden Age (cf. 1048ff., 1072-75).

Phaedra's declaration of love takes the form of inviting Hippolytus into her sea-world of passion and fantasy. "If you had entered the Cretan strait with your father, for you my sister (Ariadne) would rather have spun her thread" (661f.):

> si cum parente Creticum intrasses fretum
> tibi fila potius nostra nevisset soror.

She would have Hippolytus enter both her Cretan sea and her Cretan palace. The erotic dimension of this imagined journey is made clear from her comparison of Hippolytus to the youthful Theseus: she first glimpsed the latter in the bloom of his youth, "when he saw the dark house of the Cnossian monster and gathered in the long threads along the curving path" (648-50):

> cum prima puras barba signaret genas
> monstrique caecam Gnosii vidit domum
> et longa curva fila collegit via.

Retrospectively she would lead Hippolytus into the dark chambers that are the play's mythical locus of illicit sexuality. The movement from the "vast strait" of Crete as a political power ("great mistress of the vast Ocean," 85) to the "Cretan strait" of her erotic fantasies (661) continues her identification with the Crete of Pasiphae and its sinful enclosures, rather than with the Crete of Minos and its political and moral authority (cf. 85-88, 149f., 245).[18] This identification marks the moment of her fullest surrender to her fantasies.

III
SEA AND SEXUAL DISASTER

Phaedra's gradual invasion of Hippolytus' world radically sexualizes the imagery of the sea as receptive "hollow" (*sinus*).

---

[18] The play, understandably, does not mention the severely moral role of Mi-

In her first, ambiguous declaration of love to him she fantasizes him as his father's successor who would "receive (her) in his *sinus*" and protect her as his "slave and suppliant" (*sinu receptam supplicem ac servam tege*, 622). The ambiguity of *sinus* here keeps her discourse still perched at the razor's edge between propriety and crime.[19] Yet the hope of a loving and sexual enclosure has already been undercut by his use of *sinus* some fifty lines before, where he denounced all women with a hyperbole about the sea's hollows (570f.): "Sooner shall Hesperian Tethys bring forth bright day from her farthest hollows (*ab extremo sinu*) than I be won over and bear a gentle spirit toward a woman."[20] In the account of Hippolytus' death the monster's arousal from "the turgid sea" gives the word *sinus* an ominously sexual meaning: *nescio quid onerato sinu / gravis unda portat* ("The heavy wave bears something in its burdened womb," 1016).

Phaedra, echoing both this passage and the language of reception and concealment in her first confession of love (*receptam, tege*, 622), carries the sexual implications farther. Her passion here reaches its final, self-destructive stage (1159-63):

> me, me, profundi saeve dominator freti,
> invade et in me monstra caerulei maris
> emitte, quidquid intimo Tethys sinu
> extrema gestat, quidquid Oceanus vagis
> complexus undis ultimo fluctu tegit.

> (Neptune), cruel master of the deep sea, Send forth into me, me, the blue sea's monsters and whatever remotest Tethys bears in her deepest womb, whatever Ocean in his embrace of wandering waves conceals in his furthest flood.

nos as a judge of the underworld (cf. *Ag.* 23f., *Thy.* 22f., *Herc. Fur.* 733); but perhaps the audience's knowledge of that fact adds to the fantasy-element in Phaedra when she counters the Nurse's evocation of Minos with her own view of a complaisant father (*mitis Ariadnae pater*, 245).

[19] Cf. also the word *sinus*, used of the folds of Phaedra's garment, in 390, discussed above, sec. I.

[20] These "hollows," however, soon return to the female as the reservoir of a monstrous sexual violence that Phaedra will evoke at the climax of her tragedy (1159ff., discussed below).

Defining Tethys' *sinus* in terms of the monstrous, Phaedra gives a phantasmagoric twist to Hippolytus' assertion of 570f.: "Sooner shall Hesperian Tethys lift bright day from her furthest hollow than I, overcome, bear a spirit kindly toward woman" (*ante ab extremo sinu / Hesperia Tethys lucidum attollet diem* . . .). Where he spoke of "furthest hollow," she speaks of "deepest hollow" (*extremo sinu, intimo sinu*). She views the sea in terms of depth and enclosure rather than horizontal extension. She also replaces his neutral "lift up" (*attollet*, 571) with the more procreative *gestat*, "bears" (1162). To his sea-goddess, defined in terms of geographical extension, (*Hesperia Tethys*, 571), she adds a male counterpart, Oceanus, a sexual partner who gives the embrace and enclosure that Hippolytus had refused her (cf. *complexus, tegit*, 1164; *sinu receptam tege*, "enclose me in protection, received in your bosom," 622). The contrast between his single Tethys and Phaedra's heterosexual pairing of fertile primordial divinities recapitulates the division between them at this point of its finality.

It is characteristic of this contrast that the imagery of Hippolytus' struggle against the monster shortly before presents the sea as the place of civilized man's combat with wild nature: the Messenger uses a simile (adapted from Euripides) of a pilot in a heavy sea (1072-75). This pilot does not lose control of his ship, as Phaedra's does in her simile of 181-83 (see below), but he fails nonetheless.

Phaedra's description of the sea's monstrosities in 1159-63 completes a sustained pattern of images wherein the sea focuses the conflict between her desire and the repressive authority of the father-figures in her background. In her first line of the play she associated the sea with female power in her Minoan past ("Great Crete, mistress of the vast sea," 85), with penetration (86-88), and with the release of the passions that the Father represses. But the Nurse, reminding Phaedra of her father's authority, soon places the sea under paternal control (149f.):

quid ille lato maria qui regno premit
populisque reddit iura centenis, pater?

What of him who holds down the seas in his broad rule and gives judgments to (Crete's) hundred peoples, your father?

Phaedra, however, affirms the power of her love in the simile of a ship and sailors impotent in the raging unmastered sea (181-83). The conquest, rule, and mastery of which she now speaks are just the opposite of the Nurse's paternal *regnum* or *dominatio* in 149f.: "Mad passion has won the victory and rules, and this god in his power over my whole mind has the mastery" (184f.: *dominatur deus*, 185).

The first choral ode, on Amor, extends the force of love even to the sea's lowest depths and to their king (*rex*, 336), the divine father-figure whose power from the waves will later overwhelm the guilty son. In the ode, however, Phaedra's desire is still in the ascendant, and the language develops the erotic implications of her opening lines (335-37):

> spicula cuius sentit in imis
> pervius undis rex Nereidum
> flammamque nequit relevare mari.

> (Amor) whose darts the king of the Nereids, who gives passage to (or with) the waves, feels in the lowest depths, and he cannot lighten the flame with the sea.[21]

When Phaedra passes once more under the power of the Father and his laws (in this case, the incest taboo), she reverses the meaning of her sea-imagery. She transfers the subjugation of the sea from female to male (from *dominatrix freti* in 85 to *dominator freti* in 1159) and from her homeland to the enemy kingdom of her marriage (cf. 89f.). The sea of Phaedra's opening lines is a political and commercial entity. It is dominated by Crete, delimited by shoreland, and traversed by ships: "*Mistress of the ocean, Crete, whose numberless ships on every shore* have

---

[21] I keep ms. E's reading in 336, with Grimal, instead of ms. A's *caerulus undis grex*. Cf. Phaedra's description of the sea dominated by the Minoan Empire in 88, the sea cut by "Nereus who gives passage to the prows" (of ships), *Nereus pervius rostris secat*. Cf. also 93f. and below, chap. 8, sec. VI, ad fin. For the importance of the first ode in the play as a whole, see now Davis (1984).

held the sea" (85-87). By contrast, her despairing cry of 1159-
63 portrays the sea as a deep, womb-like hollow, fertile in monsters (1160). But this monstrosity is no longer merely the abyss
of released female sexuality; it is also the form taken by the violence of repressive patriarchal authority as Phaedra imagines it
(1159f.).

IV
POETIC IMAGERY AND ETHICAL GENERALIZATION

So far we have examined some psychological implications of
Phaedra's language. A characteristically Senecan feature of this
psychological atmosphere is the combination of emotional intensity and gnomic generality. In the *Phaedra* Seneca creates a
dialogue, and sometimes a disjunction, between the figurative
language of the heroine's passions and the philosophical argu-
mentation of the Nurse. This counterpoint between poetic imagery and moral precept is especially marked in Phaedra's first
scene, where it helps define the deeply emotional nature of her
trouble.

The Nurse uses abstract ethical injunctions like "desire what
is honorable" (*honesta primum est velle*, 140) and warnings
about the fears and anxieties produced by guilt even when the
crime goes undetected (162-64). Initially she speaks the voice
of reason, society, sanity, and the laws of nature. But at another
level her diction and imagery turn Phaedra back upon the symbolic correlates of her desire. Thus she judges Phaedra as even
more culpable than Pasiphae, for the latter's crime was due to
"fate" whereas Phaedra's derives from moral character (*fatum,
mores*, 143f.). Yet the language of literal and figurative monstrosity (*monstro, monstra*) and the reference to the Minotaur
lead back to the imagery of sinful hollows, emptiness, longing
(cf. 122, 649, 689-93, 1171).

When the Nurse mentions Theseus "held and hidden in Lethean death" (147f.), she weakens the force of her warnings about
the remote father-figures in the sky, Neptune and Jupiter, distant substitutes for Theseus' patriarchal authority. In this play

the power belongs to the lower, subterranean realm that holds
Theseus below and allows Phaedra a free hand. Against Phaedra's belief that her "crime is safe and *empty* of fear" the Nurse
sets a "mind *full* of guilt" (*animus culpa plenus*, 163). "Check the
flames of an unholy love," she reiterates (165; cf. 131); "drive
out the dreadful crime from your chaste mind" (169). But that
image of outwardly directed action (*expelle*) brings with it,
nearly in the same breath, the exemplar par excellence of female
lust and ominous enclosure, the "strange beddings of (her)
mother," Pasiphae (170).

In elaborating on her warning exemplum, the Nurse in fact
strengthens the links between the guilty enclosures of Phaedra's
house, her sinful sexual desires, and the mythical emblem of female lust, the labyrinth (170-74). Even as she warns Phaedra
against "mingling the bedchambers of father and son" and "receiving in unholy womb a brood confused" (171f.), she evokes
another image of a sinful interior, the empty room of the monster, the Minotaur's prison (174): *cur monstra cessant? aula cur
patris vacat?* ("Why do monsters cease? Why does your father's
hall stand empty?").[22] This interior emptiness, especially in
combination with the fires of passion in the previous line ("Go
and overturn nature with your criminal fires"), takes us beyond
the delusive emptiness of a crime free of fear (*vacuum metu*,
146) and back to the sexual imagery of inner space in 101ff.

Phaedra's reply reasserts the force of her love-madness (*furor*)
and the flames of passion that the Nurse would have her extin-
guish (187; cf. 313 and 165). As in her opening lines about
Crete, her imagery absorbs the external world into the inner
realm of her passion. She begins with an intellectualist vocabulary that closely follows her Euripidean model: *quae memoras
scio / vera esse, Nutrix*, "I know, Nurse, that what you say is true"
(177f.). As she moves from the objective truth of what she can
recognize in the Nurse's words to the subjective truth of her

---

[22] I keep the reading of ms. E, with Grimal, in 174. Ms. A has *fratris*, preferred by Giardina, which is unnecessary as the reference is to the Minotaur in
any case.

own feelings, she shifts to the quasi-personification of the love-madness (*furor*) which compels her to follow the worse (*sed furor cogit sequi / peiora*, 178f.). At that point her mind too (*animus*) becomes a quasi-independent being, alive amid violent forces. It is still an intellectual entity, "knowing" (*sciens*, repeating *scio* in 177), but it also "goes into a headlong plunge" (*vadit animus in praeceps sciens*, 179). In the next verse her language entirely forsakes the ratiocinative vocabulary of "truth" and "knowledge" for the emotionally colored image of a heavily freighted ship amid stormy waters that drive it to ruin (181f.). When *ratio* returns in the language of abstract reasoning, it is now the despairing admission, *quid ratio possit?* ("What power can reason have?" 184). After this, *furor* returns as an omnipotent force, almost a living being, in fact a divine being: *vicit ac regnat furor, / potensque tota mente dominatur deus* ("the love-madness has conquered and rules and a powerful god is lord in my whole mind," 184f.).

When the Nurse suggests that Theseus may not be irrevocably trapped in Hades, she is opposing reality to Phaedra's fantasies. Yet reality becomes curiously blended with fantasy as the Nurse champions the likelihood of a mortal returning from Hades, traditionally the most inflexible of all realities.[23] Even the checks to Phaedra's passion have something of an unreality about them. Phaedra fortifies her hopes with another fantasy, that Theseus will be a complaisant husband tolerant of his wife's amours (225).

At this point Phaedra's thoughts, as before (112-18), shift to the world outside. Turning away from Theseus, she evokes the object of her fantasies, Hippolytus and his hunting, groves, and mountains (233-35).[24] The outward reaching of her love, as she prepares to "follow (Hippolytus) over the very seas if he should

---

[23] E.g., Pindar, *Pyth.* 3.57ff.; Eur., *Alc.* 962ff.
[24] The motif of Phaedra's longing for the forests also appears in Eur., *Hipp.* 221; see Henry and Walker (1966) 230; also Knox (1979) 207f.; Segal (1965) 130; Glenn (1976) 439f. Cf. also Ovid, *Her.* 4.73f. and 77. The power of love has just the opposite effect on Hercules, whom it causes to exchange the masculine (and phallic) weapons of club and arrows for the woman's distaff (316-24).

flee" (241), is checked momentarily by the Nurse's logic. Determined to die, Phaedra now exercises will and reason. Reversing the pattern of 179ff., she shifts from the language of desire to words like *ratio, decerno, quaero, constituo* ("reason," "decree," "search for," "decide," 253, 258, 265). But the Nurse astutely recognizes in this outburst only another face of *furor* (cf. 268). The ensuing ode, on the power of "the goddess born from no gentle sea" (*diva non miti generata ponto*, 274), confirms this movement back to the imagery of passion, with its seething and its fires (cf. 102f. and 274-75) and her wish to pursue Hippolytus "through the very seas" (241).

As in her first speech, vast geography contracts to the narrow limits of interior pain. The ode on love alternates the sea of Venus' mythical birth (274) and the expansive geography of Cupido's dominion over the whole world (183-90) with the inner flames of love-madness that "slips into all the marrows as the hidden fire ravages the veins" (*labitur totas furor in medullas, / igne furtivo populante venas*, 279f.).[25] "Love's blow does not have a broad expanse," the chorus continues, "but deep within devours the concealed marrows" (*sed vorat tectas penitus medullas*, 281f.). This generalized description of love's effects is realized specifically for Phaedra as she repeats many of these same terms in her declaration to Hippolytus (640-44, cited below). The fire "submerged in (her) deepest entrails and hidden in her veins" (642f.) then forms part of another contrast between interior and exterior space, emotional and geographical reality, when she speaks of Greece, Scythia, and a journey across the Cretan sea in clarifying her passion (659ff.; cf. 85ff.).

V

FIRE

Besides the sea, Seneca uses the familiar metaphors of the inner fires of love to suggest the psychological rhythm of passion, the fluctuation between advance and stasis in the hopelessness

---

[25] Lines 279f. are omitted in A. For their authenticity, see Grimal (1965) ad loc.

of Phaedra's obsession.[26] He combines Euripides' objectified, anthropomorphic crystalization of love as a divine power, "of shimmering wing and golden light"[27] with the subjectivizing, psychological vocabulary of Virgil.[28] He thereby creates an atmosphere of a demonic interiority of both body and soul that has no equivalent in Euripides and is only adumbrated in Virgil.

In her opening speech Phaedra compared her passion to "steam in the Aetnean cavern" (102f.). The Nurse had warned her of the patriarchal authority symbolized by Jupiter's Aetnean thunderbolt (*fulmen Aetnaeum*, 156). Phaedra replies by reaffirming the power of those subterranean fires of passion: "Love's fire overcomes even Vulcan who tends the raging furnaces in Aetna's ridges" (*furentis semper Aetnaeis iugis / versat caminos*, 190f.). Jupiter and Vulcan, the wielder and the maker of the celestial fire, are themselves subject to the baser fires of love (187-91; cf. 681f., 959f.).[29] Even as she utilizes the celestial myths of the Olympians, Phaedra imbues them with the atmosphere of her own heavy passion, the pain of love that weighs upon her (99; cf. 142). For all the lightness of his flight, the winged god of love, says Phaedra, is "heavy (*gravis*) to sky and earth alike" (194).

The motif of fire helps effect the transition from the chorus on love to the crisis that develops within Act II. The chorus sings of "old enmity yielding to the fires (of love)" (353f.) and then asks the Nurse, "Is there any limit to her savage flames?" (359). The Nurse's reply makes these flames even more vivid (360-66):

spes nulla tantum posse leniri malum
finisque flammis nullus insanis erit.

[26] Cf. 99-102, 358-66, 640-43. For fire imagery in the play generally, see Pratt (1963) 220ff.; Ruch (1964) 358f.; Campos (1972,) p. 205 with note 75 and p. 222 with note 154.

[27] Eur., *Hipp.* 1270f., 1275; *Phaedra* 276-78.

[28] In 274ff. Seneca is also drawing on Euripides' first stasimon in *Hipp.* 524ff., 558ff., and also on 447ff.

[29] Compare Eur., *Hipp.* 452ff. and Sen., *Pha.* 186ff. Euripides' lines have none of Seneca's developed fire-imagery, which, however, does occur in the next ode (*Hipp.* 530ff., 559ff., and cf. 684).

torretur aestu tacito et inclusus quoque,
quamvis tegatur, proditur vultu furor;
erumpit oculis ignis et lassae genae
lucem recusant; nil idem dubiae placet
artusque varie iactat incertus dolor.

There is no hope that so great a suffering can be softened;
and her mad fires will have no limit. She is parched by a
silent seething heat; and the love-madness too, concealed
though it be, is betrayed upon her face. The fire bursts forth
from her eyes, and the weary orbs refuse their brightness. Of
ever-shifting mood, she takes no pleasure in the same thing,
and an unsteady pain tosses about her limbs in different
ways.[30]

These inner fires contrast with the fire of "Phoebus' torch" and
the celestial fire of her grandfather, the Sun, with which her eyes
used to shine (379f.). Now tears, not flames, come from her
eyes (381-83). The language again echoes Phaedra's first speech
(99-102, especially 102: *ardet intus qualis Aetnaeo vapor*). But
the enclosed fire is here nearer to bursting forth (*erumpit* 364;
cf. *proditur*, 363) as the doors of the palace open to reveal the
lovesick queen in her hopeless passion.

The stage action of showing the queen languishing in her palace interior enacts the process of revealing the mystery of passion hidden in her soul. After the Nurse has described Phaedra's
emotional state in 380-83, the palace doors open in 384 (*sed en
patescunt regiae fastigia*) to show the queen putting off her oriental silks, perfumes, jewels (384-93).[31] Both the metaphors of
Phaedra's inner flames in 360-66 and her external appearance in
387-96 call attention to her physical presence and her subjec-

[30] Fantham (1975), 6f., points out the echoes of *Aen.* 4.66-69 in 362-65, but
Seneca's stress on the interior nature of this *furor* is stronger (his *inclusus*, 362,
does not occur in Virgil). There is doubtless an echo of Virgil's Dido in the reference to oriental luxury in 387ff. At the same time Seneca is also drawing on
the mystery of what is hidden beneath the queen's sick body in Eur., *Hipp.*
138f., 170-75, 179f., 267-69.

[31] On *fastigia*, which seems to indicate an upper story, perhaps a higher plat-
form on the stage, see Grimal (1965) ad loc.; also below, note 36.

tion to her physical being. The langorous immobility of 387-95 belies her energetic ambitions in 395-403, hunting and throwing her hair to the winds (395ff.). She is still bound to that interior world of luxury and sensuality.

When she comes to confess her love openly to Hippolytus, she combines the imagery of fire with that of submersion in her previous response to the Nurse (219-21). She addresses Hippolytus as follows (641-44):

$$
\begin{array}{ll}
\text{pectus insanum vapor} & 641 \\
\text{amorque torret. intimis furit ferus} & 642 \\
\text{visceribus ignis mersus et venis latens} & 643 \\
\text{ut agilis altas flamma percurrit trabes.} & 644
\end{array}
$$

The vaporous steam of love burns my maddened breast.
Wild fire submerged in my inmost vitals seethes there and hidden runs through my veins, just as the nimble fire runs along the lofty beams.[32]

Here Phaedra's passion is no longer only an inner flame but resembles a fire that leaps upward to the "high beams" of the house (641-44). Instead of being part of a simile, as in her first speech (99-102), this fire is the reality of her psycho-physiological torment of love: hence the coordinate construction of *vapor* and *amor* (*pectus insanum vapor / amorque torret*, "heat and *love* parch my mad breast," 641f.).[33] As Phaedra lets her passion out into the open, the dark house which kept her prisoner and symbolized the repression of her sexual desires is overcome by an

---

[32] With Otto Zwierlein, "Interpolierte und eche Liebesglut: Zu Senecas Phaedra 640-44," *Hermes* 103 (1975) 252-55, I follow Leo in deleting line 642 which Grimal (1965) attempts to retain, reading *penitus medullis atque per venas meat*. But in that case the repetition of *venas . . . venis* remains awkward; and in any case the line repeats 282. For the bursting forth of enclosed fire Zwierlein offers a close parallel with Virgil, *Georg.* 2.303ff. Rozelaar (1976), 510, notes that these lines on fire come at the very center of the play. Line 644 may also owe something to Lucretius 2.191f.: *nec cum subsiliunt ignes ad tecta domorum / et celeri flamma degustant tigna trabesque . . .* ("Nor when the fires leap up to the roofs of the houses and with their swift flames taste the timbers and the beams").

[33] On the development of the similes, see Primmer (1976) 220f.

enclosed violence that breaks forth to the outside (643f.). Now
it is not Theseus who is submerged in darkness (220f.) but the
savage fire that is submerged in her own body. Once more the
imagery of enclosure shifts from external reality (Theseus in
Hades) to subjective emotional state. That emotion, however,
is now catalyzed as action; and once more the imagery expresses
a dynamic transformation from one stage to another.

As Phaedra grows bolder, she declares herself ready to pursue
Hippolytus through fires and maddened sea (700).[34] Pursuit
through fire now replaces her earlier desire to follow him
through cold and snowy mountains.[35] In her remorse at the
end, however, her pursuit through lakes of fire (*per amnes igneos
amens sequar*, 1180) gives her erotic journey a mood and a purpose very different from her earlier fantasies.[36]

VI
THE OUTSIDE WORLD: THESEUS

In contrast to Phaedra, Theseus is always defined in terms of
his external orientation to the house. She, feeling imprisoned
(99f.), perceives him as wandering in Hades, not held back (*te-
nuit*, 97), and seeking new loves (*quaerit*, 98). After the scene
with Hippolytus she locks herself more deeply into the house,
whereas Theseus approaches from outside (829ff.) and stands
in limine ipso, "on the very threshold" (852). Earlier in the play
the doors open from inside to display her lovesick condition
(384-86). Later Theseus approaches the doors from outside

[34] Cf. the combination of fire and sea in Hippolytus' adynaton rejecting
women in 568. Cf. also 241 and 364. See also the end of sec. VI, below, on the
imagery of the "torch" of death and life.
[35] Cf. 233-35, 613-16; also 242. For the motif of "following through snow,"
see Henry-Walker (1966) 237f.; Paratore (1957) 67; Segal (198–). Seneca is
utilizing here the traditions of Roman amatory poetry, perhaps to add to the
mood of hopelessness and elegiac fantasy. The mss. at 702 are divided between
the readings *sequar*, "I shall follow" (A), and *agar*, "I shall be driven" (E). With
Grimal (1965) ad loc., I prefer *agar*, which is more expressive and avoids the
close repetition of *sequar* at the end of 700. It is arguable, on the other hand,
that the repetition is appropriate to Phaedra's insistence and desperation at this
crisis.
[36] Cf. also her view of Theseus' descent to the Underworld for an erotic
crime. With 1180 cf. also Theseus' words at 1226f. and see below, chap. 9.

and must force them open to see the trouble within (860ff.). For him the sources of evil and corruption lie not in the inner chambers but in the remote, barbarian places of the far North (906-14). The doom he calls down on the house is to come from outside too, from the natural forces of sky and sea (954-58).

Although in her opening lines Phaedra associates herself with the vastness of the sea ruled by her homeland, Crete, she regards the sea as passive, traversed (*pervius*, 88), and penetrated (cf. *secat*, "cuts," 88) by innumerable ships. It is Theseus, on the other hand, who strives successfully to make his way from dark enclosures to the light, "through the deep shadows of the pathless lake" (*invii lacus*, 93f.) or to "find the paths that have been refused" (*solus negatas invenit Theseus vias*, 224). This energy in finding paths through dangerous places is related to his sexuality and its freedom. Phaedra, in her seductive speech to Hippolytus, casts Theseus' conquest of Ariadne into the form of a journey along a path of darkness into light (cf. 650f.); and Theseus himself reasserts his possession over Phaedra by an initial gesture of opening gates (858ff.). In the rhythm of advance and staticity that characterizes Phaedra's tragedy, however, the opening of the house only closes her more deeply into the interior darkness of her desperation (835ff., especially 860-65).

The end of the play restates these spatial contrasts in a powerful configuration. Although Phaedra and Theseus both confront Hippolytus' torn body before the palace, Phaedra's moral and emotional struggle is defined by the inner chambers of the house and all that they signify for her life as wife and woman (1184-87). Though she calls on all Athens to hear the truth (1191), her last movements are toward a dark interior space, "the appeased hollows" of Hades which she asks to be spread open (*pande placatos sinus*, 1190). Even her death takes the form of opening the gates of a "house" and reentering an interior realm in terms of which she has been defined (89ff., 99ff., 384-86).

When Theseus reenters the house, however, he still belongs to the space outside. When he calls to the servants, "Here, carry here, the remains of the dear body" (*huc, huc reliquias vehite cari corporis*, 1247), he implies its movement from sea and forest where the death occurred up to, but not into, the house before which he now stands. When he speaks of "house," he describes not going inside the palace but travelling to the remote realm of Hades (1238-43; cf. 1201ff.), a metaphorical "eternal house" (1241) which from the beginning has been associated in his case with distant wanderings rather than enclosure (91-98).

His final command, "Throw open the house bitter with funereal slaughter" (1275), shows him as an outsider approaching a closed interior (829ff.; cf. Phaedra in 1190). His next instructions, "Prepare the pyre" and "Search out the parts of the body scattered among the fields" (*per agros corporis partes vagas / inquirite*, 1278f.), again set his exterior-directed space over against Phaedra's interiority. His concerns are with movement and with the large places of the outside world, the open air implied by the pyre, the fields to which he sends his servants.[37]

At the first access of grief he had asked to be submerged (*mersum*, 1203) beneath the earth; but he combines the stationary verb, *premite* ("press down") which he applies to Phaedra at the end (*premat*, 1279), with the active motion of *rapite*: *impium rapite atque mersum premite perpetuis malis* ("Carry me off, unholy, and press me down submerged with eternal woes," 1203; cf. 1206). Like Phaedra, he asks the underworld to open up for him: *dehisce, tellus* ("Gape open, earth," 1238; cf. 1190, *pande placatos sinus*). But whereas the imagery of the opened hollows (*sinus*) suffices for her, he adds words of journey and travel: *via*, "road" (1239); *sequor*, "follow" (1240); *venimus*, "come" (1241); *exiturum*, "go forth" (1242).

Even in his closing thoughts of death he organizes his world in terms of motion outside (1276-79), hers in terms of enclosure and stasis (1279f.). In the same breath, the same line, he consigns Phaedra to the ultimate form of enclosure: burial beneath a heavy weight of earth (1279f.): *istam terra defossam premat, / gravisque tellus impio capiti incubet* ("As for her, let the

[37] Cf. *vehite*, 1246; *inquirite*, 1279; also *agros, vagas*, 1278.

earth press her down, and let the soil *lie heavy* upon her unholy head"). Nearly every word of this curse, the last two lines of the play, fixes her in oppressive immobility.

Even the grammatical construction stresses Phaedra's passivity in contrast to the energetic movement that Theseus enjoins upon his attendants: they are the subjects of second-person active verbs, *patefacite, apparate, inquirite*; she is the direct object of the verb "press down" and the indirect object of the verb "lie upon." In the change from the accusative *istam* to the dative *impio capiti* she is not only moved farther from direct action but also reduced metonymically to a part of her body, degraded and reified.

Theseus' imprecation harks back to Phaedra's opening speech (cf. 99), and the circularity in the structure reinforces the mood of futility in her tragedy. In this circular pattern the marriage torch (*iugalis fax*) with which in fantasy she would conceal her crime (597) becomes the funeral torch that in a single blaze consumes "the pyre of a son and the bier of the marriage-bed" (*funebres una face / ut concremarem prolis ac thalami rogos*, 1215f.).[38] Replacing love with death, a union of bodies with a union of doomed destinies (*fata*, 1183f.), Phaedra fuses the rites of marriage with the rites of the funeral (cf. 1184-90). It is funerary ritual that ends the play. The heaviness of desire becomes the heaviness of earth in the funeral formula of 1279f.

VII
HEAVINESS

Phaedra initially described her passion with an image of weight: "But another greater pain lies upon me in my sadness" (*maior alius incubat maestae dolor*, 99). Elsewhere in the trage-

---

[38] On the "torch" of marriage and death, see Skovgaard-Hansen (1972) 121f., who also suggests a connection with the *ambusta sudes* of Hippolytus' death, 1098. Cf. also the pure torches of the choruses honoring the Eleusinian goddesses and Minerva, from which Phaedra feels cut off, 105-9, and the now dulled torches of fire in her eyes, 379f. Campos (1972), 231, cites a close parallel with *Oed.* 54f. The collocation of the torch of marriage and the torch of the funeral is a commonplace of funerary epigrams for those who die young: see G. B. Conte, *Il genere e i suoi confini* (Torino 1980) 99f. For literary adaptations cf. Ovid, *Her.* 21.172 and *Fasti* 2.561f.

dies Seneca uses the verb *incubare* with associations of death, fear, and destructive wrath.[39] Phaedra's troubled spirit echoes that of Virgil's Dido in the first stage of her equally fatal love (*Aen.* 4.82f.):

> sola doma *maeret* vacua stratisque relictis
> *incubat.*

> Alone she grieves in the empty house and lies on the abandoned coverlets.

In Virgil, however, it is the queen herself, subject of *incubat*, who lies on the bed, whereas Seneca, with a characteristic concretization of the emotional reality, makes *dolor* subject: it is the grief of love that "lies upon" Phaedra (*incubat maestae dolor*, 99).

Phaedra takes up the image a little later as she views her house as the victim of Venus' wrath that "lays the weight (*onerat*) of crimes unspeakable upon the whole race" (126f.). The Nurse turns the imagery of heaviness in a different direction: "Why do you weigh down (*aggravas*) your infamous house and surpass your mother" (142f.). The active verb implies the power of moral choice and the exercise of will. But when Phaedra uses the image again, it is once more in a passive sense and to convey her helplessness: in the sea of her passion she is like a heavily freighted ship (*gravatam ratem*) whose crew can do nothing against the elements (*cedit in vanum labor*, 181-83).[40] In this simile the ships of Phaedra's first lines (85-88) have lost their mobility as vessels that traverse the open sea of the Minoan empire. Instead, they confront the sea as an obstacle to movement, something that weighs on them as they try to push through (*sic cum gravatam navita adversa ratem / propellit unda*, "as when the sailor drives forth his heavily freighted ship against the opposing wave," 181f.).

[39] *Thy.* 401-3, 733f.; *Oed.* 47. See also Grimal (1965) ad 99; Ruch (1964) 356; Henry-Walker (1966) 228.
[40] For the Virgilian and Lucretian echoes, see Grimal (1965) ad 179f.: Lucr. 2.1164ff.; Virgil, *Georg.* 1.201ff. See also Davis (1983) 121.

The only active force against that weight of *dolor* is suicide, and Phaedra uses a related word when she contemplates that form of resisting her passion: "Shall I end my life with the noose, or shall I lie upon the sword?" (*an ferro incubem*, 259). She thus foreshadows the Dido-like consequences of her love. The Nurse picks up the word once more as she impels Phaedra's love on its disastrous course (267f.): *si tam protervus incubat menti furor / contemne famam* ("If so headstrong a madness *lies upon* your soul, scorn reputation"). She thus brings us back to the heavy *dolor* of Phaedra's first speech (*incubat maestae dolor*, "grief sits upon me in my sadness, 99),[41] but aggravates the *dolor* to the more dangerous *furor*.

This "heaviness" surrounding Phaedra contrasts sharply with the freedom and movement that the Nurse would instill in Hippolytus. In her plea on Phaedra's behalf she tries to turn him away from the "heavy punishments" of his ascetic life (*poenis gravibus*, 439) toward Bacchus who would unburden his heavy cares (*curas Bacchus exoneret graves*, 445). Youth, she argues, flees with nimble steps (446), and he should race after it with full speed lest it flow away (450f.). He has need of lively freedom (*vegeta libertas*, 460). Hippolytus, however, is devoted to a freedom of another kind, and responds with praise of the life of the country, free and lacking vice (*libera et vitio carens*, 483), open to random wandering in fresh air (501f., 505ff.). When sleep "presses down" (*premit*) the limbs, it bestows a tranquillity untouched by anxiety (*secura*, 522), in contrast to Phaedra's care-ridden, sleepless nights inside (cf. *curis*, 101). He explicitly rejects dark interior chambers for the open sky (522-25). His confidence in his rustic life will prove to be misplaced, but in any case the Nurse's efforts here widen rather than narrow the gap between him and Phaedra.

Respite from oppressive sadness is only momentary; the motif of heavy weight comes back with Phaedra's return to the stage. Collapsing in Hippolytus' arms and then regaining con-

---

[41] The echo between 99 and 268 is noted without comment by Grimal (1965) ad loc.

sciousness, she asks, "Who gives me back to grief and calls back the *heavy* surges to my spirit?" (*quis me dolori reddit atque aestus graves / reponit animo?* 589f.). Caught in her tragedy, Hippolytus, instead of lying carefree on a grassy riverbank (504ff., 520ff.), will lie dead in tearful doom (*flebili leto occubat*, 997); and his death is part of the ill-fortune that "weighs down (*aggravet*) the shaken house" (996). At the end he will be the dead weight of an inert body and a random heap of limbs (*corporis pondusque et artus temere congestos*, 1247f.).[42] This is all that Theseus, in his repentant sorrow, has left to "fall upon" (*incumbens*) and embrace (1255). *Incubare*, finally, shifts back to Phaedra in the play's last lines, Theseus' imprecation that the earth "lie heavy" on her head (*incubet*, 1280).

VIII
SKY

Both Phaedra and Hippolytus suffer the disintegration of their desires, values, and aspirations as a closing in of expansive horizons. The imagery that presents Hippolytus' doom as a fall from the celestial brightness of his ostensibly innocent life (1090-92, 1111f.) also links their suffering. Whereas Euripides' imagery of the sky is related to mythical patterns of adolescent passage,[43] Seneca develops the psychological implications of entrapment.

In Hippolytus' first encounter with Phaedra's desire through the intermediary of the Nurse, he opposes wandering beneath an open sky (501f.) to being covered (*tegi*) by a hall with a thousand columns (496f.). His idealized mode of life searches "for no thievish deeds in inner chamber or in secret bed of shamelessness," but rather "seeks the aether and the light and lives with the sky as his witness" (522-25). But Phaedra's offer of an-

---

[42] Grimal (1965) ad loc. notes that *pondus* has often troubled commentators and been frequently emended; Zintzen (1960), 125, aptly cites Eur., *Ba.* 1216f., Cadmus' instructions to his attendants as they return from Cithaeron with his grandson's body, "Follow me, bearing the miserable weight of Pentheus" (φέροντες ἄθλιον βάρος Πενθέως).

[43] See below, chap. 5; also Segal (1979) passim.

other vision of life sends him to the opposite extreme: he prays
to Jupiter for the closing in of the sky (674f.): "Let all the aether
collapse and hide the day in black clouds" (*atris nubibus condat
diem*, 675). Phaedra, ironically, makes her false accusation
against him with an invocation to the heavenly gods and "the
shining flash of the aether's light, from whose risings our house
claims its origins" (888-90). Those origins, however, also belong to subterranean darkness (cf. 122, 649). In another reversal of the pattern, Theseus, believing Phaedra, echoes Hippolytus' oath of 674-75 when he utters his imprecation against his
son (955f.):

nunc atra ventis nubila impellentibus
subtexe noctem, sidera et caelum eripe.

Now weave a veil of night, as the winds bring on black
clouds; snatch away the stars and the sky.

As a place of divine vengeance the sky supposedly protects the
desexualized world that Hippolytus has shaped for himself (cf.
671ff.). But the sky of the chorus's first ode is ruled by Amor
and Venus, who degrade Olympian gods to shameful metamorphoses (186f., 198-201, 294ff.).

In the choral ode after Phaedra's declaration of her passion
the sky reflects the violence and destructiveness of Hippolytus'
ostensibly innocent or harmless life (cf. 502).[44] "Should it
please you to scatter your arrows, Parthian-like, into the sky,"
the chorus sings, "none will fall back without its bird; buried
deep in the warm entrails (*tepido viscere condita*), they will bring
the prey down from the midst of the clouds" (*de mediis nubibus*,
816-19). The contrast between the airy distance of *nubibus mediis* (819) and the physiological interior of the birds' *tepido viscere* (818) praises the archer's strength, but also conveys the pathos of the victim (cf. *viscera* in 53). The next chorus extends
that violence in the celestial regions from the microcosm of the

[44] For other aspects of this ode, see below, chap. 3, pp. 67-72.

individual personality to the macrocosm of the governance of the universe.

"Is this the face that shone with celestial light?" Theseus laments at the end over his son's body (*haecne illa facies igne sidereo nitens*, 1269?). The celestial light that has gone out of Hippolytus' eyes is also the fire of the Stoic world-soul of which a portion burns in the human spirit. What has been extinguished in Hippolytus is not just the individual life but something that has implications for the order of the world, as we see from comparing 1123ff. with the chorus on the governance of the universe, 959ff.[45]

The dimming of celestial fire links Hippolytus' fate with Phaedra's tragedy, for her eyes too, "once were wont to bear the starry signs of Phoebus' torch" (*qui ferebant signa Phoebeae facis*, 379). Now they lose that radiance in the malady of love, as those fires are dampened by the moisture of her tears (381-83).[46] Associated not only with the divinely governed order of the heavens but also with the emotional violence of the three major characters, the motif of the sky and the celestial fires links the breakdown of order in the microcosm with the flawed order of the macrocosm; it connects cosmic disorder with disorder in the individual soul. For all of Seneca's Stoic doctrine of a divinely governed providence, what elicits his most powerful poetry is the violence of passion, be it the force of love or the life-destroying anger of the father on earth and the father in the heavens.[47]

As a philosopher, Seneca is on the side of reason and reason's control of passion. As a poet, he is concerned with shaping a compelling representation of the psychological forces that reason must repress. Whether Seneca's own unconscious desires

[45] Compare also 972ff. and 1128ff. Croisille (1964), 283f., sets out the discrepancies between this pessimistic view of Fortuna and orthodox stoicism. See also Dingel (1974) 99f. and Boyle (1985) 1300ff.

[46] The phrase *signa Phoebeae facis* in 379, "the signs of Phoebe's torch," also connotes the luminosity of celestial bodies, as *signa* often refers to constellations.

[47] Cf. 671ff., 888ff., 903ff., 955ff.

and unsublimated sexual energies are also engaged in sympathy for Phaedra is a question that it is tempting to answer in the affirmative.[48] For Seneca *qua* poet, in any case, as for Euripides before him and Racine after him, the power of the myth lies in the ultimately unresolvable and therefore tragic conflict between the irrational power of sexual drives and society's insistence that those drives be sublimated.[49]

[48] See below, chap. 10, sec. III.

[49] See Orlando (1973) 74ff. = (1978) 176ff.; also (1978) 17ff., 22ff., for this view of the relation between the emotional power of poetry, with its roots in the unconscious, and the ideology enunciated in the rational superstructure of the work. Karl Reinhardt, "Die Sinneskreis bei Euripides," in *Tradition und Geist: Gesammelte Essays zur Dichtung*, ed. Carl Becker (Göttingen 1960) 236f., criticizing Wilamowitz's reduction of Phaedra to a bourgeois heroine afraid of scandal like an Ibsenian figure, remarks, "Das psychologische Drama des 19. Jahrhunderts suchte das Individuelle; das Individuelle war ein Wert an sich, mochte es jedes Individuum nach seiner Erfahrung sich bestätigen. Das Antike zeigte das Heroische, wie es im Lichte der neuen Erkenntnis in Splitter bricht" (237).

THREE

The Forest World

The emotional violence that Phaedra releases from Hippolytus' ostensibly peaceful landscape reveals the contradictions in his character and the precariousness of a personality that uses violence as a defense against sexuality. Seneca owes the basic structure of the situation to Euripides, but he develops it with a density and consistency of imagery that produce an entirely new way of presenting character.[1]

Phaedra is the only Senecan tragedy to begin with a lyrical solo part.[2] Although formally detached from the action of the play, this passage, Hippolytus' hunting song, has an important function. It is not merely a pretext for an elaborate description of a favorite pastime of Seneca's contemporaries nor a showpiece of vignettes of natural scenery. It reveals Hippolytus in and through the landscape appropriate to him.

The "shady woods" of his first line strike a pastoral note. But he is addressing his hunters, whom he exhorts to scour the countryside for prey, "Go and gird the shady woods" (*ite umbrosas cingite silvas*, 1). The following lines add further details to the appearance of rustic tranquillity (9-16):

hac, hac, alii, qua nemus alta
texitur alno, qua prata iacent
quae rorifera mulcens aura
Zephyrus vernas evocat herbas,
ubi per graciles levis Ilisos
labitur agros piger et steriles
amne maligno radit harenas.

---

[1] See Snell (1964) 27; Mugellesi (1973) 43ff., 53ff., 63; Tschiedel (1969) 56.

[2] On the originality of the song, see Barrett (1964) 35; Leeman (1976) 203; Friedrich (1953) 113. Its importance seems to me underestimated by Zwierlein (1966) 105, and Heldmann (1974) 77-82.

Here, here you others, where the grove is woven of the tall
alders, where lie the meadows which Zephyr soothes with
his dewy breezes as he calls forth the grasses of spring,
where the gentle Ilissus slips lazily through the meager fields
and with its scant stream grazes the unfruitful sands.

Spring blossoming gives way to sluggishness and sterility. The
flow of the Ilissus' stream is reduced (cf. *piger, steriles, maligno*
in 15f.), and the soil is thin (*graciles agri*, 13). The destructive
side of this landscape comes into its own as soon as the hunters
go to work.[3] Too long, Hippolytus reflects a little later, has the
country around Sunion been free (*diu vacat immunis*, 25). Far
from identifying with the potential peace and leisure of this sylvan setting, Hippolytus appears as an intruder and a violator.
He describes the places "where the suckling mother-does, accompanied by their small herds, seek nocturnal foliage" (18-
20); but the sympathy evoked by "small herd" (*gregibus parvis*)
contrasts with the hunter's determination to track and hunt
down these nursing does and their young fawns. The does seek
their pasture at night (*nocturna petunt pabula*) precisely to escape a predator like Hippolytus.[4]

Hippolytus' pent up violence is already hinted in his description of the river "lashing" the banks of the Thriasian valley (*ver-
berat*, 7). It is expressed more openly in such phrases as the
"boar made familiar by many a wound" (*vulnere multo iam notus
aper*, 30), the Spartan dogs' "greed" for their prey (*avidum ferae*,
36), the beasts terrified by the beaters closing in (*picta rubenti /
linea pinna vano cludat / terrore feras*, "let the painted rope, with
its red feather, hem in the beasts with empty fear," 46-48).

Like her "companion" (54), Diana is a destroyer of the life of

[3] See Henry and Walker (1966) 232. Herington (1966), 450, undervalues
the darker touches in the landscape. Heldmann (1974), 77, observes the
"impression of sterility and unreality" in Hippolytus' world, but can also find
the song "governed by an entirely bucolic-lyric mood" (85).

[4] Some commentators (e.g. Grimal 1965) interpret 18-20 as referring to
ewes and lambs, but the reference to *pabula nocturna* makes this unlikely. *Grex*,
feta, and *pabula* are all used of wild as well as domestic animals. Stähli-Peter
(1974), 102f., cites Pliny, *Nat. Hist.* 8.117.

the forests.[5] "Her arrows seek the wild beast that drinks the cold
Araxes and plays in the stiff and frozen Ister" (57f.). The verb
"plays" (*ludit*) creates sympathy for the hunted beast and also
suggests the contradictions in Hippolytus' relation to the wild.
For all the pastoral touches in his opening song, his wood is a
place not of pastoral innocence but of determined and relentless
killing. It contains not the rustic leisure and solitude of poets
and philosophers but strenuous activity in the service of death.[6]
The hidden places of his earth (*pars terrarum secreta*, 55f.) are
not the mysterious hollows of an opulent, nurturant deity of female fecundity, like Tellus on the Ara Pacis, but the places
where his mannish huntress-goddess, like Hippolytus, strikes
terror into the wild inhabitants of her forest world (cf. *metuit*,
72 and *terrore*, 47). The spatial openness connoted by *vacuis
campis* ("empty fields," 71) only stresses the animals' total subjection to Diana's rule (cf. *vacat*, 56), her unerring missiles
(56f.), and the fear that these inspire (72).

   Hippolytus is proud of the geographical extent of Diana's
pursuit of her prey (57ff.), but his expansive list of her remote
hunting grounds contrasts with the entrapment of animals
"bound" in the nets, "closed in" by the encircling hunters (*vinc-
tas*, 74; *cludat*, 47). The small detail, remarked almost in passing, that no feet of the trapped animals "break the snare" (*nulli
laqueum* / *rupere pedes*, 75f.) again arouses our sympathy for the
victims. Hippolytus began his song with live creatures, free and
running, feeding their young, defending themselves (cf. 18-20,
29f., 31ff.). Following the inexorable movement of the hunt itself, he concludes with the immobility of trapped beasts and inert corpses. No longer individual beings, the animals are a col-
lective object, *praeda*, "prey," a dead weight carried on the
groaning wagon (*fertur plaustro* / *praeda gementi*, 76f.), "Groan-

   [5] "A divinity not of life but of death," suggests Boyle (1985) 1292. See
Stähli-Peter (1974) 57f.
   [6] One thinks of the setting of Plato's *Phaedrus*, the songful woods of Theocritus and Virgil, or Maternus' woodland retreat in Tacitus' *Dialogus*.

ing" (*gemens*) strikes a doleful note, in contrast to the joyful description of vernal nature at the beginning (1-16).

Dwelling on the pride of victory as his long train returns in triumph (78-80), Hippolytus harks back to the bloodthirsty violence of his pursuit. He had already anticipated the joy of victory in the image of the successful huntsman cutting loose the entrails with his curved knife (52f.). Now he turns from the hunter to the hounds: "The dogs bear muzzles red with abundant blood (*tum rostra canes / sanguine multo rubicunda gerunt*, 77f.).[7] Such is the glory of the woods that he extolled early in his song (*si quem tangit gloria silvae*, "if the glory of the woods touches any one," 27f.). He then bids his goddess a hasty farewell as the hounds' baying summons him (81-84) to a sport that, as we now know, begins with fresh meadows and ends with disemboweled carcasses and bloody snouts.

How different is the entrance of the Euripidean hero. While the Senecan Hippolytus invokes his goddess just after the climactic buildup from the nets to the curved knife that cuts out the entrails (52-54), Euripides' character begins with mystical communion. His opening prayer to "celestial Artemis" is echoed by his followers (*Hipp.* 58-72), after which he describes at length a symbolical "uncut meadow" of Modesty (73-83). His first dialogue is about the manner of worshiping and addressing the gods (88ff.). He makes no explicit reference to Artemis as huntress but instead honors her with songs and wreaths as a celestial divinity whose voice mysteriously answers his prayers (54ff., 73ff., 85). His own hunting remains unobtrusive (cf. 109-13); and it is only the hostile Aphrodite who describes him as destructive ("With his swift dogs he removes the beasts from the land," 18).

Seneca's harsher and more determined huntsman may derive from Euripides' lost *Hippolytus Veiled*; but even so Seneca's choice of this type of hero remains significant. He holds our

---

[7] Stähli-Peter (1974), 188f., suggests a comparison with the bloody lioness of the Pyramus-Thisbe story in Ovid (*Met.* 4.96f.) but regards the detail of the bloody snouts as merely "ein weiteres Stimmungsbild" (188).

sympathies in reserve for a worthier object. In fact he gradually increases the tone of harshness in the opening song: the setting moves from shade, sweetness, and dewy places (1, 11, 23) to fierceness (69), from spring to winter (10-14, 57-59), from inhabited to desolate places (cf. 66ff.), and from Greeks to remote barbarians (57ff.).

Blurring Diana's realm with Venus', Phaedra evokes a fantasy-picture of Hippolytus: not a virginal recluse, but a desirable and available sex-object, like the Endymion and Hylas of whom the chorus sings just after her sexual fantasies reach a catastrophic end. The shifts in imagery show her gradual re-alignment of the forces in Hippolytus' world and her destructive impact on it. She annexes his virginal realm in exploiting the erotic implications of hunting, throwing javelins, letting her hair flow loose in the winds.[8] In her fantasies of pursuing him through the forests 233-35), she would invade his sylvan retreat. When she echoes the closing words of his aria, "I am called to the forests" (82), in a picture of herself as an Amazon ("In such form I shall be borne to the forests," 403), she is also invading his past, remaking it in her own image, for this is her image also of the mother of austere Hippolytus (*talis severi mater Hippolyti fuit . . . talis in silvis ferar*, 398 and 403; cf. *vocor in silvas*, 82).[9]

In the preceding scene the Nurse invoked the Amazon race as the certain foreclosure of Phaedra's amorous hopes: "You should know his Amazon origins" (232). Phaedra replied with her first figurative invasion of Hippolytus' forest: in fantasy she will pursue him through grove and mountain (233-35). With the obsessive repetition dictated by her desire, she renews the maneuver in 394ff. But the psychological impossibility of mak-

---

[8] See 233-35, 241, 394-404 and cf. Eur., *Hipp.* 198-238. Seneca, however, omits some of Euripides' more or less explicit sexual innuendos, such as the dewy spring (*Hipp.* 207, 226), the grassy meadow (*Hipp.* 210f.), and riding (227ff.). See in general Henry-Walker (1966) 229f.; Vretska (1968) 158, 163f., 166; Solimano (1980) 168. Cf. also the forest imagery of Ovid, *Her.* 4.73, 85ff., 166.

[9] Although present in all the mss., line 398, *talis severi mater Hippolyti fuit*, has been harshly treated by editors: Heinsius, Leo, Richter, Miller delete it; others have transposed it after 404. Grimal (1965) retains it, rightly in my opinion.

ing herself over into a replica of Hippolytus (a lustful Amazon is itself a contradiction in terms) adds another piece to the inevitable disastrous outcome. The contradiction is underlined by the incongruity between her Eastern silks and perfumes and the strenuous northern activities of her fantasies (398-413). Her conflation of the passionate Cretan stepmother and the celibate Amazon mother pushes the motif of incestuous desire closer to the surface. Psychologically it is also the most threatening invasion of Hippolytus' emotional life. She would replace the cherished image of the sexually pure mother that protects Hippolytus from his own sexuality (or, more accurately, enables him to repress his sexuality) with exactly the figure that Hippolytus has most avoided, the one image that he is least able to accommodate to the world he has constructed for himself: a mother who is also a fully sexual woman, desiring and desired.

Hippolytus' echo of Phaedra's words in his own call to the forest at the crisis of the action, therefore, makes clear the meaning of Phaedra's threat to his life. As he rushes wildly offstage after her declaration of passionate love, he cries out, "O forests, O wild beasts" (*O silvae, O ferae*, 718). This is his final stage utterance. He will not return alive.[10]

Hippolytus' opening song locates at least some of the responsibility for the disaster in his own ferocity. The first choral ode more drastically challenges his woodland refuge as a possible retreat from love. The chorus sees a different aspect of the wild: it is not a pleasance where "sweet sound murmurs as the stream slips among fresh flowers" (*per flores novos / fugiente dulcis murmurat rivo sonus*, 512f.) but a battleground rampant with intense sexual conflict (*tum silva gemit / murmure saevo*, "then the forest groans with the savage murmuring," 349f.).[11] As the chorus subsequently extends that savagery to stepmothers and then to the flames of love (*saevas novercas*, 356; *saevis flammis*,

---

[10] See Friedrich (1953) 131; Stähli-Peter (1974) 194.

[11] Although Hippolytus enjoys the sweet sound of murmuring streams (512f.), song is noticeably absent from his sylvan world. No Virgilian rustic, he prefers more strenuous pursuits.

358), it further eroticizes Hippolytus' virginal refuge. Even the shepherd-singer of the first ode is a victim of love: Apollo, in love with Admetus, puts aside his lyre for the herdsman's pipe and tends his beloved's cattle (296-98).[12] Here Hippolytus' own goddess "burns" with passion (*arsit*, 309). The men of the Hippolytus' "first age" of the world "mingled with gods" (*mixtos deis*, 526) in different ways from these Olympians who abandon divine dignity to chase mortal lovers (299-316).

In his opening lyrics Hippolytus had sung (25-27):

> pars illa diu vacat immunis
> qua curvati litora ponti
> Sunion urget.

Too long exempt from tribute (of the hunt) is that region where Cape Sunion presses the shores of the curving sea.

Now the chorus, near the end of its first song, places a different power in this landscape (353-55):

> nihil immune est, odiumque perit
> cum iussit Amor; veteres cedunt
> ignibus irae.

Nothing is exempt from him, and hatred perishes when Love commands; ancient anger yields to his fires.

Nothing could be further from Hippolytus' forest world, subject to the aggressive hunting of Diana and her devotees, than this forest where aggression surrenders to Amor.

Phaedra, entering soon after, utters her desperate wish to go hunting in Hippolytus' forest. The Nurse then prays to Hippolytus' own goddess, Diana as queen of mountain and woodland, to soften his austere celibacy (406-23).[13] Having annexed

---

[12] We may recall also the destruction of the pastoral world at the appearance of the sea-monster: *fugit attonitum pecus* ("the flock, thunderstruck, flees," 1050ff).

[13] Vretska (1968), 167f., followed by Primmer (1976), p. 218 with note 19, would assign the prayer of 406-23 to Phaedra rather than the Nurse. But in the Nurse's mouth the prayer is an important transition for her scene with Hippolytus, and at this point Phaedra is still partially resisting her passion: see Fauth (1958) 553 and Boyle (1985) note 38.

his image of the chaste mother in fantasizing herself an Amazon (396-403), Phaedra (via her proxy) now annexes his mother-substitute, the chaste goddess. The Nurse's closing words, *ades invocata, iam fave votis dea*, "Be present to my call, goddess, and show kindness now to my prayer" (423), echoes both the beginning and end of Hippolytus' invocation in the prologue:

> ades en comiti diva virago ("Be present to your companion, mannish goddess," 54).

> en diva faves ("Look, o goddess, where you are showing favor," 81).[14]

The Nurse is calling on Diana for an enterprise just the opposite of Hippolytus' (417): "Let him return to the laws of Venus." "Turn your force here," the Nurse goes on; "so may your countenance carry you forth (*lucidi vultus ferant*), and may you go through the sky breaking the clouds with your horns (of light) pure" (417-19). But as she calls on Hippolytus' goddess, the Nurse changes her. She implies Diana's vulnerability to witchcraft (420f.) and to love for the mortal Endymion (422).[15] This is an aspect of Diana that Hippolytus totally suppresses, just as Phaedra's Nurse suppresses the aspect of the goddess that is a *diva virago*.

The chorus after Phaedra's confession of love reveals an even greater flaw in the imagined serenity of the forest world. The peaceful springs and streams of rustic ease (502-14) turn into an insidious landscape of desire where lecherous nymphs lie in wait for good-looking young men and draw them into their forest pool (777-84):

> quid deserta petis? Tutior aviis
> non est forma locis: te nemore abdito
> cum Titan medium constituit diem,
> cingent turba licens, Naiades improbae,

---

[14] On the ritual flavor of the invocations, see Vretska (1968) 161 and Grimal (1965) ad 423, citing Virgil, *Ecl.* 8.105f.

[15] For the power of witchcraft in winning Hippolytus' love, see also 412ff. and 236f. The motif appears also in Eur., *Hipp.* 478-81 and 509-18. See also Vretska (1968) 161. On Endymion and Hylas, see now Davis (1983) 115-17.

formonsos solitae claudere fontibus,
et somnis facient insidias tuis
　　lascivae nemorum deae,
Panas quae Dryades montivagos petunt.

Why do you seek remote places? Beauty is no safer in
pathless spots. When the Titan (Sun) fixes the middle of the
day, a licentious band will gird you round in hidden grove,
forward Naiads who are wont to close handsome boys in
their pools; and the lecherous divinities of the groves will
lay ambush to your slumbers, the Dryad-nymphs who chase
the mountain-wandering Pans.

The passage utilizes the Ovidian *topos* of a forest retreat that suddenly shifts from virginal seclusion to sexual vulnerability. This
is the landscape of *deluded* innocence, of purity about to be lost
to sexual violence in the background. That vulnerability of innocence, clearly focused on young masculine beauty through
the allusion to Hylas, is already implicit in the simile of the lilies
that droop with pale petals (765-68) and in the raging heat of
the noon hour at the summer solstice, the proverbial time of las-
civious behavior.[16]

All the features of Hippolytus' ideal landscape—the deserted
place, hidden grove, pools or springs—recur, but their meaning
changes from purity to sensuality. The midsummer heat (*vapor*,
765), previously identified with Phaedra's passion (102, 640),
despoils the fresh meadows of Hippolytus' virginal youth (cf.
764-68, 779). His pure forests are now tinged by the imagery
of entrapment in the enclosing warmth of passion. In his reply
to the Nurse's first overtures he idealized wandering in the
empty countryside and under an open sky (*sed rure vacuo potitur
et aperto aethere / innocuus errat*, 501f.). The ode after Phaedra's

---

[16] For the lily, see Virgil, *Aen.* 12.68f.; Propert. 1.20.35-42; Ovid, *Met.*
10.190f., 212f.; and in general Segal (1969) 35; R.O.A.M. Lyne, *G & R* 30
(1983) 59f. For the summer solstice, see Hesiod, *Erga* 582ff.; Alcaeus frag. 347
Lobel-Page. Skovgaard-Hansen (1972), 107, observes the play's movement
from the freshness of dewy morning in the prologue to the ominous noon heat
here.

overt declaration presents the vulnerable youth's danger in that countryside as a sexual threat of "enclosure" (*claudere*, 781). The sexuality of this image harks back to the the monstrous sexuality in Phaedra's house of origin (*conclusit*, 122; cf. *claustra*, 1171). In his opening lines, Hippolytus gave orders to "gird the shady forests" as his companions "wander" in the mountains (*cingite*, 1; *vagi*, 3). As the hunter becomes the hunted, it is the young men who are "girt about" or "surrounded" in the woods (*cingent* 780) by Nymphs who "wander" over mountains in search of a prey of love (cf. *montivagos*, 784). Hippolytus' light sleep on a grassy hillock is now an opportunity for lustful goddesses of the woods (782). These female divinities are in fact bolder than usual. Horace's nymphs run away from the amorous Faunus (*Faunus Nympharum fugientum amator*, *Odes* 3.18.1); these hotly pursue Pans on the mountains (784).[17]

Now too the erotic aspects of Diana come to the fore. Comparing Hippolytus' swift flight to the violent fires of a comet that rushes on its course through the sky (*ocior cursum rapiente flamma*, 738), the chorus anticipates the disturbance in Diana's ostensibly chaste forests (cf. 788ff.). Her light in 743-46 is a sign not of divine serenity but of her mortal worshipper's agitation (cf. 736-38). The motif of fire recalls the flames of Phaedra's excitement; and the goddess's blushing face, in this eroticized context (cf. 747), recalls the fevered face of Phaedra that betrays her love (cf. 363). The reddish tinge of the full moon in 747, *vultus rubicunda Phoebe*, should suggest Diana's impervious remoteness; but the simile in which this detail occurs describes the masculine beauty (*pulchrior forma*, 743) that is to cause Hippolytus' death (cf. 820f.). We recall too how love dims the "Phoebean torch" of Phaedra's eyes in 379f., another

[17] Cf. also Ovid, *Her.* 4.49f. and 171-74, whose erotic tone Seneca has deepened here. On the rustic deities in *Heroides* 4, see Jacobson (1974) 152. For the text of 784, see Grimal (1965) ad loc., whose defense of the reading of E I accept. The reading of A, *montivagive Panes*, would make the Pans as well as the Naiads chase Hippolytus. Grimal ad 782 also notes that Hippolytus' noon sleep is the inverse of the sleeping Nymph accosted by Faun or Satyr, a common motif in the art of the period.

paradoxical link between Phaedra and the heavenly Diana. (cf.
Phoebe, 747). Diana herself, in her love for Endymion-Hippolytus, "has just now blushed, and yet no cloud stood in her way
to soil her shining countenance" (788; cf. 747). The lines echo
the Nurse's prayer, "May your bright countenance carry you
forth, and, now that the cloud is broken through, may you pro-
ceed with pure horns" (*sic te lucidi vultus ferant / et nube rupta
cornibus puris eas*, 418f.). In the comparison of Hippolytus'
beauty to the full moon, Diana/Phoebe's "horns" are no longer
described as "pure" (*coeunte cornu*, 745). When she blushes for
love of Endymion-Hippolytus, no obscuring cloud accounts
for the reddening of her orb (*nullaque lucidis / nubes sordidior
vultibus obstitit*, 788f.). These small changes offer a measure of
the goddess's decline from her virginal lunar pallor.[18]

These intimations of blemishes in the pure sky and in the
pure goddess are part of another pattern of celestial imagery
linking Diana and Hippolytus. The fall of Hippolytus as an unsuccessful Phaethon in 1090-92 corresponds to a fall of a different kind for his virgin goddess. In the choral ode at 309-16 she
burns with love and in order to indulge her passion for Endymion hands her chariot over to her brother Phoebus. As in the
Phaethon story the horses and chariot are unaccustomed to the
difference in weight (313-16).[19] In the later ode, where Diana's
love for Endymion is more fully developed, the details of the
chariot recur (746f.); and now, exactly like Phaethon, "she will
not be able to steer the white (horses of her) car" (*currus non
poterit flectere candidos*, 787), just as Hippolytus, far more disastrously, will not be able to control his chariot (1082ff.; also
1055f., 1068-77).[20]

[18] Cf. also the later chorus, *tractam Thessalicis carminibus rati* ("thinking that
you were drawn down by Thessalian spells," 791) with 421, *detrahere
numquam Thessali cantus queant* ("May Thessalian enchantments never draw
you down to earth").
[19] As Grimal (1965) notes ad 316, Seneca borrows his language here from
Ovid's account of Phaethon's fall in *Met*. 2.161ff. He imitates the same passage
later in comparing Hippolytus, not Diana, to Phaethon, 1088-92. See also
Skovgaard-Hansen (1972) 97ff.
[20] Cf. 316, *dum tremunt axes graviore curru* ("while the axles tremble with

In Seneca, as in Euripides, part of Hippolytus' tragedy lies in the ultimate remoteness of his goddess. For all her vulnerability to earthly love (at least as the chorus sees her), Diana remains secure in her celestial realm, safe even from the Thessalian witchcraft that would pull her down (cf. 420-22, 785-94). Hippolytus, though figuratively associated with celestial movements (736-41, 743-52), is also entrapped in low-lying places on the earth, both in fantasy (780-83) and in reality (1085ff., 1102ff.). He is a Phaethon who crashes heavily to the ground (1090-92), a youth of godlike beauty whose celestial fire is extinguished (1269), leaving behind the mere "weight" and "randomly gathered limbs" of the tortured mortal flesh (*pondus et artus temere congestos*, 1248f.).

The myths and images of this second choral ode (736-823) illustrate how radically Seneca reconceives the meaning of the Euripidean gods. They are no longer even symbols of clearly demarcated emotions or instincts and projections, longings and fantasies. Diana and her myths function as a kind of auxiliary imagery, without the religious or cultic reality that Artemis and Aphrodite have in Euripides. Seneca's gods become part of the psychological landscape. Their very remoteness and the literary artifice in the allusions to them depict the precariousness of boundary between fantasy and reality in the chief characters.

This chorus has an important place in the play's dialogue between voices of fantasy and voices of reality. By this point each character has fully projected a private world, somehow insulated from the "real" world. Only a few lines before the choral ode, however, a public voice, carrying the implications also of a public reality, makes itself heard for the first time: *adeste, Athenae* ("Come hither, Athens") the Nurse cries out (725). She is summoning the "trusty band of servants" ostensibly for aid, but in fact to bear witness to the false accusation that she is preparing against Hippolytus. That call to the "public" realm

---

heavier chariot") and 1088f., *sensere pecudes facinus et curru levi, / dominante nullo, qua timor iussit, ruunt* ("The horses felt the deed, and with lightened chariot, as no one ruled them, they rush wherever fear commands").

reminds us of the Athens that lies outside the erotic fantasies of
Phaedra's house and the Athens also excluded from Hippolytus'
life as hunter and worshipper of Diana. Escapism and lovesick
delusion are momentarily, and ominously, recalled to responsibility for a larger society. Against the elaborate mythological artifice of the following ode this momentary call to Athens stands
out in sharp but isolated relief. The corresponding ode in
Euripides' play, for all its escapist geography and motif of flight,
remains in closer touch with the physical reality of Phaedra's approaching death and with the mood of concern for her (*Hipp.*
764-75). Seneca's ode is more a continuation of the subjective,
interior, fantasizing mood of the first half of the play than an
independent comment on the action.

In thus crystallizing alternative imaginary worlds, the first
three lyrical passages—Hippolytus' opening song and the two
choral odes that follow—reveal Hippolytus' ideal and its landscape as a personal construction that must compete with other
visions of life. His world has no greater claim to ultimate reality
than those other visions. The Diana-Endymion-Hylas ode creates an alternative image of his world, filtered through more seductive and also more dangerous images of myth and place. The
eroticized landscape of Phaedra's passion and the monstrous
landscape of the sea-creature that Theseus calls forth (1007ff.)
transform Hippolytus' *locus amoenus* of fantasied innocence and
the sensual idyll of the second chorus (cf. 777ff.) into the characteristically Senecan *locus horridus* of nightmare, analogous to
the dark groves of sinister happenings in the *Thyestes* or the *Oedipus.*[21]

From Hippolytus' perspective the catastrophe to his forest
world is the metaphorical equivalent of reversing his self-image
from chastity to criminal lust: "That dweller in the forests, still
rough, chaste, virgin, of rude simplicity," Theseus begins, as he
works himself up to curse his son for raping his stepmother (*silvarum incola / ille efferatus, castus, intactus, rudis,* 922f.). The
monster that Theseus calls up in his wrath does to Hippolytus'

---

[21] *Thyestes* 650ff., *Oedipus* 530ff. On the Senecan *locus horridus*, see Mugellesi
(1973) passim, especially 43ff. and 53ff.

forests what Theseus does to Hippolytus' definition of himself as chaste hunter. Land is overwhelmed by sea; the "dew" of the peaceful woodland becomes the "dewy spray" that reaches the highest peaks with the monster's apparition (*rorat*, 1027; cf. *rorifera aura*, "dew-bearing air," 11; *roscida tellus*, "dewy earth," 42). "All the earth trembles" (1050); shepherd and flock flee in terror (1051f.). "Every wild creature flees; every hunter shudders, bloodless, by his own element." Theseus calls forth aspects of this world that Hippolytus had not seen.

Another nightmarish inversion is also operative here, for the effect of the sea-monster on the forest world is not so far from that of Hippolytus and his huntress-goddess on the animals they pursue (cf. 1053f. and 60-72). The monster not only destroys Hippolytus' existence; it also reveals that existence for what it is in the dark mirror of its most savage and aggressive meaning. There is a grim poetic justice in the reversal of the hounds' role: instead of relentlessly tracking down small game and returning with bloody muzzles (77-80), they now "sadly track down their master's limbs" (1108; cf. 31ff.).[22] The noose that Hippolytus' men are to prepare for their prey (*laqueus*, 46; cf. 75) reappears as the "clinging noose" of the reins that strangle Hippolytus as he loses control of his horses (*laqueo tenaci*, 1086).[23] The "wandering," "searching," and "hunting" of the opening song now change to the passivity of the corpse tracked down by the servants who wander through the fields and by the hunting dogs (1105, 1108). Hippolytus' initial "wandering through fields" is fragmented into the "wandering parts" of his body that have to be "searched out" for burial at the end (*at vos per agros corporis partes vagas / anquirite*, 1278f.; cf. 3, 13-15, 41). The "shade" with which he opened the play (*umbrosas silvas*) is now tinged with the underworld "shades" that weigh heavily on the last scene.

Even Hippolytus' modesty or chastity (*pudor*, cf. 1196), re-

[22] For the reversals in the motif of the hunt, see Henry-Walker (1966) 232; Davis (1983) 114f.
[23] See Davis (1983) 117; Segal (1984) 324. Cf. also the noose with which Phaedra threatens suicide in 259.

habilitated after Theseus' insults of 914 and 920, is no longer so
simple as it once was. Phaedra reestablishes him as *pudicus, insons* ("chaste, guiltless," 1196; cf. Hippolytus' *innocuus*, 502).
But she thereby recalls his aggressive *pudor* (cf. *impudicos . . .
amove tactos*, "keep away your unchaste touch," 704). Her more
complex *pudor* at the end, *O mors pudoris maximum laesi decus*
("death, greatest glory of injured shame," 1189), interweaves
them both in the tragic conflict of *amor / pudor* (cf. 1188f.) and
evokes the whole course of the passion that has destroyed Hippolytus' world (cf. 1189 and 261).[24]

Phaedra's absorption of Hippolytus' forest world is part of a
larger tragic pattern, already present in Euripides, wherein opposing qualities of the two protagonists come together not only
for their mutual destruction but also for the revelation of a paradoxical fusion of opposites in their common doom.[25] All three
poets who treat the myth, Euripides, Seneca, and Racine, develop that symmetry of correspondences and contrasts.

Both figures, in their emotional violence, destroy the boundary between reason and madness, *ratio* and *furor*.[26] Both are described in metaphors of animal savagery. Hippolytus is consis-
tently called *ferus, efferatus, silvester, ferox, torvus, saevus,
intractabilis, immitis*.[27] Phaedra is heir to her mother's passion
for the wild, savage, and fierce bull (*efferum saevi ducem . . . torvus, impatiens, iugi*, 116f.). Her love, too, like her mother's
"knows how to sin in forests" (*in silvis*, 114). The fire of her love
is also savage (*ferus ignis*, 641f.). It is as if she sees in Hippolytus
not only the handsome young Theseus with whom she once fell
in love (646ff.) but also the wild bull, the fantasy of unbridled
lust that harks back to the sexual crimes of her heredity (115-
18).

[24] The echo between 1187 and 261 (*castitatis vindicem armemus manum*) is
noted by Grimal (1965) ad loc. On *vindex*, see Boyle (1985). Seneca is perhaps
drawing on the ironical interweaving of Phaedra and Hippolytus in death at the
end of Euripides' play (*Hipp.* 1429f.), on which see Segal (1978/79) 138f.

[25] See in general Frischer (1970).

[26] *Ratio* and *furor*, for Hippolytus: 565-67 and cf. 1070; for Phaedra: 184,
253, 259.

[27] Cf. 229-32, 240, 271-73, 414-16, 461, 580. Also 573, 576, 798, 913f.,
922f. See in general Skovgaard-Hansen (1972) 104.

As part of the tragic *coincidentia oppositorum*, each protagonist finds in the other his or her monstrous double. Phaedra finds in the chaste Hippolytus the wild bull of her mother's lust.[28] Hippolytus finds in Phaedra both the evil stepmother and the licentious, seductive mother, the most repulsive of all women (cf. 558, 564, 686-97). As Phaedra viewed the savagery of her love in terms of the mythical aspect of her past—Pasiphae, the bull, the Minotaur (115-18)—so Hippolytus does the same for the fierceness of his hatred, evoking the example of Medea beside that of Pasiphae (563f. and 686-97).

The bull that destroys Hippolytus is a distorted emanation of his own repressed sexuality, a monstrous projection of his own violent hatred of a part of himself.[29] It is also a symbol of Phaedra's expressed sexuality and therefore a manifestation of the tragic impossibility of the bond between himself and Phaedra, the point of precarious, unstable juncture between her fantasies and his terrors. When the Messenger describes the bull as resembling the leader of a wild herd (*feri dominator . . . gregis*, 1039), he is echoing Phaedra's description of Pasiphae's bull in Phaedra's first scene: *pecoris efferum saevi ducem* ("wild leader of a savage herd," 116). This creature destroys Hippolytus' pastoral and venatic shelter (1050-54), but Phaedra sees its power to destroy her world too, for she begins her suicide speech with the prayer that Neptune, savage ruler of the deep sea, may send the same monster against her 1159-63).[30]

[28] Euripides had already developed the motif of Pasiphae's bull: *Hipp.* 336. Ovid too was doubtless in Seneca's mind: *Her.* 4.55ff. and 165ff. See above, chap. 2, note 10.

[29] See Leeman (1976) 203: "And when in the end the hunter is himself hunted and killed by a monstrous animal, we feel that he falls victim to his own great overpowering *furor*."

[30] There are other resemblances too between Pasiphae's bull, the Minotaur, and the monster from the sea in the Messenger's account, 1080f.: *nam toto obvius / incurrit ore corniger ponti horridus* ("It rushed against him with its whole head, horned, fearful creature of the deep"). Cf. 1172, where Phaedra, lamenting over Hippolytus' body, asks whether the Minotaur killed him, *taurus biformis ore cornigero ferox* ("a bull, two-formed creature, savage, with horned head"). The sea-monster too is called *torvus* (1063), like Pasiphae's bull and like Hippolytus. The simile of the loss of control over a ship also links Hippolytus' *furor* (1070) with Phaedra's: cf. 1072-75 with 181-83. On the *furor* linking both fig-

Theseus, in his anger, finds Hippolytus savage in another way: thanks to Phaedra's lie he accuses this wild dweller in forests (*silva incola* / *ille efferatus*, 922f.) of a licentiousness that surpasses that of the beasts (913f.):

> ferae quoque ipsae Veneris evitant nefas
> generisque leges inscius servat pudor.

> Even wild beasts avoid this horror, and an unconscious modesty preserves the laws of the species.

But near the end, lamenting over his son's torn body, he accuses himself of having practiced a savage killing (*exitia effera*, 1221), as bad as the cruel tortures of Sciron or Sinis (1223-25). Like Phaedra he calls down on his own head the monstrosity and savagery that he had released against Hippolytus (1222-25). Twenty lines later the chorus applies Theseus' word "savage" to the rending that has mangled his body (*dispersa foede membra laniatu effero*, "the limbs horribly scattered by the savage rending," 1246).[31] In the release of each character's inner violence and animality, the savagery of the father answers what was called forth by Phaedra from the son.

The savagery of the bull thus serves as a link between the potential savagery of each of the three main characters. The imagery of the wild, opening into the psychic borderland of fantasy, dream, repressed fears and desires, serves as a screen on which each projects his or her vision of a hidden self in the shape of the monstrous double: for Phaedra, Pasiphae's lust; for Hippolytus, the sea-monster that ravages the woods and destroys all living creatures; for Theseus, the violent outlaws whom he has subdued in the wild places of Greece but not in his own soul.

---

ures, see Henry-Walker (1966) 226f.; Leeman (1976) 204; also above, notes 25 and 26.

[31] The echo between Theseus' *effera exitia* in 1221 and the chorus's *effero laniatu* in 1246 is noted without comment by Grimal (1965), who also points out (ad 1221) the Lucretian association of the adjective.

FOUR

The Golden Age and Nature

I

When confronted by Phaedra's desire, Euripides' Hippolytus retreats to a utopian vision of sexless, or rather womanless, reproduction. As an alternative to procreation from women, he desiderates the acquisition of offspring by leaving gold, silver, or bronze in the temples of Zeus (*Hipp.* 616-24).[1] Seneca's hero, confronted with Phaedra, takes refuge not in an imaginary social order outside of time or in a timeless present, but in a historical construction, an idealized image of the Golden Age (483-564).

In one respect at least the interiorizing mood of Senecan tragedy is heir to the subjectivizing of experience that runs from Hellenistic poetry through Catullus, Virgil, and Roman elegy. A character often reveals himself through a vision of the past, a past which is simultaneously personal and historical. A poem like Catullus 64 or 68 not only projects personal experience upon a historical-mythic past as a general paradigm for experience,[2] but actually absorbs the mythical into the personal life, fuses the exemplary past with the individual present, and recasts the mythical past as the vehicle for intensely emotional experience.[3] So here Hippolytus projects his emotional needs not only upon an imaginary landscape but also upon an imaginary reconstruction of human life. The Greek tragedians occasion-

---

[1] For Hippolytus' utopian fantasy of a womanless world, see Barrett (1964) ad loc.; Friedrich Solmsen, *Intellectual Experiments of the Greek Enlightenment* (Princeton 1975) 73ff.

[2] This is the way of classical Greek literature: see Hugh Parry, *The Lyric Poems of Greek Tragedy* (Toronto and Sarasota 1978) 27-29, 36-41, on what he calls "hypomnesis."

[3] On this aspect of Catullus 64, see P. W. Harkins, "Autoallegory in Catullus 63 and 64," *TAPA* 90 (1959) 102-16; M.C.J. Putnam, "The Art of Catullus 64" *HSCP* 65 (1961) 165-205, especially 196-98. For recent criticism, see Richard Jenkyns, *Three Classical Poets* (Cambridge, Mass. 1982) 88.

ally create such retrospective, personalizing landscapes: one thinks of the meadows of childhood innocence to which Sophocles' Deianeira and Ajax look back momentarily in the *Trachiniae* and *Ajax* respectively.[4] Hesiod and Plato use the myth of the Golden Age to reflect on the human condition in general.[5] But classical Greek literature does not, on the whole, so directly correlate a vision of the past with an individual's personal vision of himself and his world.

Viewed psychologically, Hippolytus' Golden Age is a retreat to childhood, to a lost purity and innocence that he will defend, at all costs, against the demands of growing up. Like all Golden-Age constructions this paradise necessarily exists in a state of latent or overt tensions with reality and is therefore fraught with contradictions. The sharpest of these is the fact that such a world exists only as a denial of another way of life, be it the complexity of urban life or the reality of the sexual drive in the individual.

Hippolytus' speech falls into two main sections (483-525, 525-64). The first praises the simple life of the ancient ways (*ritus priscos*, 485); the second gives a quasi-historical sketch of the development of civilization in its decline from primitive ease and innocence to the corruptions of modern life.[6] The theme is a familiar one in classical literature, and Seneca draws heavily on Lucretius' fifth book, Catullus 64, Virgil's Fourth *Eclogue* and Second *Georgic*, Horace's Second and Sixteenth *Epodes*. In his philosophical writings too Seneca frequently

[4] Soph. *Trach.* 144-47; *Ajax* 558f.; see J. de Romilly, *La tragédie grecque* (Paris 1970) 99f.

[5] For an attempt to find such personal aspects of the Golden Age in Hesiod, see Peter Smith, "History and Individual in Hesiod's Myth of the Five Races," *CW* 74 (1979/80) 145-65; yet they remain only a remote possibility for the text at a high level of generality.

[6] For the motif of purity and the Golden Age, see I. S. Ryberg, "Vergil's Golden Age," *TAPA* 89 (1958) 112-31; Patricia A. Johnston, *Vergil's Agricultural Golden Age, Mnemosyne* Suppl. 60 (Leiden 1980), especially Chap. 1, with further bibliography in F. E. Brenk's review, *Gnomon* 53, (1981) 763-66; C. Fantazzi, "The Golden Age in Arcadia," *Latomus* 33 (1974) 280-305; Bodo Gatz, *Weltalter, goldene Zeit, und sinnverwandte Vorstellungen, Spudasmata* 16 (Hildesheim 1967).

contrasts the purity of the Golden Age with contemporary decadence.[7]

By shifting from an idealized, atemporal praise of simplicity to a specifically historical account, Seneca makes clear Hippolytus' movement backward in time, *à la recherche du temps perdu*.[8] His macrocosm of Golden-Age humanity overlays the microcosm of his personal search to reclaim and maintain an idealized childhood. His account stops with strife and violence within the family, specifically with evil (step)mothers (555-64). Medea, who stands for the whole "accursed race" of women, is his closing example (563f.).

Hippolytus' speech makes ontogeny coincide with phylogeny, for violence within the family marks the end of both Hippolytus' childhood innocence and the innocent childhood of the human race. The overtures of Phaedra have for him something of the horror attaching to a fall from primeval purity. Her act forces him to confront the reality of a mother-figure who is a fully sexual being. For him this is an experience laden with the horror of pollution and monstrosity (688, 704f., 713f.). Face to face with Phaedra's sexual desire, he must rediscover and relive his suppressed knowledge that the family is a place not of purity, shelter, and innocence but of sexual desires, temptations, conflicts, anger, and hatred. When he cries out in response to her declaration of love, "I am guilty; I have deserved to die; I have been pleasing to my stepmother" (*sum nocens, merui mori: / placui novercae*, 683f.), he reenacts in his own life those first "crimes that entered every house" when the Golden Age came to an end (553ff.).

At the close of his denunciation of Phaedra he again invokes the image of Medea, the archetypal evil stepmother. As Phaedra is worse than the sexually depraved mother-figure, Pasiphae

---

[7] E.g. *De Ira* 2.9, *De Benef.* 5.15; *Epist.* 90.4f., 97. See in general Herrmann (1924) 484f., 502f.; Friedrich (1953) 123f., and the notes of Grimal (1965) on specific lines.

[8] Seneca prepares for this shift prepared by repeating *ritos priscos*, "ancient ways," at the beginning of the first section (485) in *ritu* at the beginning of the second part (526).

(688), so she is "a greater bane" than the maleficent stepmother, Medea (*Colchide noverca maius haec, maius malum est*, 697). Harking back to Medea as the example of the accursed race of women at the end of his Golden-Age speech ("Medea alone, the wife of Aegeus, will render women a race accursed," *dirum genus*, 563f.), Hippolytus implicitly experiences Phaedra's overture as the destructive invasion of his personal Golden Age.

His first action in the play is, in effect, to reenact his construction of his Golden-Age, sex-free paradise. In his opening lyrics he recreates verbally the shady mountains, rushing streams, and snowy hills (1-8) where his only companions are his fellow hunters and the *diva virago* whom he worships (54).

He projects this ideal, however, not only upon a timeless present or a utopian future, as does Euripides' hero (*Hipp.* 616-24), but also upon a temporal axis, a historical schema for the development of human civilization. By this step Seneca gives the landscape of Hippolytus a further dimension of psychological significance. It becomes a symbolic condensation of his emotional world.

The symbolical landscape associated with Phaedra also has its temporal dimension: her past associations with the palace of Minos, the labyrinth, Pasiphae, the Minotaur, Ariadne. These places and persons are part of the dangerous heredity that she carries with her.[9] Just as her inward space is the complete antithesis of Hippolytus' forest world, so the temporal dimension of her emotional world is the opposite of his. He looks back to an idealized Golden-Age paradise of innocence and peace; she looks back to a polluted kingdom of violent passions, criminal loves, overpowering sexual desires. Already for Virgil this Minoan past symbolized the corruption of monstrosity and guilty sexuality, the "memorials of accursed love" that mark the point of transition from the old Trojan world to the hopeful New World of Italy and the West (*Veneris monumenta nefandae*, *Aeneid* 6.26; cf. *Ecl.* 6.45ff.).

[9] For the family curse and Phaedra's heredity, see chap. 2, note 10.

These oppositions express the contrasting ways of structuring the world that lie behind the hopelessness of Phaedra's love. The spatial contrasts, however, extend even further in the correspondences of marginal geography for the two protagonists. Crete and Scythia in the respective backgrounds of the two main characters are each at the opposite fringes of the Hellenic world.[10] In the first act the Nurse tries to dissuade Phaedra from her passion by labelling it "a crime which no barbarian land (*barbara tellus*) has ever perpetrated, not the Getae wandering on the Steppe nor the inhospitable Taurian nor the widely scattered Scythian" (167-69). The three examples of a barbarian land are all in the far North from which Hippolytus' Amazon mother came. Immediately afterwards the Nurse appeals to the warning exemplar of Phaedra's Cretan past, Pasiphae and the bull (171-77), and concludes, "Will Nature depart from her laws each time a Cretan woman falls in love?" (176f.).

This juxtaposition of Scythia and Crete as the two extremes of barbarism then recurs in Phaedra's fantasy-reconstruction of her personal "Golden Age": Hippolytus' blend of Scythian austerity and Greek countenance and his imagined "entrance to the Cretan Sea" (660f.). The two lines in fact juxtapose the geographical epithets, "Scythian" and "Cretan," with their similarity of sound, in identical metrical positions (660f.):

in ore Graio *Scythicus* apparet rigor . . .
si cum parente *Creticum* intrasses fretum . . .

On a Greek countenance appears Scythian austerity . . .
If with your parent you had entered the Cretan Sea . . .

In Phaedra's fantasy Hippolytus is the ideal blend of civilized Greek and severe, he-man barbarian. Hippolytus, of course, is nothing of the kind. The two sides of his nature—Greek and barbarian, urban and savage, "soft" and "hard" primitivism—are at war rather than in harmony with one another.

---

[10] This is a theme which Seneca could have found in Euripides' lost *Hippolytus*. There are perhaps suggestions of it in the extant *Hippolytus*, 732-51, 752-63.

His *rigor* or austerity (660) is in fact closer to the unpitying ferocity of his exaggerated puritanism, and that is the sense in
which he uses *rigor* some twenty-five lines later (686). His definitive response is the murderous gesture of sacrificing her to
his goddess of that sylvan world which symbolizes both his innocence (cf. 502) and its ambiguity.

Phaedra provokes his brutal act by an image of the wildness
of nature in her, something that corresponds to the latent violence of his supposedly Golden-Age purity. At this crisis of the
action she would follow him, she says, "even through fire,
through the *mad* sea, over *rocks* and through *rivers* in the rage of
their seething waters" (699-701):

> sed mei non sum potens.
> te vel per ignes, per mare insanum sequar
> rupesque et amnes, unda quos torrens rapit

Her sea-imagery (85ff., 181ff.) now mingles with the rocks and
streams of his forest world (e.g. 1-7, 16, 23).

Her love contains a kind of private, emotional Golden Age
that corresponds to his historical vision. But her overheated
imagination interacts with his for their mutual destruction. She
projects upon her present love the happy time when she first
saw and loved Theseus, and in her fantasy improbably amalgamates the puritanical huntsman and the womanizing, monster-
slaying adventurer (646-66).[11] His response of disgust and horror brings her abruptly back to reality, that is from the image of
a happy Crete that he might have "entered" (661) to the darkness of that Minoan realm and all it contains.

After his terrible imprecation against her and just before she
abandons herself to her passion in the lines cited above (699-
702), she recognizes what her Cretan abode means for him and
what is likely to result from this love (698f.): *et ipsa nostrae fata
cognosco domus: | fugienda petimus* ("I myself recognize the doom

---

[11] The references to Ariadne in this passage recall the erotic side of Theseus'
adventurousness, another area where Phaedra's fantasied amalgamation of father and son completely misses the mark.

of my house; I pursue what I should flee"). Still she goes on, "But I have no control over myself. . ." (699ff.). This tragic recognition (anagnorisis), coupled with her continued pursuit of love, links past and future in the inevitability of her doom. At this point she is aware that her Golden-Age fantasy will cancel out the positive side of his. In the symmetry of correspondences and oppositions between them, the geographical, cultural, and psychological marginality of each can come together only disastrously. From Hippolytus' Golden-Age vision of himself Phaedra will elicit only the huntsman's murderous savagery.

II

As traditional images of the Golden Age fluctuate between a paradisiacal simplicity and a primitive rudeness, just so Hippolytus' images of childhood fluctuate between innocence and domestic murder, between safety and destruction. The primitive side of his refusal to compromise takes the form of his fierce violence. Like the primordial world of his fantasies, he too swings between bucolic joy and bloodthirsty killing.

The very unreality of the Golden Age, its function as a fantasy refuge from the actuality of human life, with its responsibilities and complexities, makes it well suited to symbolize the disequilibrium in the character of Hippolytus. The abruptness of the change from idyllic peace to virulent hatred gives us an important clue to his instability (cf. 483ff. with 559-73). His idealization of a life of supposed innocence in rude nature leaves him less capable of civilized man's inhibitions against violence and therefore more a prey to the darker side of the "natural man" in himself.[12] Seneca has been able to draw on a long literary and philosophical tradition of the ambiguities of the Golden Age and is able to condense these into a single description of an idealized landscape that enriches the cultural and psychological meaning of his character.

---

[12] See Leach (1975) 225. Croisille (1964), 285, points out that the Stoic idea of living in accordance with nature does not necessarily mean a return to primitive simplicity.

Hippolytus' account of the Golden Age, to which we must now turn in greater detail, is strongly regressive. He places the more primitive life of hunting and foraging above the settled, stable economy of farming. Thus his view of rustic simplicity veers between the "hard" primitivism of bare survival ("shaking apples from forest trees" and "tearing berries from small bushes," 515-17) and the "soft" primitivism of an original benignity of nature when "the fields by themselves fertile fed people who asked for nothing, and the forest gave the wealth it bore there and the dark caves gave their natural homes" (537-39).[13]

Hunting contains the greatest ambiguity in Hippolytus' ideal construction. The little exception that he has to make for his favorite activity is an important clue to the problematical innocence of his Golden Age. He eliminates the bloody altars of sacrificial ritual: his original forest-dwellers wander over the countryside *innocui* (502), without doing harm to anyone or anything (498-502):

> non cruor largus pias
> inundat aras, fruge nec sparsi sacra
> centena nivei colla summittunt boves;
> sed rure vacuo potitur et aperto aethere
> innocuus errat.

> No abundant flow of blood floods upon the holy altars,
> nor do a hundred snowy oxen lower their heads, sprinkled
> with the sacred grain; rather, he possesses an empty
> countryside and wanders harmless and unharmed beneath
> the open sky.

The implicit criticism of the bloodiness of sacrifice in contemporary religious practices in contrast with a simpler life of the past may owe something to Lucretius (1.82-101, 5.1201f.; cf.

---

[13] On the motif of the "spontaneous" nurture of the Golden Age, see Hesiod, *Erga* 117-19; Virg., *Ecl.* 4.39; for other contradictions in Hippolytus' Golden Age, especially in 473 and 515ff., see Henry-Walker (1966) 234f. and Segal (1983b) 244ff.

2.352ff.); yet the addition of "empty countryside," *rure vacuo* (501), suggests desolation rather than peace. We may compare this *rus vacuum* (501) with the sluggish flow and barren fields of the Attic landscape of the prologue (15f.). In the opening song too he enumerated the places of Attica that "are too long free and exempt" from his pursuit of its wild inhabitants (*pars illa diu vacat immunis*, 25). When he uses *vacare* again thirty lines later, it is to describe Diana's power to kill rather than foster the creatures in her realm (*cuius regno pars terrarum / secreta vacat*, "for whose reign part of the earth is free, set apart").

Hippolytus' Golden-Age landscape is in fact not innocuous to all of its inhabitants (502-4):

> callidas tantum feris
> struxisse fraudes novit et fessus gravi
> labore niveo corpus Iliso fovet.

> Crafty snares for the wild animals only does he know how to devise, and tired with the heavy toil he refreshes his body by the snowy Ilissus.[14]

The Ilissus (whatever the appropriateness of its epithet here) again takes us back to the context of the opening song (13). Even apart from the echo of Hippolytus' hunting there, the present passage would at once put the educated audience on guard. Craft or trickery (*fraudes*, 503) is generally banished from the Golden Age and certainly from its most famous representation in Latin, Virgil's Fourth *Eclogue* (cf. *Ecl.* 4.31). Here, emphasized by the adjective *callidus*, these crafty tricks of the hunter have a prominent place. The addition of *tantum*, "only," in 502 calls attention to Hippolytus' special pleading. In the ode on the disorder of human affairs after Theseus' curse, trickery, (*fraus*) marks the fallen, chaotic state that in fact an-

---

[14] There is perhaps another latent tension within this Golden Age in that the image of the youth resting in verdant pleasance after the exhaustion of the hunt can suggest the erotic dangers of the country developed by Ovid, e.g. *Met.* 2.417ff., 3.175ff. and 407ff., 7.808ff. See Segal (1969) 15ff., 40ff. Hippolytus' language at 519-21 also verges toward the erotic.

swers Hippolytus' Golden Age: *fraus sublimi regnat in aula*
("trickery rules in the lofty hall," 982; cf. 496-98, 522f.). Just
such *fraus* will entrap Hippolytus (cf. 828), in this case too the
hunted instead of the hunter (cf. 778-84).

Amid the pacific idleness there is still heavy toil (*gravis labor*,
504), due, as the context suggests, to unlimited opportunities
to trap and kill. The altars may not be stained with the blood of
snowy oxen (*nivei boves*, 500), but the hunter's tired body, lying
by snowy Ilissus (504), will be stained by the blood that needs
washing off. That, at least, is a possible implication of *niveo corpus Iliso fovet*, where the verb *fovet*, as Grimal points out, can
have the meaning "purify," "wash."[15] We may again recall Hippolytus' opening song with its strong emphasis on the bloody
traces of his hunting (77-79). Hippolytus praises early man's
vegetarian diet of fruits and berries (515f.), but such vegetarian
fare does not seem probable for the one who sets out his crafty
snares and then dozes in exhaustion on the Ilissus' banks (502-
4).

The two contiguous sentences of 499-502 and 502-4 immediately juxtapose sacrifice and hunting. This contrast is part of a
familiar antithesis in Greek culture, taken over in part by the
Romans, that carries a strong hierarchical valuation. Sacrifice is
the institution of civilized life, whereas an economy based on
hunting is the mark of a primitive existence, the "beastlike life"
which man leaves behind him as he progresses to the "higher"
and more developed social organization of which he is inher-
ently capable.[16] In substituting hunting for sacrifice, Hippolytus is in fact regressing not to bucolic leisure (in any event undercut by the *gravis labor* of 503f.) but to primitive savagery.

[15] See Grimal (1965) ad 504, citing Virg., *Georg.* 4.230. Grimal suggests a
contrast with the luxury of the warm baths of urban opulence, but the repetition
of *niveus* in 500 and 504 (an adjective that has troubled editors, as Grimal notes)
also suggests the contrast of snowy whiteness and blood, undercutting Hippolytus' claims for the purity of his Golden Age in 499f.
[16] See Segal (1981) 31ff., 130, 300ff. with further references; Eugene Vance,
"Sylvia's Pet Stag: Wildness and Domesticity in Virgil's *Aeneid*," *Arethusa* 14
(1981) 127-38, especially 132ff.

Hippolytus would not permit the blood of bulls to flow upon the altars (498f.), but he is quite ready to pour out Phaedra's blood as a sacrifice on the altars of Diana (708f.):

iustior numquam focis
datus tuis est sanguis, arquitenens dea.

Never has blood more just been offered to
your altars, my bow-bearing goddess.

Instead of banning animal sacrifice, he reverts to the barbarism of human sacrifice. This is the hidden savagery in his Golden-Age world, stripped of its defensive trappings. Invoked as the justifier of his own latent violence (cf. *iustior*, 708), Diana appears here not as the divinity of a paradise where the lion lies down with the lamb but as the goddess of a savage barbarism like the Artemis of Euripides' *Iphigeneia among the Taurians*, a goddess who might accept human sacrifice.

The last stage of degeneration within Hippolytus' Golden Age is the polluting "flow" of spilled blood (*cruor*) that "pours forth and has stained (*infecit*) every land," making the sea red (551f.). For all his concern with purifying himself from Phaedra's polluting touch (690, 713ff.), Hippolytus is blind to the blood that, in the name of justice, he himself would shed (708f.). In his ideal account of hunt versus sacrifice in the Golden Age he repeats the epithet "snowy" (*niveus*) twice within five lines (500, 504): contrast his exultation in the red and bloodied muzzles of his hunting dogs in his opening song (77-79).

When Hippolytus describes his Golden-Age simplicity as free of the disturbances of both sea and fire, he is unknowingly revealing his incapacity to deal with just those forces that he excludes. His imitation of the simple life of old, he claims, is free of the flaming passion of greed (*non illum avarae mentis inflammat furor*, 486). Later he cites the disruptive effect of "the unholy madness for gain (*lucri furor*), abrupt anger, and lust that drives on inflamed minds" (*succensas agit / libido mentes*, 540-

42). These images, along with *furor*, occur throughout the play to describe Phaedra's passion.[17]

In Hippolytus' historical scheme abrupt anger (*ira praeceps*) brought an end to the pristine harmony of that remote time (541). He himself now enacts that anger and along with it the disintegration of his own Golden-Age fantasy. When the Nurse, a few lines later, sees her initial assessment (414-17) of Hippolytus' irremediable savagery confirmed, she compares his obduracy to a harsh reef battered by wind and wave (580-82).[18] The marine landscape is no longer the untraversed surface of a peaceful time before ships but a place of irreconcilably warring elements: "The *harsh* reef . . . sends far back the *harassing* waves." The sea, initially identified with Phaedra's regal status as the heir of Minos' empire (85-88), now reflects female sexual aggressiveness as it encounters harsh intransigence.

In Hippolytus' account of human history, the stepmother's crimes mark the last stage of the world's collapse into evil. "As to the stepmother," he begins, "I keep silence; she is no gentler than the wild beasts" (558). The stepmother is the starting point for his general denunciation of women, culminating in Medea: "Let the others be kept in silence," he says, rounding off this subsection with an echo of his opening phrase (*sileantur aliae*, 563; *taceo novercas*, 558); "Aegeus' spouse alone, Medea, will render women a race accursed" (563f.).

The link with the Golden Age here becomes even clearer when one compares Seneca's *Medea*, where the heroine's potential violence is defined by the background of evil intruding into a world of pristine innocence. The voyage of the *Argo*, first ship to sail the ocean, introduces the sailing and commerce that end the Golden Age and also bring Medea from her barbarian home to Greece (*Medea* 301-79, especially 360-69).[19] Later, when

---

[17] Even Hippolytus' similar description of the rushing waves that pour forth from the abundant spring of his pleasance (*fons largus citas / diffundit undas*, 512f.), may carry echoes of those more dangerous "waves" of Phaedra's passion. Cf. 103, 182, 394.

[18] Cf. *Aen.* 4.438-40, 7.869ff.; see Fantham (1975) 3f., 7.

[19] See Regenbogen (1930) 197f.; see Lawall (1979) 421-23; Segal (1983b) 237ff.

Hippolytus denounces Phaedra as the worst of women (cf. 687 and 564), he again invokes Medea, now surpassed in evil by his own stepmother. Medea is part of the recent Athenian past, but she also has associations with the loss of a remoter Golden Age, a Golden Age that Hippolytus is now losing, figuratively, in his own life experience.[20] As he is forced to confront corruption in his own house, he swings from a fantasy of total innocence to accusations of total depravity. He thus eliminates the middle ground, the ground of reality where the imperfect and compromised nature of human life must be lived.

Hippolytus ostensibly blames himself as well as Phaedra for his loss of purity: "I am guilty, I have deserved to die" (683). The former phrase, *sum nocens*, cancels out his Golden-Age innocence (*innocuus*, 502), just as the figurative reincarnation of Medea in Phaedra seals off his happy childhood (cf. 697 and 564). But in 683 he is far from any real conviction of his own fault. Far from behaving as though deserving to die, he nearly puts Phaedra to death (706). He remains as blind to the sources of violence in himself now as he was to the destructiveness of his Golden-Age innocuousness earlier (502).

In Hippolytus' history of civilization, the stage before the evil stepmother belongs to violence. The wars that rage on land and sea (550-52) soon infect the domestic realm with crimes of kin against kin (553-62). The whole passage requires close scrutiny (550-62):

> Invenit artes bellicus Mavors novas
> et mille formas mortis. Hinc terras cruor
> infecit omnis fusus et rubuit mare.
> Tum scelera dempto fine per cunctas domos
> iere, nullum caruit exemplo nefas.
> A fratre frater, dextera gnati parens
> cecidit, maritus coniugis ferro iacet
> perimuntque fetus impiae matres suos.

---

[20] Note too the verbal similarity between *Pha.* 697, comparing Phaedra to Medea, and *Med.* 362, on the *Argo* and its dangerous passenger marking the end of the Golden Age and the beginning of corruption.

Taceo novercas: mitius nil est feris.
Sed dux malorum femina. Haec scelerum artifex
obsedit animos; huius incesti stupris
fumant tot urbes, bella tot gentes gerunt
et versa ab imo regna tot populos premunt.

Warlike Mars invented new arts (of war) and a thousand
forms of death. From here blood poured forth and stained
every land, and the sea grew red. Then, as all limit was
removed, the crimes marched through every house; no sin
lacked an example. Brother was killed by brother, parent by
the hand of son, husband lies (slain) by a wife's sword, and
unholy mothers destroy their own offspring. As to
stepmothers I am silent: they are a thing no gentler than
wild beasts. But woman is the leader of evil deeds. This
clever deviser of crimes lays siege to our minds; because of
the sinful licence of this corrupted being so many cities
smoke (in ruins), so many peoples wage wars, and
kingdoms overturned from their foundations lie heavily
upon so many peoples.

There is a curious mingling of domestic with civil violence.
Hippolytus shifts abruptly from war to evil women (*bellicus Ma-
vors*, 550; *impiae matres*, 557) and then again from evil women
to war (*novercas*, 558; *bella*, 561; cf. 550). His close conjunction
of war and domestic (especially maternal) violence reveals again
the personal dimension of his Golden-Age fantasy, his fusion—
and confusion—of phylogeny with ontogeny.[21]

The list of violent deeds within the house in 553ff. culminates
in the crime of mothers against sons: "Wicked mothers kill their
own offspring" (557). "Stepmothers" occurs in the next line
(558); and the evil stepmother par excellence, Medea, "wife of
Aegeus," is cited at the end for her attempted murder of her
stepson, Theseus (563f.). As wife of Aegeus, Medea becomes

---

[21] Cf. Empedocles 31 B137 Diels-Kranz, where such a vision of violence
within the house—fathers killing and devouring sons and vice versa—is the correlative of cosmic and social, rather than personal, disorder.

part of the family background of Hippolytus himself, so that the degeneration of the Golden Age moves from primordial myth to his present life. As wife of Aegeus too, she has presumably accomplished her vengeful crime of killing her own and Jason's children and found not only refuge but also regal status at Athens. The movement from mothers killing children in 557 to stepmothers in 558 may suggest that Hippolytus already has the filicidal Medea in mind. The female archcriminal, she is successful in past evil and still plots future crimes. The status of stepmother obviously alludes to Phaedra too, but it is part of Hippolytus' blindness and of Phaedra's heroism that Phaedra will ultimately refuse to be another Medea. She carries out the first stage of criminal vengeance, prepared for her by the Nurse, to protect herself; but she turns back, as Medea does not, from completing the crime. She punishes herself when she might have escaped.

Mothers killing children in 557 is the only crime in which the act of murder has an active verb. Brothers and fathers both "fall" at the hand of their killer; the husband "lies slain" (*iacet*) by the wife's sword. Only the mothers actively "destroy" their offspring, and the verb comes first in the carefully worded line (557): *perimuntque fetus impiae matres suos.*[22] The wife who kills her husband is also the only murderer whose weapon is explicitly named (*maritus coniugis ferro iacet*, 556). This emphasis pinpoints Hippolytus' greatest anxieties. On just the other side of his artificial paradise lie the infantile terror of a fully sexual and murderous mother and the fear of a woman powerful and determined enough to kill her husband.[23]

As the emissary of the erotic and seductive (step)mother, the Nurse elicits the full force of Hippolytus' defensive strategies. The sequel will attack Hippolytus' Golden Age at its psycholog-

[22] *Fetus suos*, "their own offspring," includes daughters as well as sons, but the masculine pronominal adjective tends to keep "sons" in the foreground.

[23] One could also explain Hippolytus' rage against bad mothers and stepmothers as the anger he feels toward the mother who has abandoned him. Lines 578-80 would justify such an interpretation.

ical roots. Theseus' accusation transforms the chaste realm of his Amazon mother (cf. 575-79) into a subhuman savagery of lustful prostitution (909-15). Hippolytus' search for ancient ways (*prisca et antiqua appetens*, 916; cf. 484) becomes a deceitful cover for lust, shameless boldness, and criminality (916-22). Like all the fantasies in the play, that of the Golden Age, for all its superficial appeal of freshness and beauty, turns into its nightmare opposite.

Blind to what his fantasy conceals and excludes, Hippolytus imagines all the worst crimes in the family except the one that actually applies to him. He lists brother killed by brother, father by son, husband by wife, child by mother, but not son killed by father. The crimes of kindred blood that he does evoke are the opposite of the actual crimes perpetrated in the play. Instead of son murdering father (555), a father will murder his son (cf. *natum parens*, 998). Instead of wife killing husband (556), a husband has killed his wife (Theseus and Antiope, 926-29). Just after the "Golden Age" passage Hippolytus neutralizes this homicidal aggression in the family when he describes Antiope as *matris amissae*, "a mother lost" rather than a "mother killed." This silence too passes over the violence done not by women but by men. It parallels his inability to see his own violence, for instead of a mother or stepmother killing her sons (557), he is himself a son who comes close to killing his stepmother (707-12). He would use against a woman the weapon that, in his view, a wife used against husband (*ferrum*, "sword," 556; *ensis*, 706, 714, 729, 796; *ferrum*, 728, 891).

"About the stepmother I keep silence: she is no gentler than the beasts" (558): the silence of Hippolytus in fact points to his greatest fears and most exaggerated anger. His rhetorical figure of *praeteritio* here is far from keeping silence. For seven verses he expatiates on the bad stepmother's nefarious doings (558-64), whereas three lines suffice for all the other kinfolk combined (555-57). He repeats the motif of silence at the end to name Medea: "Let the others be held in silence (*sileantur aliae*); alone Aegeus' wife, Medea, will make woman a race accursed"

(563). His emphasis on his silence only points up the things he does not say. He cannot put into words the crimes that touch him most closely and in fact mark the real end of his Golden Age, the incestuous desire of a sexual mother and the murderous anger of a wrathful father. Had he been able to lift his veil of silence around them, he might have been able to accept the end of the Golden Age and live in the real world on the other side.

The final destruction of Hippolytus' Golden-Age childhood comes, after all, not from the evil stepmother, but from the wrathful father. Theseus' anger is a triple blow. First, his murderous curse on his son realizes in Hippolytus' own life that slaying of kin by kin that Hippolytus associated with the corruption of the Golden Age (555-64). Far from living in a private age of innocence, he is forced to confront the violent emotions among which he lives. Second, Theseus' acceptance of Phaedra's accusation directly attacks Hippolytus' emulation of the pristine simplicity of the men of old (915-17):

ubi vultus ille et ficta maiestas viri
atque habitus horrens, prisca et antiqua appetens,
morumque senium triste et affectus graves?

Where is that countenance and feigned majesty of the man? Where his shaggy dress, aiming at pristine and ancient manners? Where is that elderly severity of morals, that solemn bearing?

Hippolytus's whole way of life is transformed into a sham, concealing hidden lust behind a fine show of chastity (918-22). His sylvan simplicity now appears as sylvan savagery (922-24). Ironically, Theseus' denunciation of Hippolytus' lustful Amazon ancestry and licentiousness concealed beneath a chaste exterior (907-24) is in fact far more appropriate to Phaedra, with her heritage from Pasiphae and her lies to protect her position as a chaste wife (*pudica*, 874; cf. 891-93).[24]

---

[24] On the theme of deceptive appearance here see Seidensticker (1969) 150.

Theseus' third and greatest blow is to tarnish the image of the pure mother on whose loss Hippolytus has founded his hatred of all women. The Nurse had made the first attack by suggesting that even the realm of his (Amazon) mother was subject to Venus' yoke of love (574-77). Theseus leaves that maternal purity in shreds. In his eyes the Amazons are degenerate barbarians rather than noble savages (906-8).[25] For him the chastity that Hippolytus takes as his model hides a more culpable sexual licence and passion (*furor*, 909): the Amazons, he charges, "hate the (marriage) covenants of Venus and prostitute their long-chaste bodies to (all) peoples" (*odisse Veneris foedera et castum diu / vulgare populis corpus* (909-11). This attack on Hippolytus' mother indirectly shatters Phaedra's fantasies too, for she had idealized Hippolytus as a blend of the best in Greek and Scythian (658-60). With Theseus' appearance and the intrusion of hard realities on all sides, the northern influence of the Scythian or Amazon corrupts the Greek.

These Amazons illustrate the characteristic ambivalence of primitive life, shifting between Golden-Age purity (Hippolytus' vision) and subhuman savagery (Theseus' accusation).[26] Shunning the covenants of Venus (*Veneris foedera*, 910), that make sexuality a part of legitimate marriage, they are even worse than the beasts, for they replace these laws of Venus with a crime of Venus (*Veneris nefas*, 913) of which even the wild beasts are ashamed. This total reversal in the meaning of his mother's landscape exactly parallels the reversal of Hippolytus' forest world in the previous ode (784ff.).

The collapse of Hippolytus' forest world at Theseus' accusation in fact fuses Hippolytus' idealized childhood, based on the

[25] Grimal (1965) ad loc. gives a good paraphrase: "Les Amazons fuyaient le mariage mais, pour assurer la continuité de leur espèce, s'offraient aux étrangers qui traversaient leur pays." There is perhaps a further undercutting of Hippolytus' Golden Age vision in Theseus' bitter accusation of reversion to a degenerate *primam stirpem* (908), in contrast to Hippolytus' *prima aetas* (526f.). On the savagery of the Amazon cf. also *Tro.* 243 and *Herc. Fur.* 242ff., 542ff.

[26] For the ambiguous place of the Amazon in the classical image of civilized peoples see Segal (1981) 30; Page duBois, *Centaurs and Amazons* (Ann Arbor 1982) 32ff., 69ff.

image of a chaste mother, with its apparent opposite, the criminal passion of the archetypally lustful mother, Pasiphae. Early in the play the Nurse warns Phaedra against a "crime (*nefas*) which not even any barbarian land has ever perpetrated, not the Getae wandering on the plains, not the inhospitable Taurians or the sparsely settled Scythians" (166-69). Two of the three peoples recur in Theseus' accusation (*Taurus aut sparsus Scythes*, 168; *Taurus Scythes*, 906). For the Nurse too, these remote races are potential perpetrators of *nefas*, the sinful violation of moral law, but even so they abstain from the crime that she sees Phaedra meditating. For Theseus, implicitly, they are now the actual perpetrators of such a crime, and Hippolytus shares their heritage (906-9). Theseus, moreover, adds the point that even the "wild beasts avoid (such) a crime against Venus" (*ferae quoque ipsae Veneris evitant nefas*, 913). The degeneration of the remote world of Hippolytus' mother thus worsens in two respects: Scythian and Taurian are actual rather than potential criminals; and the key term in the rhetorical comparison, "Not even X would do such things," has moved from men to beasts.

"Remember your mother," the Nurse warned Phaedra (*memor matris*, 170). These memories are full of monstrous lust (170-77). Hippolytus evokes them later when he shrinks from her touch and accuses her of an evil greater than her mother's (688-93). But now his childhood past, viewed through Theseus' accusing eyes, seems to contain the same corruptions and the same propensity toward sexual crime (*Veneris nefas*, 913; *nefandum*, 921; cf. *nefas* describing Pasiphae and Phaedra in 143 and 166).

The movement, on the psychological level, between fantasy and nightmare (preserving a sexually pure mother and accusations of incestuous rape against one's own mother) corresponds, on the cultural level, to the shift between "soft" and "hard" primitivism. The personal Golden Age of childhood and the historical Golden Age of the human race both revert to a savage, lawless state. Thus, on the cultural or historical plane, Hippolytus' account of the historical Golden Age fluctuates between Nature's spontaneous profusion in fertile fields (*arva per se feta*, 537; cf. 525-27) and a rude existence of bare survival sustained by berries, wild fruits, and life in forests and caves (515-17, 539).[27] The corruption of his personal Golden Age is complete when Theseus recasts the Amazon mother as promiscuous rather than virginal (909-14), as barbarian degenerate rather than noble savage (cf. 660 and 906ff.).

Earlier in the scene the Nurse had urged him to imitate the farmer's fields that luxuriate in rich crops (454-56), whereas he is in fact to prove harsh and savage (*truculentus et silvester*, 461), barren like the hard rock (*dura cautes*, 580), sterile despite the vigor of his youth (*sterilis iuventus*, 479), like the sterile fields through which flows his sluggish Attic river, the Ilissus, in his opening song (*agros steriles*, 15; contrast *arva feta*, "fertile fields," 537). Phaedra, herself prone to draw his idealized image of the Amazon mother into her own love-fantasies (cf. 660), is the catalyst for releasing the savagery pent up in the unstable fictions out of which he has constructed his world-view. Thus she awakens in him not images of the pure Amazon of the undefiled North as she had hoped (cf. 398-403) but the impure mother-figures of the fallen world that he associates with female sexuality, Medea and Pasiphae, the criminal stepmother and the sexually insatiable mother (687-97; cf. 559-64).

Proven worse than a savage, worse than a beast (913f.), Hippolytus is destroyed not only in a monstrous reenactment of the end of the Golden Age but also in a regressive movement back toward savagery. His physical destruction by the monster from the sea, as we have noted, reverses man's control over nature. The monster itself is the leader of a *wild* herd (*feri dominator gregis*, 1039), scatters domesticated flocks, puts to flight the hunter, and figuratively makes the sea overwhelm the pilot (cf.

---

[27] Seneca's description may also have been influenced by Virgil, *Georg.* 1.127f., *ipsaque tellus / omnia liberius nullo poscente ferebat* ("The earth by itself, under no one's demands, brought forth all things freely"). Seneca, however, has changed the emphasis to underline the simplicity of early man's needs. For other borrowings (Lucretius, Ovid, Tibullus) see Grimal's notes ad 525-39, passim. See above, note 13.

1048f., 1050-54, 1072-75, 1082ff.). The reins that should control his horses become the "snare" that entraps the hunter (cf. *laqueus* in 1086 and 46).

The only remaining source of civilized order is the king, famed for destroying monstrous evil-doers. But Theseus too, aware at the end of all his own cruel and savage potential (cf. 1221, 1246), feels that he deserves death from those very outlaws whom he exterminated in his civilizing exploits (1223-25). Negating his ascent from Hades, he would attach himself to the worst of the sinners punished below (1229-37). His self-lacerating remorse vindicates his son, but it also takes us to a world-view that is at the furthest possible extreme from the idealized innocence in Hippolytus' Golden-Age world.

III

These fluctuations between innocence and chaotic violence appear on a more general level in the conception of Nature (*Natura*) in the play. *Natura* is an important concept in Seneca's moral philosophy. In its broadest terms it refers to the divinely governed world-order which is both the model for and the source of the fixed laws for man; it is the source of man's true happiness, which consists in living in conformity with those laws.[28]

Within the play, however, *Natura* too is subject to the movement between order and chaos reflected in the lives of the mortal characters. The Nurse cites Nature, with all her laws, to oppose the monstrosity toward which Phaedra's passion is leading (176). But in the next ode "Nature" means the power of love as an elemental force which "claims as her own all the beasts," including those of Hippolytus' supposedly pure forest world (*vindicat omnes natura sibi*, "Nature claims them all for herself," 352). The verb *vindicat* here also carries a hint of Nature's

---

[28] E.g. *Cons. Helv.* 8 and 20, *Epist.* 90. See in general Croisille (1964) 285; Hadot (1969) 100f., 147ff. Boyle's study of *Natura* (1985) complements mine: he stresses the close association of Nature with Diana and the contradictions in them both.

power to avenge or punish infringements on her claims.[29] "Nature" has a similar meaning in the following scene, where the Nurse urges Hippolytus to "follow nature as the guide of life" (*proinde vitae sequere naturam ducem*, 481). But her notion of "nature" includes the freer life of the town (482) as well as the instinct of procreation given us by "the greatest parent of the world" so that we may replenish the world as the old pass away (466-74).[30]

The role of *Natura* in Hippolytus' intemperate hatred of women establishes a correspondence between the order of the individual soul and the order of the world. The ideal of "following nature" in 481 is drastically undercut by the unnaturalness of his attitude to women (566-73):

> Detestor omnis, horreo, fugio, execror.
> Sit ratio, sit natura, sit durus furor,
> odisse placuit. Ignibus iunges aquas
> et amica ratibus ante promittet vada
> incerta Syrtis, ante ab extremo sinu
> Hesperia Tethys lucidum attollet diem
> et ora dammis blanda praebebunt lupi
> quam victus animum feminae mitem geram.

> I loathe, shudder at, flee, curse, all women. Let it be reason, let it be nature, let it be fearful madness: my resolve is to hate them. Sooner will you join water with fire, sooner will Syrtis promise friendly waves to ships, sooner will Hesperian Tethys lift up bright day, and sooner wolves offer

[29] With Grimal (1965) ad loc. I keep the ms. reading in 352: "La 'nature' est précisément cette puissance d'amour." On *Natura* and its shifts of meaning see also Henry-Walker (1966) 233; Boyle (1985) passim; Davis (1983) 125-27.

[30] Seneca probably has in mind the praise of Venus genetrix, the sexual instinct as the renewing force of life, in passages like Eur. *Hipp.* 447ff., frag. 898 Nauck, Aeschylus' *Danaids* (frag. 44 Nauck), or Lucretius' proem: see Grimal (1965) ad 469. Though the Nurse mentions Venus here, she is also careful to add the masculine ruler of the universe, *maximus mundi parens* (466), a wise precaution in addressing a devotee of the goddess not of sex and procreation but of her antagonist.

soft and gentle face to does than I, conquered, bear a spirit kind to woman.

In this passage he invokes the normative cosmic order of Nature (cf. also 176, 959ff.) for an idiosyncratic antipathy that flies in the face of *natura* (cf. 350-52, 1115f.). His vehemence of feeling is so great that he can treat *natura* as an equivalent of reason on the one hand and of madness on the other (*ratio, natura, furor*, in 567). Appropriately his rhetorical figure in the next lines is an adynaton, i.e. an assertion of emphasis by a deliberate violation of nature. The contradictions between nature and the unnatural in both subject and style match the contradictions that Hippolytus' world-view has to span in order to maintain itself.

Both protagonists depart from the laws of Nature, albeit in opposite directions, and suffer accordingly. Thus Hippolytus' irrational blurring of reason and madness also draws him paradoxically into the language of Phaedra's conflicts (cf. 184, 253, 259). The unnatural joining of water and fire in his hyperbole of 568, *ignibus iunges aquas*, has the same effect. In the destructive symmetry of likeness and opposition that runs between them, his defiance of Nature in 568-73 finds an echo in Phaedra's suicide speech (cf. 1161-63).

The laws of nature are the subject of the ode just after the peripety. Nature, "great parent of the gods," shares with Jupiter the rule of the heavenly motions and the seasonal rhythms (959-71). But Theseus has just let loose the forces of sea, sky, and wind against his son (954-58). The orderly Nature of the ode is a foil to the disorder increasingly apparent in the human world, where the evil prosper and the good fare badly (972-77).[31] Fortune, not Nature, the chorus concludes, "governs human affairs with no order at all, scattering her gifts with blind hand, fostering the baser cause (978-80).

After the catastrophe Nature reasserts her power as a moral

---

[31] Boyle (1985) discusses the ode of 959ff. as a message of "unrelieved despair." See also Dingel (1974) 99f.

force for a moment in the natural grief that Theseus, as a father, feels for the loss of his son (1114-17). But even so the bonds of nature do not cancel out the murderous violence of his justice. "Not because I destroyed him, but because I have lost him, do I lament" is his ambiguous closing statement of the scene (1122).[32] The following ode on Fortune, the last choral song in the play, qualifies the blindness of Fortune in the previous ode and suggests some order in the alternating destinies of the mighty and the humble. But it still does not reinstate Nature as a universal power above or against Fortune.[33]

The chorus' bleak vision in both of these odes corresponds to the darkening of Hippolytus' Golden Age as lust, violence, and hatred intrude into family life (555-73). The world that these odes imply (especially 959ff.) is just the reverse of the rustic simplicity idealized by Hippolytus. He had fantasied a life far from "the winds of popular favor and the mob that puts no trust in good men" (488), untainted by the luxury of the columned and gilded hall (496-98). The chorus describes a state in which "trickery reigns in the lofty hall and people take joy in bestowing the fasces of authority on the base" (982-84). Hippolytus attributed the end of the Golden Age to limitless "desire" (*libido*, 542) and the rule of vice (540ff.). The chorus here essentially does the same (981-88), with *dira libido*, "accursed desire," strongly in evidence (981). The echoes confirm the collapse of Hippolytus' fantasies but also carry the fall of the Golden Age from a remote, historical past into the present scene of action.

The chorus closely identifies *Natura*, "great parent of the gods," with Jupiter, ruler of the heavens (959ff.). This anthro-

[32] To keep consistency with 1117, line 1122, *quod interemi non quod amisi fleo*, should mean, "Not because I killed him, but because I lost him do I weep." Grimal (1965) ad loc. points out, "Mais la construction est volontairement ambiguë, *non* pouvant aussi bien être reporté sur ce qui suit, *non quod amisi.*" Miller, in the Loeb edition, follows the latter possibility, "Not that I lost, but that I slew, I weep," but does not mention the other meaning. For the importance of the ambiguity see also Skovgaard-Hansen (1972) 122.
[33] So Skovgaard-Hansen (1972) 95f.

pomorphization of *natura* suggests for a moment an analogy between the governance of the world and a human family. But, as we have seen, the destruction of order on the individual level, for both Hippolytus and Phaedra, takes the form of the destruction of the family (cf. 553-64). The first half of the play stresses the corruption of the mother-figure by the criminal acts of Pasiphae and Medea in the background. The second half of the play extends that disorder to the father, both in the heavens and on earth. The ode on the power of love made no exception for the gods, including the "very god who fashioned the sky and the clouds" (299f.), the "ruler of Olympus" who is later paired with *Natura*, "great parent of the gods" (959-63).

At the same time the chorus has a view of *Natura* that is more inclusive than that of any of the individual characters. The Nurse can use *Natura* as it serves her purposes, now to check Phaedra's lust (176), now to excite Hippolytus' ardor (481). The chorus includes both the forests of Hippolytus' sylvan world and the agrarian domain of Ceres in their praise of *Natura's* power (966-71). Although they now look upon a world disordered by violence, their words point at least in the direction of an equilibrium where both barrenness and fertility have their due season. Within the play, however, such harmony seems improbable as we witness monstrosities past or present, figurative or literal: monstrous births that result from an excess of procreative energy on the one side, sterility in an aggressive virginity and delight in killing on the other.

In tragedy generally the fecundating power of life—here celebrated in the first choral ode—cannot take its "natural" route to physical union and the procreation of children, but instead follows a darker course. The fire that sets Phaedra ablaze with love is the same fire, figuratively speaking (and the figure is Seneca's), that kindles the funeral pyres.[34]

This fusion of love and death, of the fires of passion and the funeral pyres, runs counter to *natura* in the limited sense of the

---

[34] On the torch see above, chap. 2, note 38.

"natural instincts" of self-preservation. But in defying the life-
instincts which are also part of *Natura* in its larger meaning, the
governing principle of the cosmic order (*magna parens, Natura,
deum*, 959), this course of action is ambiguous. The play works
out its ambiguity in terms of the ironical inversions in the lives
of the major characters: Phaedra's willed fusion of love and
death; the collapse of Hippolytus' aspirations and the corruption of his idealized Golden Age; Theseus' wish to reverse his
ascent from Hades to the upper air (1213ff.). The focus of the
tragic action, however, early centers upon Phaedra and remains
with her to the end. As the bearer of the full force of love, she is
also the focus of its fully tragic dimension in its fusion with
death.

IV

This tragic element in the play resides in large part in the
emotional complexities surrounding the suicide of Phaedra;
and these ultimately go beyond a one-dimensional philosophical explanation in terms of obedience to Stoic *Natura*. Hippolytus' refusal to accede to the compelling *natura* of the sexual
drive (as the Nurse perversely interprets *natura* in 481) is narrow and superficial in comparison to Phaedra's victory over this
aspect of *natura* by her suicide.[35] She refuses to return to those
"chambers of her husband" which she defended by incriminating Hippolytus. "Shall I then seek the bedroom of a spouse des-
ecrated by so great a crime?" she asked in her death-scene (*coniugis thalamos petam / tanto impiatos facinore?* 1185f.) Theseus on
his return had addressed her as *socia thalami*, "consort of my
bedchamber" (864), and it was to preserve that title that she
carried through the accusation of Hippolytus that the Nurse
had already prepared by her quick and resourceful response to
the situation (719ff.). But in refusing to return to that bed-

---

[35] The Nurse's "following nature as leader" (*sequere naturam ducem*) seems in
fact closer to the Epicurean *dux vitae dia voluptas* (Lucretius 2.172, "divine
pleasure as leader of life"). For the perverted use of the argument from Nature
(from the Stoic point of view) see Grimal (1965) ad 481f.

chamber, Phaedra relinquishes her honorific title, her good name, and life itself for the truth of her love. She thereby establishes a truer union with Hippolytus than was ever possible, realistically, in life.

Her choice of suicide over a successful crime also checks the moral disorder that the chorus warns against in their praise of Nature as the ordering force of the human and natural realms (959-88; contrast 481f., discussed above). That ode ends with the ill-gotten gains that accrue to evil men in a world alienated from Nature (985-88):

> tristis virtus perversa tulit
> praemia recti: castos sequitur
> mala paupertas vitioque potens
> regnat adulter: o vane pudor
>   falsumque decus.

> Turned upside down are the rewards that severe virtue wins for righteousness. Grim poverty pursues the chaste, and the adulterer, powerful through his crime, rules. O empty modesty and false glory.

Phaedra's self-chosen death rejects just such empty modesty and false glory. She will not become the chorus's adulterous ruler, powerful through her crime (986f.).

Yet the vehemence of the passion surrounding her suicide also renders ambiguous her moral triumph. She herself admits this double perspective: she dies as chaste for her husband but as unchaste for love (*morere, si casta es, viro; / si incesta, amori*, 1184f.). Her talk of "joining minds" (or "hearts") with Hippolytus (*animos iungere*) in the line just preceding seems to favor *amor* over *virtus*.

Her death is a tragic version of the *hieros gamos*, the "sacred marriage" that was once part of the myth.[36] This mythical motif also undercuts the philosophical triumph of her suicide. It con-

---

[36] See most recently Walter Burkert, *Structure and History of Greek Mythology*, (Sather Classical Lectures 47, Berkeley and Los Angeles 1979), 99ff.; further references in Segal (1979) p. 159, note 19.

firms Hippolytus' sterility and simultaneously confirms both
Phaedra's intensity of love and its utter impossibility. She dies
out of fidelity not so much to love as to the fantasy of love. In
her closing words she calls Hippolytus a *sanctus vir* (1198), a
term that may imply a kind of sanctified union (cf. *vir* in the
sense of "husband" in 1184 and the hint of ambiguity in *virum
sequamur*, 254);[37] but it is a union purchased at the price of further union with her living husband (cf. 1185).

It completes her tragedy that none of her painfully won efforts toward a purification of her passion are visible to Theseus.
He can only curse her, in his closing lines, as impure and defiled
(*impio capiti*, 1280). He is as one-sided against her as he was earlier against Hippolytus. Thus, paradoxically, the Nature Ode's
bitter reflection on unrewarded virtue may apply to her almost
as much as to Hippolytus: "Turned upside down are the re-
wards that severe virtue wins for righteousness" (985f.).

The continuing tensions in Phaedra between remorse and
fantasy, between a purified and a still purblind love, make the
play more than a moralistic condemnation of irrational passions. Seneca maintains to the end a depth and clarity of insight
into the folly and the beauty of desperate love. Beneath the philosophical themes of *ratio* and *natura* lies a rich mythic structure,
taken over from Euripides but surrounded with Seneca's own
aura of intense emotionality: the loss of a Golden-Age world of
childhood innocence, the corrupted past symbolized by the Minoan labyrinth, the contrasts of chastity and monstrous births,
of Amazon and Pasiphae, the figurative and literal descent to
the subterranean darkness of the Underworld, the battle to
overcome chaotic monsters, the emulation of a heroic father,
and its failure.

"If the way of Greek tragedy led to a humanization of myth
that finally destroyed myth," Otto Regenbogen observes, "this
new time, which could no longer create myth, symbolized its
way of life and its feeling about life in ancient myth which it ac-

---

[37] See Henry-Walker (1966) 231, 238. For the ironies of 1198 see below,
chap. 9, sec. III, ad fin.

cordingly chose, reformed, and refilled from within."[38] Seneca effected that transformation of Greek mythic tragedy through the poetry of the emotions which he inherited and developed from Catullus, Virgil, Ovid, and the elegists.

Quid ratio possit? "What power might reason have?" (184). Whatever Seneca thought he was doing in the service of Stoic rationalism by reproving the passions, the force of his poetic language cuts deeper than the moralism of his ideology.[39] His rhetorically encrusted imagery simplifies the old myths and flattens out their religious dimension, but the poetry of his psychological landscape enables them to speak to us still of the dark truths they contain. The power of this play, as of Senecan tragedy in general, comes not from the victory of *ratio*, however necessary and laudable, but from the emotionally convincing portrayal of the monstrous shapes beneath the surface of the moral life.

[38] Regenbogen (1930) 216.
[39] On the conflict of knowledge and passion see Giomini (1955) 44f.; Vretska (1968) 169; Lefèvre (1972) 370ff.; Leeman (1976) 209ff.

FIVE

Rivalry with the Father: Initiation and Failure

I

In Greek myth the youthful hero's initiatory passage from adolescence to adulthood often has a double component: martial deeds (rivalry with or imitation of the father) and a sexual adventure, trial, or temptation. Familiar examples, with success (overt or implicit) in both areas, are the stories of Bellerophon, Peleus, Meleager, Telemachus, Theseus (in Bacchylides 17) and in displaced form the tales of Orestes and Perseus. Failures include Actaeon, Adonis, Hylas, Pentheus, and the "flower children," Narcissus, Hyacinthus, and Cyparissus. The myth of Theseus (along with that of Perseus) is the success story par excellence.[1] This pattern is still present in the substratum of Seneca's play, but it is transformed from initiatory ritual to psychological meaning and conveyed through the suggestive imagery of monstrosity in the background, especially the Minotaur in the past of Phaedra and of Theseus.

In the preceding chapter we have seen how the Golden-Age imagery of Hippolytus' forest world reflects a fantasy of prolonged childhood innocence. Rather than grow up and accept the civic and domestic responsibilities of the adult male, he remains a marginal figure whose attachments keep him in his mountainous or sylvan setting. Unsuccessful transition from this savage realm of the hunter to the city is the mythical equiv-

---

[1] For the initiatory themes in Theseus' adventures, see Henri Jeanmaire, *Couroi et Courètes. Essai sur l'éducation spartiate et les rites d'adolescence dans l'antiquité hellénique* (Lille and Paris 1939) 273-75, 314ff., 324ff.; Angelo Brelich, *Paides e Parthenoi*, Incunabula Graeca 36 (Rome 1969) 376f.; also Segal (1979a) 23ff. and (1982) 166ff., 189ff.

alent of failure to progress from adolescence to manhood.[2] Life exacts neurosis as the price of failure to mature; myth and literature inflict the more dramatic penalty of death by dismemberment, drowning, or decapitation in the wild.

In order to grow up, the young hero must supplant his father. In the myth of Hippolytus, as in many Oedipal narratives, rivalry with the father is heavily overdetermined: it is worked out both in the foreground of the events unfolding in the present and in the mythical background. The latter is the characters' immediate past, but to the audience it has the fabulous aura of myths within myths: the ancestry of Phaedra, the stories of Minos and Pasiphae, or Theseus' conquest of the Minotaur. The discontinuous retracing of this mythical past in the course of the play corresponds to the psychological effort of reaching back to remoter or more archaic strata of the self and laying bare more primitive layers of motivation.

Phaedra began her confession of love with her memory of Theseus defeating the Minotaur, his most famous exploit (649-55). Her emphasis on Theseus' beauty and the mention of Ariadne's thread (with the erotic connotation of 650) imply that Theseus won a woman and a heroic victory in a single exploit. This is a victory in which, paradoxically, he "pleased his enemy" (*placuit hosti*, 656). As Phaedra uses this achievement of the youthful Theseus to convey her love for the youthful Hippolytus standing before her (654ff.), she also joins sexual competition with the father in the incest motif to implicit martial competition against the father as heroic monster-slayer. Theseus combined sex appeal and heroic effectiveness, but for Hippolytus the former will be disastrous, as the chorus sings at the end of the next ode: "Scarce are the men—survey the centuries—to whom good looks (*forma*) were without penalty" (820f.).

---

[2] See Marcel Detienne, *Dionysus Slain*, trans. M. and L. Muellner (Baltimore 1979) 24ff.; Segal (1978/79) 134, 138f.; Neumann (1954), chap. 2, especially 50ff.

Hippolytus responds indignantly to Phaedra by likening her to her "monster-bearing mother," Pasiphae (688-94). He then congratulates Theseus on having had to deal only with Medea (694-97):

o ter quaterque prospero fato dati
quos hausit et peremit et leto dedit
odium dolusque! genitor, invideo tibi:
Colchide noverca maius hoc, maius malum est.

O three and four times given to a happy fate are those whom hatred and guile dispatched and destroyed! Father, I envy you: this is a greater thing, a greater evil, than the Colchian stepmother.

The rhetorical figure of the beatitude is a literary echo of *Odyssey* 5 and *Aeneid* 1.[3] Hippolytus is recalling the heroic wish for a noble death in war when his own concerns are narrowly personal and his enemy is not a hostile army but a woman. It is Theseus, of course, who receives the grandiose epithet of epic heroism when Phaedra salutes him as "great-spirited Theseus" (*magnanime Theseu*) on his arrival (869).[4]

The father's heroic triumph over the monster shifts to the son's confrontation with the sexuality of the mother. Theseus drew his sword against a dangerous male foe; Hippolytus, confronting a greater evil (697), draws against a helpless woman at his feet (706ff). The comparison with Medea in 697 enables Hippolytus to present himself as somehow greater than his father. Ironically, his "evil" is indeed greater, more powerful, for him than the Minotaur was for Theseus. Hippolytus' rejection of Phaedra's advances is a moral victory; but the violence of his

[3] Virgil, *Aen.* 1.94-101 (a passage Seneca himself quotes in *Epist.* 67.8); Homer, *Od.* 5.306ff.

[4] The epithet occurs only here in the play and only four other times in Seneca's tragedies, always in respectful address to men of recognized achievement: Hercules (*HF* 310), Theseus (*HF* 647), and Oedipus (*Oed.* 294 and *Phoen.* 182).

response also reveals the qualities that stand in the way of his reaching adult status.

Between Hippolytus' flight from Phaedra and Theseus' arrival from Hades the chorus sings an ode full of the mythical exemplars of failed generational passage. It compares Hippolytus not only to the handsome young gods, Bacchus and Apollo, but also to Hylas and Endymion, beautiful adolescents of vulnerable beauty who remain trapped in the marginal world of forest and mountain (777-84).[5]

Turning from Hippolytus' erotic attractions to his athletic prowess, the chorus praises the manly severity of his face: *quam grata est facies torva viriliter* ("How pleasing is your face, rough in its manly way," 798). Yet the adjective *torva* ominously suggests the "savage" quality that he shares with the Minotaur's bestial sire (117), with the wild beasts that he hunts, and with his own Amazon mother (658f.). When the chorus goes on to praise his ability to dare contests of strength (*viribus*) against the gods and to "equal Hercules' muscles" (804-7) or to rival Mars and Castor and Pollux (808-15), the overreaching of the hyperboles begins to undercut the praise. It is, in fact, ambiguous male beauty (*forma*, 820), not manly strength (*vires*, 805), that sets him apart.

Hippolytus' failure to reach manhood leaves him suspended ambiguously between male and female. Hence his *decus* is not the masculine honor or glory of heroic exploits but the physical beauty that is more frequently praised in women than in men and is a dangerous possession for the latter (820ff.). This beauty, singled out for praise by the chorus (*forma*, 761ff.), is the subject of lamentation at the catastrophe. The Messenger bewails the ruined "honor of the son's handsome form" (*formae decus*, 1110). "Only just now," the Messenger continues, "he shone forth like a star as the radiant companion and certain heir of his father's kingdom" (*clarus imperii comes et certus heres,*

---

[5] For Hylas and Endymion, see the references cited above, note 2. See also above, chap. 3, pp. 67ff., with notes 15 and 16.

1110-12).[6] The *decus* of the family's male lineage (900) and the *decus* of the handsome son are both destroyed when the idealized father changes to the monstrous emanation of the father's wrath (cf. 894 and 1110). This change begins with Theseus' demand to know the one who overturned his honor (*decoris eversor*, 894). The effect of Phaedra's desire on the house of Theseus is to involve the masculine *decus* of honor in the female values of modesty or shame (*decus* as *pudor*). At the end her only remaining *decus* is death: "death, greatest glory of an injured modesty" (*o mors pudoris maximum laesi decus*, 1189).

The closely associated themes of sexual trial, sword, and forest should confirm the son's inherited nobility as a high manifestation of civilization (cf. 899). Instead they indicate the degeneration of the race and a reversion to barbarian savagery and feral promiscuity (909ff., 923ff.). Instead of passing through the wild forest in his first trial of young manhood and his first loss of *pudor* (920; cf. 913), Hippolytus is fixed as "that savage inhabitant of the forest" in the most pejorative sense: *silvarum incola / ille efferatus*. So Theseus, at the height of his fury, calls him (922f.). Instead of showing the glory of the race (*decus generis*), Hippolytus shows the stain of an unspeakable race (*genus infandi lues*, 905f.). Not Athens, but Scythia or Colchis nurtured such a son (906f.; cf. 900); and the race (*genus* again, 907) reverts to the corruptions of its original stock (907f.). When this father recognizes the son by the sword, the son is expelled from the city, fails to attain sexual maturity, and is defeated by the evil monster. Instead of leading Hippolytus on to success in heroic *labor* (1067), the father insures his hopeless failure to grow up and accomplish noble deeds.

II

In his last known utterance, Hippolytus claims for himself the father's power as a conqueror (*vincere*, 1067). In narrating

[6] The chorus at the climactic moment of Hippolytus' imminent destruction compares his beauty favorably with "all the beauty of old" (*decus omne priscum* 741).

his death-scene, the Messenger quotes his boast that "this empty fright breaks not my spirit, for it is a labor of my father to *conquer* bulls" (*haud frangit animum vanus hic terror meum; / nam mihi paternus* vincere *est tauros labor* (1066f.). His role in the play, however, is defeat, not victory; and we have already noted the reversals from trapper to trapped, hunter to hunted in the Endymion passage and in the use of snares (*struxisse fraudes*, 503; *instruitur . . . fraude feminea dolus*, 828). Despite his theoretical preference for a pacific Golden Age over "warlike Mars' new arts" and "thousand shapes of death" (542-51), he assimilates hunting to war (46-50), idealizes a glory of the forest (*si quem tangit gloria silvae*, 27f.), praises as a *victor* the hunter eviscerating the slain beast (52), extols his goddess as commanding a *regnum* (55), and compares the return of the rustic throng to the long procession of a triumph (*longo triumpho*, 79f.). The ode that follows his drawing of the sword celebrates his "conquest" in athletics and war (804-19; *vincere*, 806), but the chorus's praise of his beauty and comparison of him to the victims of female sexual passion come closer to the truth.[7] The helplessness of the young male victimized by female passion is their first concern immediately after the ode (824f.):

> quid sinat inausum feminae praeceps furor?
> nefanda iuveni crimina insonti apparat.

> What act of daring would the woman's headlong madness leave untried? She makes ready evil crimes against the guiltless youth.[8]

"Trickery is being plotted with every scheme of woman," they add three lines later (*instruitur omni fraude feminea dolus*, 828).

For Hippolytus, the Minotaur is the ultimate monster (cf. 688) and simultaneously the one monster that he cannot overcome, for it constitutes the final proof of the powerful maternal sexuality that he would deny. Only in his fierce outcry against

---

[7] Cf. 777-94, 820f.; also 824-28.
[8] Contrast the chorus's praise of Hippolytus' daring in deeds of strength against the gods in 804f.: *tu licet asperos / pugnacesque viribus audeas. . . .*

Phaedra can he specifically name the sexual reality of the mother. He is anatomically explicit, if general, about the womb or belly (*venter*) that gave birth to Phaedra as it gave birth also to the Minotaur: *ille te venter tulit* ("That womb bore you," 693). For him the dark labyrinth is the fearful abyss of female sexuality and especially maternal sexuality (cf. 99-102), for in Phaedra's criminal lust the reproductive aspect is stressed equally with the erotic (so especially 170-72 and Hippolytus himself at 687-93).

Theseus, the potent father, could enter that dark enclosure and emerge victorious, combining both martial and sexual prowess (646-63). Such is the image of the conquering hero with whom Phaedra fell in love, as she says, when her sister, Ariadne, invited and guided Theseus within (cf. 649f., 655f.). Now Phaedra wants a Hippolytus who resembles his father (646ff.) and like him could follow "the long thread on the curving path" through those dark passages to triumph (*et longa curva fila collegit via*, 649). "How radiantly he shone then!" she exclaims in her next line (*quis tum ille fulsit*, 650).[9] For Hippolytus the Minoan labyrinth holds no such radiant prospect (687-93).

Hippolytus' inability to match his father's strength against bulls is followed by another failure. The chorus compares his loss of control over his horses with Phaethon's fall from the chariot of his father, the Sun, when the horses recognized that "the day was entrusted to a false Sun" (*Solique falso creditum indignans diem*, 1091). The analogy with Phaethon suggests a parallel between the problematical domestic order of the father-figure, Theseus, and the world-order of the gods.[10] The Mes-

---

[9] There is probably an erotic sense latent in Phaedra's words about the curving path in 650f.: see Adams (1982) 89, with the examples there cited. Cf. also Ovid, *Her.* 4.59f. and also above, chap. 2, sec. II, ad fin. Seneca's phrasing is perhaps indebted to Virgil, *Aen.* 6.29f., where "Daedalus himself unloosed the winding deceptions of the building, guiding the dark tracks by a thread" (*Daedalus ipse dolos tecti ambagesque resolvit / caeca regens filo vestigia*); but Virgil's language, as befits the guide (Daedalus, not Ariadne), lays more stress on the intellectual effort (e.g. *regens*).

[10] Liebermann (1974), 43, suggests that the Phaethon simile adds "cosmic perspective."

senger's comparison of Hippolytus' death to Phaethon's fall in 1090-92 implies, among other things, the heroic model of a celestial father (Sol: Phaethon = Theseus: Hippolytus). But this father is not the solicitous divine parent of the Phaethon myth, but more like Erich Neumann's "uroboric" father, the jealous, violent parent who swallows, engulfs, or strangles the child.[11] Chthonic darkness contrasts with celestial light, murderous anger with protective concern. The idealized father who might be a model for a heroic self, a father whose conquest of bulls Hippolytus takes as an example of his own fearlessness (1066f.), proves to be the source from which emanates the murderous violence of the sea-bull.

The chorus later explains Hippolytus' death as the change of fortune to which exalted men are liable: Father Jupiter always strikes what is high and nearest the heavens (1132-40). Here, as earlier, Jupiter is a figure of remote phallic potency, smiting with his thunderbolts (cf. 673f., 188f.). His concern for the heavens (*metuens caelo*, 1136) recalls the Phaethon-simile some fifty lines before, the tale of a son unequal to his father.

In his last words Hippolytus boasted that the bull-monster did not break his spirit (*haud frangit animum vanus hic terror meum*, 1066f.). But in Phaedra's eyes now he is not only defeated but torn apart (*divulsit*) by a bull (1169-73):

> membra quis saevus Sinis
> aut quis Procrustes sparsit aut quis Cresius,
> Daedalea vasto claustra mugitu replens,
> taurus biformis ore cornigero ferox
> divulsit.

What cruel Sinis scattered these limbs or what Procrustes? What Cretan bull, filling Daedalus' enclosure with vast roaring, a two-bodied creature, savage with his horn-bearing face, tore them apart.

His metaphorical "breaking" of spirit (*frangit animum*) becomes her grimly literal and corporeal "tearing apart" (*divulsit*).

[11] Neumann (1954) 27ff., 170ff.

He is no match for the monsters and outlaws that Theseus vanquished in a chain of victories that led to winning Phaedra's bed. Phaedra's reference to the Minotaur here reminds us again of the sexual challenge and temptation that she has posed to Hippolytus. Her description in 1171, *Daedalea vasto claustra mugitu replens* ("filling Daedalus' enclosure with vast roaring," 1171), echoes her description of her love in the first act: no Daedalus could help her flames (120), though Daedalus had closed up our monsters in the dark house (*qui nostra caeca monstra conclusit domo*, 122).

Combined with the bull-like (*corniger*, 1081) and phallic apparition of the monster from the sea, the evocations of the Minotaur in Phaedra's dirge join the two sides of the sexual threat to the son in the Oedipal triangle: the ambiguous lure of the mother's "monstrous" desire for the son (cf. 649f., 687-93), and the phallic father's threat to castrate the son who desires the mother (cf. 1170-73). At every level heroic paradigms on the father's side are answered by the son's failures. Idealized fathers are answered by monstrous or destructive males; paternal models are answered by a mother's violent and sinful past.

SIX

Parental Models: Ideal and Nightmare

I

The dramatist has to convince us that there is an iceberg of coherent human reality beneath the tip of character that we see on the stage. *Nihil ex nihilo fit* applies to effective drama as well as to physics. If a character is to interest us, the events for which he is responsible have to appear as more than arbitrary, detached, isolated gestures. They must in some way express what the novelist George Eliot called "that inexorable law of human souls, that we prepare ourselves for sudden deeds by the reiterated choice of good and evil which gradually determines character."[1] Just before this sentence, the chief male character of Eliot's novel has reacted to an unexpected event in a way that reflects a pattern of behavior that we have seen building up over several years. Now he "seemed to have spoken without any preconception: the words had leaped forth like a sudden birth that had been begotten and nourished in the darkness." In the brief, condensed time encompassed by a play, in contrast to a novel, what lies in that "darkness" has to be implied, elliptically and symbolically, through skillful references to the past.

For Seneca, as for his Greek predecessors, the mythical tradition is in this respect a rich resource. He need only give a few hints to indicate the deeper stratum of personality implicit behind the present events. For both Phaedra and Hippolytus this stratum is created in part by images of powerful parental figures whose existence suggests that chronological depth and sense of pastness, growth, memory, change, and relatedness to others

---

[1] George Eliot, *Romola*, chap. 23, Penguin Books, ed. Andrew Sanders (Harmondsworth 1980), 287. The quotation that follows comes from the same page.

that belong to every human life. Seneca's Phaedra, like Racine's, is very much "fille de Minos et de Pasiphaé."

Hippolytus' character is defined by his situation between a pure mother of a remote past and a lustful mother onstage in the present, beside or behind whom stands the powerful father, Theseus, whose absence and return determine the course of events.[2] Theseus' absence from the first half of the play enables Phaedra to define Hippolytus as an object of desire, at the precarious moment when desire is possible. But Hippolytus occupies the ambiguous position of an object of desire who cannot reciprocate with desire, who himself cannot desire. This ambiguity parallels the tensions of his place between present and absent parental figures: an all too tangible Phaedra and a remote, invisible Amazon and Diana; a Theseus who is both living and dead and is capable of reaching beyond his physical presence, whether from Hades to earth or from his palace to the seashore of Hippolytus' flight, to assert the punitive potency of patriarchal authority.

II

Euripides had already created Hippolytus as a character defined by a problematical absence of desire. His story, like the life-pattern of the Euripidean hero, contains deep initial loss and a replacement of that lost original mother by the goddess Diana and her woodland realm of hunting. He redirects his sexual energy into devotion to a pure, virginal, and inaccessible mother-figure. Difference from others and aloofness—in modern terms, alienation—form one of the essential traits of his character in both Euripides and Seneca. Behind this, as both tragedians suggest, lie his abandonment of competition with his father and his transformation of his lost mother into the idealized symbolic surrogate, Diana.[3]

---

[2] On the importance of the father-figure, not just as the source of authority but also as an emblem of the defining circumstances of the past generally, see Barthes (1963) 48f.

[3] See Segal (1978/79) 134f., 136-39; also the essays of Rankin (1974) and

The play presents a plethora of father-figures: Theseus, Neptune, Jupiter, and even Minos. This overdetermination of the paternal role encourages a self-dramatizing rhetoric of allegiance to the higher powers, a language of ostentatious display of obedience to Law as something closely identified with the father.[4] Hence the recurrent exclamations to the Olympian fathers, Jupiter and Neptune, or to the celestial gods in general.

Accusing his son of rape, the Euripidean father claims that young men are no more stable than women "when Cypris stirs up the thoughts that bud in youth, and the very maleness that is in them helps them along" (τὸ δ᾽ ἄρσεν αὐτοὺς ὠφελεῖ προσκείμενον, Eur., *Hipp.* 966-70). These lines have no counterpart in Seneca's play. In Seneca Hippolytus' rejection of his sexuality imposes silence on male desire and transfers the active thrust of desire entirely to the female. On the other hand, given the repressive power of the Senecan father, Phaedra can reveal her desire only through devious and indirect modes of expression. She can make one massive, confession of desire, but then has to have recourse again to deceptive and ambiguous speech.

The early dialogues between Phaedra and the Nurse discuss the struggle between lust and repression, female desire and the Law upheld by Father Minos, Father Jupiter, and Theseus. This conflict takes the form, in part, of the Nurse's attempt to block desire by interposing a series of substitute fathers for the absent Theseus. But these attempts in the first part of the play all fail; the result is a primordial conflict of the father and son, conveyed in an equally primal symbolism.

In the first direct address to Phaedra in the play, the Nurse calls her "wife of Theseus, glorious offshoot of Jupiter" (*Thesea coniunx, clara progenies Iovis*, 129). The single verse implies the three repressive father-figures of Phaedra's life—Theseus, Minos, and Jupiter. To fortify her ethical maxims against illicit passion (132-42), the Nurse again mentions the name of Theseus

---

Smoot (1976). For the experience of "an original loss and the discovery of difference," see Lacan/Wilden (1968) 166.

[4] For some reflections on female desire and the order of language, see Gallop (1982), chap. 4, especially pp. 47ff.

(148), now given the title of "husband" (145).[5] She then explicitly names Minos, the Sun as Pasiphae's *parens* (152-55), and finally Jupiter (154-57). Minos has his full regal authority as the ruler of the hundred cities of Crete (150) and as the one "who presses down the seas in his wide rule" (*lato maria qui regno premit*, 149). The last phrase associates this Father of the Law with control over the sea (cf. 85ff.) and with oppressive weight (*premit*). Both images recall the language of Phaedra's passion in her first speech.[6] In the Nurse's mouth, however, this imagery belongs to the desire-inhibiting authority of the father. Jupiter too has his awesome authority as "the one who shakes the world and brandishes his Aetnean lightning-bolt in flashing hand, sire of the gods" (155-57).[7] None of the remote fathers cited by the Nurse, however, is a sufficient counterweight to the absence of the father-figure, "Theseus held concealed in Lethean depths" (147f.).

Phaedra's desire for Hippolytus at once opens a double and divided perspective on the return of the father: the sense of loss or absence (91f.) and the wish for his complete disappearance (145-48; cf. 93-98, 218-21). Turning the rule of the father inside out, Phaedra attributes conquest, mastery, and kingdom to *furor* and Amor (184-85):

> quid ratio *possit*? *vicit* ac *regnat* furor
> *potensque* tota mente *dominatur* deus.

> What *power* does reason have? Mad passion has *conquered and rules*, and this god in his *power* over my whole mind *has dominion*.

Amor, not the father, she will soon declare in defense of her position, holds the "greatest sway" over her: (218-21):

---

[5] *Thesea* in 148 (here the Greek accusative) sharply recalls *Thesea* (feminine adjective) in 129. In both cases *Thesea* begins the verse.

[6] See above, chap. 2, sec. III and VII.

[7] This reference to the Aetnean thunderbolt also recalls the absence that exacerbates her desire, the seething Aetnean cave of empty longing in 102.

Amoris in me maximum regnum puto,
reditusque nullos metuo: non umquam amplius
convexa tetigit supera qui mersus semel
adiit silentem nocte perpetua domum.

I hold as greatest Amor's power over me,
And I fear no return; never more
Does he reach the upper vaults who once submerged
Attains the house of silence in perpetual night.[8]

The *maximum regnum* of Amor not only means the victory of
the repressed desires in her own soul but also implies another
weakening of paternal power, the rule of Jupiter, highest father,
now overshadowed by the "greatest rule" of the impudent
young god.

By thrusting the father-figure into the subterranean depths,
she also fulfills the son's other secret Oedipal desire. The absence of Theseus in the infernal regions is in fact the central concern of their conversation: it is the enabling factor behind the
ambiguities of their words (617-33).[9] Her wish that the father
may disappear from the scene is quite literally a death-wish for
him, as his absence in this case equals being kept underground,
in the realm of the dead.

For Phaedra the god Love (*deus*, 185) has subdued Jupiter,
the highest form of paternal authority (187; cf. 154-57). The
arrows of the "boy," Amor (*puer*, 193), she says, defeat the
more powerful (phallic) missiles of Mars, Vulcan, and Phoebus
Apollo (188-94). She voices what might be the son's repressed
fantasies about his father.[10] But she characteristically eroticizes

---

[8] On the text and interpretation of 218, see Grimal (1965) ad loc. and Zwierlein (1966) 196f. On *furor* generally, see now Regina Fucito Merzlak, "*Furor* in
Seneca's *Phaedra*," *Collection Latomus* 180 (Brussels 1983) 193-210.

[9] For the motif of the absent father, see Fauth (1958) 550 and Friedrich
(1933) 41. It is generally agreed that Theseus' presence in the Underworld is
not original with Seneca, but probably reflects Sophocles' lost *Phaedra*: see Paratore (1952) 203; Barrett (1964) 12f.; Grimal (1963) 305-7; Herter (1971)
59ff.

[10] In Lacanian terms, again, her language constitutes the Discourse of the
Other with respect to Hippolytus.

the defeat of the father: the marks of the paternal power and authority (155-57) become attributes of Amor triumphant (188-91). The "small" wins out over the greater force: love's small fire proves mightier than Vulcan's raging forge where the father's lightning-bolts are made (190f.).[11] "Raging" (*furentis*) assimilates the celestial authority to the *furor* of interior passion. Boyish Amor's triumph prefigures Phaedra's outspoken preference later for the "boyish" form over the father's (*puer*, 647). The returning husband's scepter, in the Nurse's warning soon after (217), as we have seen, can do nothing against these phallic arrows of the young god, associated with Phaedra's illicit desires for another arrow-bearing youth.[12]

The Nurse makes a final attempt to invoke the father, but with no better success (242-45). To the Nurse's "Remember your father" Phaedra replies, "I remember my mother at the same time" (242). To the Nurse's threat of the arrival of husband and father (*aderit maritus . . . aderit genitor*), she hints at Theseus' own erotic exploits in the first case and at Minos' "mildness," that is, his complaisant indifference, at the behavior of another daughter, Ariadne, in the second (*mitis Ariadnae pater*, 245).[13] This alleged gentleness of Minos toward Ariadne's elopement remakes the father-figure according to her own present needs. As she imagines the celestial father as a victim of Amor, so she pictures the *paterfamilias* as either helpless or pliant at the daughter's amours. The chorus seems to reinforce her wishful images of the father a few lines later, extolling the victory of the youthful Amor's arrows (276ff.) over old and young alike (291-95).

As the invocation of the father proves futile, the Nurse aban-

[11] Cf. the reverse image in the ode on Amor, 337: Neptune's waves do not help against the flames of love.
[12] For Hippolytus' arrows, see 809-19; cf. also 48-50, 56-62, 72, and Phaedra's desire to run in his woods with the hunter's quiver, 395f.
[13] Grimal (1965) ad 245 remarks that Minos' "indulgence envers Ariane et Thésée garantit son indifférence à l'égard de Phèdre." There seems no need to punctuate 245 with a question mark, as Grimal does. Ariadne is also associated in Phaedra's mind with a woman's sexual power over the attractive young Theseus when he was the age of the present Hippolytus: see 646-56.

dons her attempt at representing paternal authority and instead reverts to her motherly role. She appeals to her own impotence in old age and to the "dear breasts" which once nursed Phaedra (*cara ubera*, 247), whom she soon calls *alumna*, "foster daughter" (255), as she urges her to give up her momentary resolve to die rather than yield to her love (250-57). In identifying now with the tender nurture of the mother rather than the implacable laws of the father, the Nurse frees Phaedra momentarily from the burden of patriarchal authority and opens the way for its destruction. She resolves to approach Hippolytus; and the ode on Amor, with its erotic defeat of the father, follows at once. After this the two female characters, Nurse and Phaedra, take an active role in expressing sexual desire openly to Hippolytus.

III

The two seduction scenes—first with the Nurse and then with Phaedra—attack Hippolytus' denial of maternal sexuality.[14] The two scenes form a progression from overt statement to symbolic representation. In the first scene the Nurse, another surrogate mother-figure (cf. 246f.), uses a variety of arguments to convince Hippolytus to abandon his celibate life. Even his Amazon-mother, she concludes, indulged in the sexual union of which he is the product and the proof (574-77):

saepe obstinatis induit frenos Amor
et odia mutat. regna materna aspice:
illae feroces sentiunt Veneris iugum.
testaris istud unicus gentis puer.

Love often puts his curbs on those who are persistent, and changes their hatred. Look at your mother's realm. Those

---

[14] Seneca may be fusing or "contaminating" the seduction scenes of Euripides' two versions of the myth, the approach by the Nurse in the extant *Hippolytus Crowned* and the direct approach by Phaedra herself in the lost *Hippolytus Veiled*.

women, fierce as they are, feel the yoke of Venus. You are a
witness to that fact, the only male-child of that race.

The effect of this little speech, however, is to raise rather than
to allay Hippolytus' ambivalent feelings about the maternal figure (cf. 578f.). Later, when Hippolytus' world is well on the
way to disintegration, Theseus reaffirms the Amazons' subjection to Venus in a grossly exaggerated way (907ff.). Possibly
this alleged promiscuity also contains a projection of Hippolytus' repressed desires. We may compare Pentheus' sexual fantasies about the sexual promiscuity of his mother's Maenad companions outside the city in the *Bacchae*.[15] In any event, the
Amazons' oscillation between the rejection of sexuality and licentiousness expresses the precarious status of Hippolytus' own
sexual drive; and his death under sentence for rape is another
form of the return of the repressed.

Not only are the Nurse's Amazons *feroces*, "savages"; not only
are they subject to "the yoke of Venus," i.e., not chaste; they are
also far from loving to their male children. Murder of sons is the
implication of the Nurse's statement that Hippolytus is the sole
male of that race to survive. Traditionally, Amazons preserved
only their daughters.

The Nurse's main objective, however, is to prove that sexual
desire is a powerful force, even in those maternal realms (*regna
materna*) of Hippolytus' remote and pure childhood. His answer is to affirm that his only solace (*solamen unum*) is hatred for
all women (578f.):

solamen unum matris amissae fero
odisse quod iam feminas omnes licet.

The only solace of my mother's loss I bear
Is then my right to hate all women.

The lack of logical connection with the Nurse's argument reveals the charged emotional background behind Hippolytus'
hatred of women.

[15] Eur., *Bacchae* 215-25, 686-88.

The love that joins the sexes can "change hatred," the Nurse said (*odia mutat*, 574f.); it can even abolish hatred entirely in the forests and among the wild beasts, as the chorus sang in the ode on Love's power (353f.):

nihil immune est, odiumque perit
cum iussit Amor . . .

Nothing is free from him, and hatred perishes when Love gives the command.

But Hippolytus, totally rejecting Amor and blocked in his vision of that union of the sexes, is left with only *odium* toward women (579).

Hippolytus' "loss of a mother" alludes to the death of Hippolytus' mother, Antiope, at the hands of his father, Theseus (cf. 926-29). This is a crucial event in his psychological background.[16] By having sex with his father and thus becoming "impure," his mother anticipates her later status as "lost" to him when she is murdered by the sexually aggressive father. The two crimes of the father against the mother, namely sexual penetration and killing, are of course chronologically separate and sequential; but psychologically they are parallel and coexistent. Having thus "lost" his mother to the phallic wound of the father, he will refuse to become the phallus of a substitute mother, a new object of desire. Instead he surrenders both phallus and desire to a fantasied mother whom he imagines as impenetrable and inviolable, the *diva virago* (54) who herself commands the penetrating force of male weapons (48ff.). His object of desire, therefore, appears as an unreachable absence, be it in the form of the otherworldliness of his goddess or the disappearance of a geographically distant and in fact murdered mother.

---

[16] Cf. 226f. (with Grimal's note ad loc.), 927-30, 1167; cf. also 906-14. The motif of Theseus' killing Antiope also appears in Ovid's *Heroides*, 4.117-22; and cf. Hyginus *Fab*. 241; see in general Zintzen (1960) 31 and Jacobson (1974), p. 156 with note 35. From another perspective this harshness of Theseus, *durus semper*, as Phaedra says (1164f. and cf. 226), is important as the background for her anxiety and perhaps for her marital unhappiness. That Theseus was capable of killing the mother of his son is suggested also by his readiness to use violence against the old Nurse (882-85), as well as by the curse on Hippolytus.

On a Freudian reading, the trauma of such a loss, caused by so potent and terrifying a father-imago, would be seen as producing the deep repression of sexual desire that Hippolytus exhibits in the play. "Hating all women" would then be the logical "consolation for the loss of a mother" (578f.). Rather than confront his hatred of the father, Hippolytus has transferred his anger from the father who has removed the mother to the mother who has abandoned him by being "lost." Through its mythical background and glimpses of Hippolytus' past the play implies the processes by which he has transformed his libidinal energies into his intense hatred of women.

The other major force in Hippolytus' character is the Oedipal conflict with the threatening father, Theseus, who has so ruthlessly demonstrated his power by killing the mother (926-29) and will demonstrate it again by castrating and killing the son.[17] At the same time the father's destructive and aggressive sexuality still remains as the son's model for behavior toward women. In confronting the sexual overtures of Phaedra, therefore, he self-righteously repulses her on the one hand but nearly repeats the father's murderous sexual aggression against the mother on the other (704-9). Yet touching the body of his father's wife with his sword awakens the Oedipal terrors of Theseus' vengeance—terrors which are realized as fact by the overdetermined agency of paternal punishment reported by the Messenger. At the critical point, then, Hippolytus abandons the sword, asks to be purified by the idealized, morally demanding Father of the Law, Neptune (716-18), and retreats again to his safe, asexual world of "forests and wild beasts" (718).

Phaedra's seductive presence onstage and the allusions to Antiope by the Nurse and later by Theseus have filled the lacuna in Hippolytus' knowledge of the maternal figure. This is the knowledge of female sexuality missing from his image of her.

---

[17] Compare Hyllus' repugnance at being compelled to marry his father's concubine in Sophocles, *Trachinian Women* 1121ff. Hercules, like Theseus, is another violent and dangerous father-figure. For the motif of incest in the myth of Theseus, see Green (1977) 150.

When Theseus hears of Hippolytus' alleged rape of his present wife, he thanks the gods that "Antiope fell struck (*icta*) by my hand" before falling victim to her son's lust (926-28). Killing by penetration (which *icta* in 927 can imply) is what Theseus inflicted on Antiope and just what Hippolytus cannot do to Phaedra (713-18).

IV

The interaction between the two characters in the central scene of the play operates at the subsurface level of the primal fears and desires of the unconscious. Phaedra begins her seduction by evoking the father as a sexually attractive and potent male, combining beauty with strength, and possibly too the strength of phallic potency (650ff.): "How radiantly he shone then! . . . In his soft arms were *strong* muscles. . . . Just so, just so, he was, when he *pleased* his enemy; so did he *carry his head raised high*." Phaedra's fantasy-image fuses and confuses the son with his virile father, but Hippolytus is unable to accept such an identification. He replies with his own, very different fantasy-image of her, the sexually threatening Evil Mother who is even worse than her own mother, the mother of the monster vanquished by Theseus in the labyrinth (689f.; cf. 649f.).

Phaedra's threat to Hippolytus' adaptive mechanisms and hence to his emotional stability is all the more dangerous as her insistence on his resemblance to his father evokes the sexual knowledge forbidden to or repressed by the child (658f.):

et genitor in te totus et torvae tamen
pars aliqua matris miscet ex aequo decus.

Your father, complete, is there in you; and yet some part of your fierce mother mingles her beauty equally.

Phaedra seems to take Hippolytus back to his childhood curiosity, and uncertainty, about where babies come from. The part of his mother that mingles (*miscet*) her beauty in his features indicates the sexual union of his mother and father that he would, at some level, deny. When Phaedra forces him to confront sexuality, it is of a monstrous birth that he speaks (688-93).

It is instructive to compare Euripides' treatment of the same theme in his play. For the Euripidean Hippolytus the birth of children from the sexual intercourse of their parents has an obliquity quite different from that of Phaedra's hint in 658f. The subject occurs in his tirade against women (*Hipp.* 616-24). He cries out reproachfully to Zeus for having brought the hated race of women into the light; then he utters the utopian wish that the god had sown (*speirai*) the race of mortals from another source. He desiderates an asexual acquiring of children by placing gold or silver or bronze in the god's temple—the bright, hard metals associated with the male world of trade and commercial valuation—so that each man could "buy the seed (*sperma*) of children in accordance with his worth." Euripides shows the same kind of psychological insight as Seneca in having this hero respond to erotic temptation with a denial of the sexual procreation of children. But in the Greek play it is Hippolytus and not Phaedra who broaches this subject (cf. *Phaedra* 658f., above), though he avoids any explicitly sexual language and uses only the conventional agricultural metaphor, "sow" or "seed" (*Hipp.* 618, 623). In raising the issue of procreative sexuality, Euripides focuses on cultural rather than personal concerns. He reflects the Greeks' misogynistic tendency, with its strong component of the male's resentment at dependency on the woman for the continuation of his line.[18]

Seneca's Hippolytus characteristically externalizes the temptations held out to him as "crimes" detected and punished by the all-powerful father-figure: "Great ruler of the gods, are you so slow to hear such crimes (*scelera*), so slow to see them" (672f.). This rhetorical outburst, addressed to the ultimate Father, condenses into a single utterance the mechanisms of

---

[18] The locus classicus is Hesiod, *Theogony* 591-612, the poet's reflection on the story of Pandora. For discussion, with further literature, see Froma Zeitlin, "The Dynamics of Misogyny: Myth and Mythmaking in the *Oresteia*," *Arethusa* 11 (1978) 168ff., and Nicole Loraux, "Sur la race des femmes et quelques-unes de ses tribus," in the same volume, 43ff.

repression that are operative in his character. He expects instant penetration by the "three-pronged torch" (*triscula face*, 681) of Jupiter's lightning bolt. This image is a direct rejection of Phaedra's torch of love (188), whose power, she said, extends over even the father-figures, Jupiter and Vulcan, the latter the craftsman of the three-pronged lightning bolt (*opifex trisulci fulminis*, 189).[19] When he says a few lines later, "I have deserved death" (683), he is addressing himself; but he also projects into the heavens an implacable superego figure, an omniscient guardian, like Blake's Nobodaddy, who scrutinizes his acts and desires.[20] Having failed to shape for himself a valid discourse of reality about father and mother, cut off from them both, he is condemned to confront both parental figures as the monstrous imagos of his unconscious. His real mother is lost to him in his childhood (578f.), and his father castrates and dismembers him through the horrible sea-creature of his curse.

About the actual father, Theseus, Hippolytus has not a word to say. The rhetorical address serves as a screen of self-representation, protecting him from what he has chosen to exclude from his life. His cry of guilt in the quasi-legal language of this passage (*nocens, merui*, "guilty," "deserved") is answered by no corresponding verbal utterance onstage; the answer comes in the murderous apparition described later by the Messenger. The self-righteous appeal to the elevated Father of the Law, "ruler of gods and men" (679), to "transfix" him changes to physical impalement when the actual father returns (compare *me fige*, 682, and *domino affixo*, 1100).

The intense emotions around guilt and fathers in this passage (671-86) have no parallel in Euripides' extant *Hippolytus*. Euripides' hero invokes his "purity," but has nothing like these impassioned appeals to the Father (*Hipp.* 601-68). The Euripi-

---

[19] Cf. also Phaedra's use of the torch of marriage to conceal her guilty love in 597. See above, chap. 2, note 38.

[20] William Blake, "To Nobodaddy":

Why art thou silent and invisible, / Father of Jealousy? / Why dost thou hide thy selfe in clouds / From every searching Eye? / Why darkness and obscurity / In all thy words and laws, / That none dare eat the fruit but from / The wily serpent's jaws? / Or is it because Secresy gains females' / Loud applause?

dean Hippolytus, in fact, makes his first outcry to "Mother Earth" (601). He invokes Zeus briefly, without epithet, in 616 for the rhetorical question, "Why did you create women?" When he mentions "father" or "Theseus" later, he refers to the sanctity of the bed and the patriarchal authority as the source of moral law (*Hipp.* 651, 658, 660f.), but he is matter of fact and gives these points no particular emphasis. He is much more emotional about the evils of women and his own purity than about the exclusive rights and dignity of the father (cf. *Hipp.* 651f. with 653-58).

After invoking the remote, punitive celestial fathers (671-84), the Senecan Hippolytus turns to Phaedra with scathing curses (685-97). For him her very act of speaking is a kind of monstrous birth: it reenacts the crime of Pasiphae, whose act of giving birth, "with its double-formed mark of infamy, revealed a crime *long kept in silence*" (*et tamen* tacitum diu / *crimen biformi partus exhibuit nota*, 690f.).[21] Phaedra's speaking both designates and enacts the nightmare fantasies of licentious maternal sexuality symbolized by Pasiphae.

The return of the repressed takes the form of a horrible castrating punishment by a monstrous surrogate of the father. Pursued by the terrible monster from the sea, Hippolytus loses control of his chariot; and, after the mangling of his handsome face (*ora pulchra*, 1095), he is left impaled through the middle of his groin by an upright stake (*medium per inguen stipite erecto*, 1099).[22] This castration is the "logical" end of his story. It is the visible enactment of his denial of his sexuality. Ironically, the hyperboles of guilt before the father in his rhetorical cries of 671-84 are fulfilled; but, in more ways than one, vengeance comes not from the sky but from the subterranean depths of sea and earth.

This form of death is also the logical result of the inversion of

---

[21] I follow Leo and other editors in reading *biformi* in 691: see Grimal (1965) ad loc. *Partus* in 691 is carefully chosen to suggest both the act of giving birth and the monstrous "offspring" itself.

[22] For the sexual elements in the scene, see below, chap. 8, sec. VII, and my remarks in Segal (1984) 319 and note 36 on p. 323. Zintzen (1960), 124, would look for parallels with the "hanging gods" of Sir James Frazer.

traditional male and female roles in the relation of sex and aggression. The power of desire has been left entirely to the woman and is thus feminized. Having gained possession of the sword, Phaedra betrays it into the power of the father, with the resultant castration of the son. She thereby converts the sword from being the sign of repulse by Hippolytus in his invulnerability to desire (710ff.) to being the instrument of her vengeance through the father. In this process she falsely re-sexualizes its meaning in the realm of female and maternal desire. Her ability to use his own sword against him is crucial to these sexual inversions. His negation of desire eventually takes the form of a double negation of the (phallic) power of the sword: his abandoning it before her in 710ff. and her turning it against him later.

Hippolytus polarizes the parental figures into the punitive celestial father on the one hand and the mother of bestial amours and bestial impregnation on the other. Ironically, it is just the nightmarish versions of these figures, their monstrous imagos, that come to life in the action of the play. The mother-figure in his present house and his actual father fulfill his darkest unconscious fears. He is left mangled, his personal identity violated utterly in a *sparagmos* that leaves him totally unrecognizable. This destruction of his physical coherence combines loss of control (helplessness to stop the chariot and check his maddened horses) with mutilation and virtual castration. His end confirms and reenacts the latent pattern of his behavior from the beginning. It blazons across the whole canvas of his world the hidden fear that, if he claims the phallic power of the father and admits the existence of the sexually desirous and seductive mother, the father will annihilate him in a vengeance of almost unimaginable horror. Phaedra's seductive discourse in her interview with Hippolytus failed to win him over; but at another level, in the play's acting out of repressed fears and desires, it succeeds all too well. And it has exactly the effect that he "knew" it would, the most horrible punishment that the father could inflict.

SEVEN

Character Structure and Symbols
of Power: Sword and Scepter

I

In Euripides' *Hippolytus* the protagonist's cultural and psychological marginality is expressed in his occupation as a hunter in the wild; his social marginality in his status as a bastard; and his religious marginality in his association with a mode of mystical worship which is at one point identified with Orphism (*Hipp.* 952).[1] As a virgin youth, he relinquishes his potential status as the founder of a family and a citizen. Remaining a hunter and athlete, he fixes himself in the role of the perpetual adolescent sportsman, avoiding the civic responsibilities that would follow from the position that his father now occupies (cf. *Hipp.* 1013-15). Since Hippolytus is also a bastard, his legal right to inherit his father's prerogatives is also in question. These elements in his life story heavily overdetermine the difficulties surrounding succession to the father's possessions and to adult status generally.

In the traditions on which Seneca drew, passage to adulthood and inheritance from the father are interwoven with the meanings of the sword. A version of the legend doubtless familiar to Seneca had Theseus find his sword, the property of *his* father, Aegeus, under a rock and bring it to Athens as proof of his identity.[2] Guided by his mother Aethra or by her substitute, Athena, he takes rightful possession of the kingdom.[3]

---

[1] See Barrett (1964) ad loc.; Segal (1978/79) 134.

[2] Euripides, *Aegeus*, frags. 1-13 (Nauck). For the plot of the *Aegeus*, see Plutarch, *Theseus* 12; schol. on Homer, *Iliad* 11.741. See in general Grimal (1965) ad 899; Dingel (1970), p. 54 with note 6; Green (1977) 157. Cf. the story told in Ovid, *Met.* 7.406-55, discussed below, chap. 8, sec. V.

[3] Cf. the fine terracotta relief from Cerveteri now in the British Museum (D 594) illustrating Theseus' lifting the rock to take possession of his father's sword, with Aethra standing by. For a good illustration, see Ann Birchall and P. E. Corbett, *Greek Gods and Heroes* (London 1974) plate 41.

Presumably Seneca has transferred to Hippolytus Euripides' detail of the very different, far happier recognition between Theseus and Aegeus in his lost *Aegeus*. In any case Theseus' response to the sword cancels out the role of the kindly human father, Aegeus (whose death Theseus has caused: 1164f.), and calls forth the dangerous and wrathful supernatural father, Neptune. In the early life history of Theseus the sword embodies the heritage of sexual, martial, and political power which the son in due course must claim as his own.[4] For Hippolytus the sword embodies not the orderly succession of paternal inheritance but the worst imaginable infraction of paternal property.

After Phaedra's accusation the hilt enables Theseus to recognize the sword as belonging to his son. This mode of recognition raises a problem of detail, minor perhaps, but interesting. How does Hippolytus come to have a sword which certainly resembles that of Theseus in the mythical tradition? Is it in fact a doublet of Theseus' sword? Are we to imagine that Theseus gave it to his son when he departed for his Underworld quest? Would he deprive himself of such a prize weapon? Are there then two such swords in the house of Theseus?[5] We cannot, of course, answer these questions; and we verge dangerously close to the documentary fallacy in raising them. The motif of the hilt, "glory of the race of Aegeus" (900), recalling the father's weapon as proof of legitimacy, I suggest, ironically superimposes Theseus' own myth of successful inheritance upon the failure of his son.[6]

Hippolytus' opening ode defines the weapons of penetration as the property of the virginal woodland goddess, a sexually pure huntress like his Amazon mother, rather than as the inheritance from the father. These weapons, therefore, are the sign of his ambiguous relation to masculine sexuality. They stand in the

---

[4] On this aspect of the patrimony, see below, chap. 8 and 9.

[5] See Herter (1971), p. 71 with note 72; also Zintzen (1960), p. 104 with note 16.

[6] Compare Telemachus' tentative essay of Odysseus' bow in *Odyssey* 21. This discreet son, who is on the verge of succeeding in the trial of the paternal weapon that would win the hand of the queen, his mother, desists at a nod from his father.

place of the regal sword, and they mark the absence of the phallus that would mean rivalry with the father. It is in the service of Diana, *diva virago*, that one wields the iron blade and penetrates the entrails of the slain prey with the curved knife (48-53).[7]

At the climax of the action the sword functions (*inter alia*) as a signifier of the phallus in the Oedipal situation. The three people whom it involves constitute a family whose situation is defined by the dramatic action as an Oedipal triangle. It is the term through which the child (the functional position held by Hippolytus in the play) relates to both the mother and father.

When Phaedra, at the first crisis of the action, makes her sexual overtures to Hippolytus, he responds not merely by repulsing her with horror, but by drawing his sword in self-righteous indignation at a criminal act: *stringatur ensis, merita supplicia exigat*, ("Let the sword be drawn and let it exact its just punishment" (706). With the drawn sword he would sacrifice her as a bloody offering to his pure goddess, Diana (708f.):

> iustior numquam focis
> datus tuis est sanguis, arquitenens dea.

> O goddess who holds the bow, never has blood more just
> been given to your altars.

The invocation to his "bow-wielding goddess" repeats in microcosm the sacrifice that Hippolytus has already made to Diana, the sacrifice of his phallic sexuality to this weapon-bearing, virgin goddess, the *diva virago* of the prologue.

Phaedra responds instantly and unhesitatingly to Hippolytus' threat of sacrificial death. She addresses him by name as she did in her initial confession of love, now for the third and last time in this scene.[8] She goes on (710-12):

> Hippolyte, nunc me compotem voti facis;
> sanas furentem. maius hoc voto meo est,
> salvo ut pudore manibus immoriar tuis.

---

[7] On the implications of Diana as *diva virago*, see Stähli-Peter (1974) 158: "speziell die männlich kühne, harte ausdauernde Jungfrau."
[8] *Hippolyte*: 611, 646, and 710.

Hippolytus, you now make me fulfilled in my prayer;
you heal me in my love-madness. This is greater than my
prayer, that with my modesty intact I might die at your
hands.

Death at his hands would resolve her conflict between desire
and morality and leave her with the *pudor* of the faithful wife.
Yet the erotic undertone speaks another language, a language of
desire, of *furor* (711) that she would have "healed" differently.
At one level her lines are a request for death; at another they are
a continuation of the seductive discourse that she has been addressing to Hippolytus since the beginning of the scene. In classical literature from at least the time of Sophocles death by the
sword of the beloved belongs to the tragic union of love-in-
death, the *Liebestod*.[9]

II

Throughout the play's central scene, the only face-to-face encounter of the two principals, the sword is a focal point for the
double meanings in language generated by sexual desire. The
sword is both a signifier of desire (for Phaedra) and a signifier
of the rejection of desire (for Hippolytus). No sooner does
Hippolytus draw it than he throws it away, for he feels it as already polluted by contact with Phaedra (713f.). As we have
noted earlier, he invokes the "great father" Neptune, the divine
father-figure on his own father's side, as the (inadequate) agent
of this purification.

There is probably a further sexual innuendo in Hippolytus'

---

[9] See Soph., *Trach.* 923ff. and *Antig.* 1235ff.; Virgil, *Aen.* 4.642ff. Although
Racine has his heroine come to a somewhat more decorous end by poison, he
preserves the erotic meaning of the sword. After her confession of love Phèdre
says to Hippolyte (II, v, ad fin.):
"Voilà mon coeur. C'est là que ta main doit frapper. / [. . .] Frappe. Ou si tu le
crois indigne de tes coups, / Si ta haine m'envie un supplice *si doux*, / Ou si d'un
sang trop vil ta main seroit trempée, / Au défaut de ton bras prête-moi ton épée.
/ Donne. [My italics]"
Robert Lowell makes the sexual symbolism unclassically explicit (and rather
grotesque) when he translates, "Look, this monster, ravenous / for her execu-
tion, will not flinch. / I want your sword's spasmodic final inch": Robert Lowell, *Phaedra and Figaro* (New York 1961) 45.

phrasing, "Let this sword, polluted, abandon my chaste side" (*et hic / contactus ensis deserat castum latus*, 713f.), for *latus* frequently means "phallus" in Latin poetry.[10] Logically, of course, Hippolytus cannot be saying, "Let the polluted sword (= phallus) abandon my chaste *latus* (= phallus)." But the double rejection of his sexuality—abandoning the sword and also declaring his *latus* to be chaste and free of pollution (= sexual activity)—is a classic example of the mechanism of overdetermination. The passage presents Hippolytus' phallic sexuality simultaneously and tautologously in two different but parallel registers just at his strongest denial of sexuality, that is, his intensest assertion of sexual purity. The double meaning of Phaedra's request in 710-12 marks the crossing between desiring and denying desire. Even in her defeat, then, she obtains a kind of victory over him: through the sword she succeeds in creating between them a paradoxical bond of desire, but a desire that includes its denial or repression as its inseparable defining quality.

The sexual implications of the sword in this exchange (710ff.) become overt in the story that Phaedra weaves around it in the next scene, for there, in her false accusation of Hippolytus, the sword is indeed the instrument of desire. It replaces the phallus metonymically as well as metaphorically. In claiming that Hippolytus has raped her in a scene that includes the sword and threats (891), she pictures the drawing of the sword in potentially murderous penetration as an act immediately prior to the violent sexual penetration. The sexual violence (*vis*) that she says her body endured follows immediately upon the threat of the violence by the sword (891f.):

temptata precibus restiti; ferro ac minis
non cessit animus; vim tamen corpus tulit.

Tried by prayers, I resisted; my spirit yielded not to the sword and threats; yet my body endured violence.[11]

[10] See Adams (1982) 49. One anonymous reader suggests the possibility of construing *castum* proleptically: "Let the sword abandon my side so as to leave it chaste." That is perhaps too strong; but in any case the assertion of purity in the sentence is overdetermined or redundant.
[11] On the ambiguity of the "violence" here, see Davis (1983) 122f.

The meaning of the sword in 710-12 and the contiguity between the threatened violence in 891 and the sexual violence in 892 (*vim tamen corpus tulit*) intertwine the metonymic and metaphoric axes, the plane of contiguity and the plane of analogy. Metonymically, the sword is the instrument whose threat precedes and makes possible the rape. It is a causal agent in the sequence of acts that constitutes Phaedra's story, and it holds a central place in the plot of that story. Metaphorically, the sword, in its close identification with the phallus (cf. 710-12), is itself a signifier of the rape. As metaphor, its presence onstage is a condensed symbolic realization of that crime. In both scenes the discourse around the sword is a discourse of hidden thoughts, imagined desires, repressed wishes: Phaedra's wish for death in place of love in 710-12 and her scenario of violent and illicit sexual consummation in 891f.

Yet Phaedra's lie about Hippolytus' violence in 891-93 contains a kernel of truth. He did indeed offer her violence. The two scenes suggest an equivalency between sexuality and violence as the one form of *vis* blends into the other. Sex and violence, we may recall, are similarly blended in Theseus' relationship with Antiope, at least as we glimpse it in the play. The movement from Phaedra's suppliant gesture of submission to love at Hippolytus' feet (666f., 703) to his twisting of her hair, drawn sword, and threats of bloodshed, as viewed in the perspective of the later scene, unmasks the latent violence in the expression as well as the repression of sexuality.

Love, the Nurse suggested early in the play, is a maker of fictions; its essence is fantasy. Lust, *libido*, fabricates (*finxit*) Amor as a god, the Nurse warns (195f.). In a kind of ring-composition, she repeats the verb a few lines later: "the love-maddened mind . . . fashions Venus' divinity" as its excuse or authority (*demens animus . . . Veneris numen finxit*, 202f.). Phaedra has fashioned a Hippolytus so overcome by passion that he cannot control himself and oversteps the most sacred bonds of the family in order to satisfy his lust for her. Such a Hippolytus, however, is created as Phaedra's own mirror-image, for it is she who cannot resist her passion, she who finally allows her lust to transgress lawful behavior. When in her lie she recreates his desire to Theseus, therefore, she possesses Hippolytus' sword as the mark of having usurped his desire. She takes for herself the instrument that overtly expresses the lust and sexual need that she wishes for him. As a woman, she cannot rape him; possessed of his sword in a situation that, at one level, acts out her fantasies, she can recreate a Hippolytus who rapes her.[12]

III

Immediately after his flight from Phaedra in the center of the play, the choral ode reenacts the symbolic abandonment of phallic sexuality that Hippolytus had made in his opening ode (cf. 736ff.). After praising his incomparable masculine beauty, the chorus dwells on his prowess in hurling javelins and shooting arrows (811-19). These penetrating "shafts" are "fixed in the warm vitals" (*tela . . . tepido viscere condita*, 816-18) where they have no generative or sexual potential: they are simply the murderous instruments of his huntress-goddess's pursuits.[13] The potential sexual energy is displaced upon killing in the hunt. The threatened penetration of the sword-scene now becomes literal action, but only in the mythical realm of Diana and only with the erotic meaning subordinated to the aggressive.[14]

When Phaedra learns the news about Hippolytus' death, she enters with his drawn sword in her hand: *strictoque vaecors Phaedra quid ferro parat* ("What is maddened Phaedra preparing with the drawn sword?" 1155). This passage echoes her earlier

---

[12] My point is hardly the sexist idea that women want to be raped, but rather the shifting and fusion of sexual roles in the movements of sexual repression and desire as reality passes into fantasy.

[13] Cf. the victorious hunter's excision of the entrails in Hippolytus' opening song (52f.): *tu, iam victor, / curvo solves viscera cultro.*

[14] As an indication of this transfer of sexual to aggressive energy we may note the increasing emphasis on dismemberment in Hippolytus' opening song: He describes the cutting out of the entrails and views the animals in terms of their capturing or captured organs: snouts, nose, breast, back, feet, horns, blood (30, 39-41, 63-65, 75-78). One may think here of Lacan's remarks on the narcissistic personality's concern with the "fragmented body" ("le corps morcelé"): Lacan/Sheridan (1977) 4f. and 11. For possible applications to a classical text, see MacCary (1982) 84ff.

approach to Hippolytus, before the sword had made its appearance on the stage, when she declared herself prepared "to give her breast to the readied (i.e., drawn) swords" (*paratis ensibus pectus dare*, 616). But now she invokes the potent Name of the Father, "Neptune, cruel master of the deep sea." "Send forth into me, me," she cries, "the blue sea's monsters and whatever remotest Tethys bears in her deepest womb, whatever Ocean in his embrace of wandering waves conceals in his furthest flood" (1159-63):

> me, me, profundi saeve dominator freti,
> invade et in me monstra caerulei maris
> emitte, quidquid intimo Tethys sinu
> extrema gestat, quidquid Oceanus vagis
> complexus undis ultimo fluctu tegit.

The "inmost womb" of Tethys of which Phaedra speaks in 1161 (*intimus sinus*) is no longer the interior sexual space burning with desire for the absent man that she described in her first scene or the receptive hollow for the sword/phallus of the son in an incestuous union (cf. 172, 710-12), but the remote depths where the dangerous sea of Theseus' immortal father, Neptune, nurtures horrendous forms of vengeance. The phallus of the desired son is replaced by the multiple terrors of monstrous penetration in the realm of the punitive father (*in me monstra caerulei maris / emitte*, "Into me send forth the blue sea's monsters," 1161f.).[15] The sexual significance of violence and penetration in the earlier occurrences of the sword now moves to the register of nightmarish exaggeration characteristic of the return of the repressed in this play. The reassertion of patriarchal authority after the release of desire once more takes the form of monsters and hyperboles of violence.

From her harsh father-figure in 1159 (*"cruel* ruler of the sea"), Phaedra moves at once to the wrath of the vengeful father, whom she addresses by his human name in the next lines:

[15] For other aspects of 1159-63, see above, chap. 2, sec. III.

"O Theseus, always hard" (*O dure Theseu semper*, 1164; contrast her *magnanime Theseu* in 869). The "hardness" of Theseus here, unlike her fantasy of the attractive *rigor* of Hippolytus (660), is destructive to his house and his women (1164-67):

> O Theseus, always hard, never returning without injury to your own! Your son and your father paid with death for your return. Always you overturn your house, harmful whether in love or in hate towards your wives.

The father's destructiveness extends back and forward, wiping out both past and future generations.[16]

The return of the repressed contains images of maternal as well as paternal violence. The creature from the sea is a monstrous tumescence that fulfils the father's wrath (1015f.); but it is also a form of monstrous female fertility. It bursts forth as if carried "by water heavy in an overburdened womb" (*nescio quid onerato sinu / gravis unda portat*, 1019f.).[17] The maternal threat is no longer the erotic aggressiveness of the seductive mother, but the monstrous fertility of an oceanic womb whose offspring is destructive to both protagonists (1019f., 1160-62).[18] In the play's shift of perspective between female desire and masculine authority, between passion and order, the sea fluctuates between images of patriarchal power and feminine *furor*. Phaedra's passion was like the heavy sea that tossed a ship out of control, heavily freighted in a hostile sea (*gravatam adversa ratem unda*, 181f.; cf. *gravis unda*, "heavy wave," 1020).

[16] The Nurse had made the same point about Theseus in the first scene: *immitis etiam coniugi castae fuit* ("Even to a chaste wife was he harsh," 226). Seneca also creates a certain impression of harshness around Theseus at his arrival on-stage, for the expressions of concern for his household—father and children—that Euripides assigns to his Theseus (*Hipp.* 794-800) are entirely absent. Instead they have been given to Hippolytus in the earlier scene of his meeting with the Nurse (*Pha.* 433-36). On Theseus' character generally, see below, chap. 9, sec. III-IV, with note 32.

[17] On *sinus* as "womb," see Adams (1982) 90f. For the image of pregnancy, see also Davis (1983) 118.

[18] For this kind of oceanic imagery and images of monstrous, engulfing female sexuality, see Durand (1976) 103-7. Cf. also Hippolytus' entrapment in the reins, 1085-87.

For Phaedra, as in a different way for Hippolytus, sexual energy swings precariously between generativity and destruction and stands in close proximity to death and aggression. The emptiness of her desire becomes the barrenness of death. At the end she leaves her husband's bedchambers empty (1185f.) and calls on Hades to spread wide its "folds" or "hollows" (1188-90): '

> o mors amoris una sedamen mali,
> o mors pudoris maximum laesi decus,
> confugimus ad te: pande placatos sinus.

> O Death, of evil love the only means of calm,
> O Death, injured shame's greatest glory,
> To you we flee. Spread open your appeased embrace.

Once more love and death share a common boundary. Not only is the sexual act denied to her, but it reappears only as a transformation into death. The inversion of male and female roles in this sexual imagery (1190; cf. 1019f. and 1159-63, above) also corresponds to the feminization of desire that, as we noted earlier, results from Hippolytus' flight from sexuality.

IV

The psychological dynamics of the play involve another symbol of paternal power, the royal scepter. Like the hilt of the royal family of Athens, the scepter is a symbol of law, kingship, adult masculinity, and patriarchal authority.[19] The scepter, like the hilt of the sword, is a blunted manifestation of the phallic power of the father. The relation of sword to hilt is analogous to that of sword to scepter. The sword points to what is aggressive and violent in the relation between father and son; the scepter and the hilt belong to the milder, less threatening aspect of paternal power, its authority as a guarantor of due succession

---

[19] For the scepter as a symbol of male generative and political power, see Soph., *El.* 419-25. For cross-cultural parallels, see Durand (1976) 137f., 322, 398.

and of social, political, and moral order.[20] In Ovid's *Metamorphoses*, for example, Jupiter "leaves behind the weighty solemnity of his scepter" when this "father and ruler of the gods" becomes the adulterous seducer of Europa (*sceptri gravitate relicta / ille pater rectorque deum*, 2.847f.).[21]

As the hilt, "glory of the Athenian race" (900), should manifest the (ac)quiescence of the son's sexuality in his Oedipal rivalry with the father, so the scepter should be the secure possession of the father, symbol of his authority over house and kingdom. But the absence of the father in the Underworld disturbs this balance. Thus when the Nurse warns Phaedra to "fear and respect the scepter of her returning husband" (*metue ac verere sceptra remeantis viri*, 217), Phaedra counters with "Love's greatest rule" over her and with the Underworld's inescapable imprisonment of whoever enters it (218-21).[22]

When Phaedra replaces the "proud and too powerful name of mother" with that of "servant" in the *servitium amoris* (609-12), she would also replace Theseus with Hippolytus as bearer of the scepter, thereby betraying to the son the two most sacred possessions of the father, emphatically contiguous in 617. She repeats her word "servant" (*famula*, 611f.) as part of a not quite logical double gift: Hippolytus is to receive her (the queen, not the servant) along with the scepter (615-23):

non, si per ignes ire et infesta agmina,
cuncter paratis ensibus pectus dare.
mandata recipe *sceptra, me* famulam accipe:

[20] One could perhaps compare the relation between the sword and the hilt, or the sword and the scepter, to the relation between the Lacanian father and the Name of the Father.

[21] The entire passage exploits the discrepancy between the patriarchal majesty of Jupiter as king of the gods and the animal form to which his lust reduces him (*Met.* 2.846-51): "Majestic power and love do not fit together very well or remain together in a single place. That father and ruler of the gods—he whose right hand is armed with the three-pronged flame and who shakes the world with a nod—leaves behind the weight of the scepter and assumes the form of a bull. Mingling with the heifers, he bellows and in his beauty treads the tender grasses."

[22] On this passage, see above, chap. 6, sec. II.

te imperia regere, me decet iussa exequi.
muliebre non est regna tutari urbium;
tu qui iuventae flore primaevo viges
cives paterno fortis imperio rege;
sinu receptam supplicem ac servam tege.
miserere viduae.

No, not even if (you order me to) go through fire and
enemy columns, would I hesitate to give my breast to the
swords ready for it. Receive the *scepter* entrusted (to me),
receive *me* as your servant. It befits you to rule kingdoms,
me to follow (your) commands. It is not a woman's role to
protect the rule of cities. Do you, who flourish in the first
flower of youth, strong with your father's rule, govern the
citizens. Receive me in your bosom, a suppliant, and protect
a slave. Pity a widow.

Phaedra has no hesitation to "give her breast to the swords
readied for it" and to entrust the scepter, symbol of the paternal
kingdom (*paternum imperium*, 621), to Hippolytus. His "vigor
in the first flower of his youth" (620) suggests to her a capacity
for more than rule over his father's kingdom (621).[23]

Hippolytus' immediate reaction here, as elsewhere, is to invoke the Name of the Father, the "highest god," as the authority for the return of the father who will reclaim wife, scepter,
and kingdom (623f.): "Let the highest god turn away this
omen; my father, safe and sound, will be here at once" (*summus
hoc omen deus / avertat; aderit sospes actutum parens*).

To the celestial father who replaces the absent father with the
Father of the Law, and to the returning father who will reclaim
his kingdom, however, Phaedra opposes the lord of the tena-
cious realm below and the silent Styx (*regni tenacis dominus*,
625) who is not likely to release the ravisher of his own bridal

---

[23] The sexual innuendoes of this passage are also prepared for by Phaedra's
words to herself at the beginning of the scene when she contemplates concealing her "crime" by the "marriage torch" (595f.). They are also aided here by the
sexual connotation of *sinus*, which Phaedra exploits later too, when the destructive force of sexuality is unleashed (1161f.; cf. 622, 1019f., 1190).

chamber (*thalami raptorem sui*, 627). In place of Theseus as a Father of the Law who rules justly and protects suppliants, she puts Theseus as a lustful and violent father who carries off others' wives. In place of the assumed presence (624) of a scepter-bearing king she sets an empty throne, a vacant house, and an available widow and queen. In place of the "real" Hippolytus she reconstructs what might be his hidden alter ego: a Hippolytus who does indeed desire what she desires but has repressed it in his Oedipal fear of the Father.[24] For a moment the stage action seems to play out her fantasies: when he offers "to fill the place of a (his?) parent" (*ac tibi parentis ipse supplebo locum*, 633), he seems to enter unconsciously into the fantasies through which she has been speaking the language of his hidden desires. Or, more precisely, he unwittingly speaks out the desires that one may plausibly suspect to have been repressed by a personality like Hippolytus'.

V

When Theseus returns, it is as the ruler of the palace and owner of everything in the house. He throws open gates and again takes possession (863). Surprised that the consort of his bedchamber (*socia thalami*) should thus receive the countenance of a long-sought husband (865), he asks that Phaedra make her right hand widowed of the sword (*quin ense viduas dexteram*, 866). His verb, *viduas*, "bereave," recalling the terms of Phaedra's offer of herself to Hippolytus as *vidua* in 623 (*misere viduae*, "pity me, a widow"), evokes once more the themes of incestuous desire. It may also suggest the deeper desires behind the "widowhood" that she offered Hippolytus in 623: the son's Oedipal wish for his father's disappearance.

In this opening dialogue with Phaedra Theseus is the first to mention the sword; but she addresses him directly, for the first time in the play, by the scepter (868-71):

---

[24] From Hippolytus' perspective, Phaedra speaks what Lacan calls the Discourse of the Other.

> eheu, per tui sceptrum imperi,
> magnanime Theseu, perque natorum indolem
> tuosque reditus perque iam cineres meos,
> permitte mortem.

Alas, by the scepter of your rule, noble Theseus, and by the
family of our sons and your return and now my ashes, allow
me death.

The scepter accompanies her initial (and temporary) redefini-
tion of Theseus as a noble hero (*magnanimus Theseus*), able to
achieve his return from Hades. The shift from sword to scepter
is also a change from the incestuous desire for his son to the
sons she has borne him, and from love to death (*mortem*, 871,
foreshadowing her address to *mors* at the end, 1188f.). She thus
moves back from the realm of hidden desires to the stable order
of the house, from private to more public symbols, and from the
subterranean world to the upper air (implied in "your return,"
870). For a moment the scepter, as a signifier of the Name of
the Father, can stand as a buffer between the fearful vengeance
of the wrathful father and the "guilty" Hippolytus.

Phaedra begins her accusation of Hippolytus, as he began his
denunciation of her, with the distant, celestial father-figures, Jupiter and her remote ancestor, the Sun (888-90): "You I call
upon as witness, creator of the heavenly gods, and you shining
ray of aether's light, from whose rising our house derives."[25]
But such appeals only set off the dangerous proximity of the terrifying father-imago, embodied in Theseus, and it is to this figure that the sword in her possession does the most direct and
effective "speaking" in the scene (897f.).

When Phaedra shows Hippolytus' sword to Theseus, she recreates for him, imaginatively, a primal scene, the visible presence of the phallus in its most forbidden place, brought forth by

---

[25] These lines ironically echo Hippolytus' similar invocations of remote father-figures in his denunciation of Phaedra, 671-683. Line 890 may also contain a reference to the source of the amorous disasters in Phaedra's house in the
anger of Sol or Helios: see Grimal (1965) ad loc.

the wife as physical evidence of violation by the son. The sword also manifests the ambiguity of this "other scene." At this point, mixing psychological truth with falsehoods about the facts, it places us at the borderline between fantasy and reality. This other scene refracts Theseus' vision of the world through his own unconscious fears, fantasies, anxieties. The language around the sword, mediated through Phaedra, becomes the only form of communication possible between father and son. They exchange no words, only a symbolic language of primal acts.

VI

Three other plays by Seneca, *Oedipus*, *Phoenissae*, and *Medea*, help illuminate the meaning of the scepter in the *Phaedra*. In all three the scepter symbolizes the political and regal authority of the father and is a focal point of conflict with that authority.

In the *Oedipus* the heinous crimes of the son against the father transform the scepter from an object of reverence to an object of horror: instead of being "holy" it becomes "bloodied" (*sancta sceptra*, 240; *cruenta sceptra*, 642f.).[26] Oedipus' crime against his father, when revealed in its first enigmatic form, appears as a "prize of savage murder" (*Oed.* 634f.), the bloodied scepter of a bloody king (*cruenta sceptra*, 642; cf. *rex cruentus*, 634). In Laius' dread prophecy, Oedipus will relinquish the scepter for the staff of old age (*baculo senili*, 657), with which, as in Sophocles, he will henceforth "feel his way by touch on the sad road" (656-58).

In this version of the archetypal father-son conflict, the scepter, as the token of paternal power, closely parallels the bedchamber (*thalamos*) where the father exercises the other prerogatives of his power (634f.). Laius' ghost calls Oedipus the "bloody king who seizes (*occupat*) the scepter as the prize of cruel murder *and* seizes the forbidden chambers of the father, a hateful offspring": *sed rex cruentus, pretia qui saevae necis / sceptra*

---

[26] Early in the play too the scepter appears as an object of respect and veneration by which King Oedipus can entreat Creon's help for their "kindred house" (*Oed.* 512f.).

et nefandos occupat thalamos patris / invisa proles (634-36). *Sceptra* and *thalamos* are both objects of violent usurpation by the son (*occupat*, a telling zeugma).[27] The adjectives "bloody," "savage," and "evil" (*cruentus, saevus, nefandus*) in these lines magnify the father's horror at being thus violated by his son. "Bloody" in particular, which is applied both to the son who attacks the father (*rex cruentus*, 634) and to the scepter stained by the crime against the father (*cruenta sceptra*, 642), stresses the primal violence of the patricidal and regicidal act. Covered with blood, the scepter lends the authority of monstrously outraged sanctities to the accusations of a relentless, condemning father.[28]

The ghost of father Laius is called forth from the "blind chaos" of Hades (572) amid eerie rites and horrible images of Furies and subterranean monsters (582-98), including the mothers who have lost or killed children (Niobe and Agave, 613-18). As the unconscious terrors break through into the realm of society, politics, and the moral order, the king and father appears only as a terrifying, wrathful voice of retribution. Laius takes no account of the circumstances of the killing or the technical innocence of Oedipus.[29] The Underworld from which Seneca's father-figure comes is the unconscious reservoir of the imagos; and his Laius is an inexorable demon of unreasoning and unreasonable guilt.[30]

[27] I call the figure a zeugma, even though the verb *occupat* has a similar meaning with both objects, because the "grasping" or "seizing" of the scepter is of a different nature from the "seizing" of the bedchamber. The one can be understood in a literal sense; the other has to be figurative.

[28] For the significant repetition of *cruentus* in 634 and 642, see D. J. Mastronarde, "Seneca's *Oedipus*: The Drama in the Word," *TAPA* 101 (1970) 300, who also calls attention to 93f., where the word describes another evil element of the nightmarish past, the "bloody jaws" of the monstrous Sphinx.

[29] Seneca's treatment of the Oedipal guilt is almost the reverse of Sophocles' in his later reflection on the consequences of Oedipus' action in the *Oedipus at Colonus*. There the guilty son, Oedipus, is now himself a paternal figure, old and possessing a commanding and mysterious patriarchal authority. He is reconciled to the maternal powers of the Underworld, who have become deities benign to him (Eumenides instead of Erinyes), and he can use the pleas of intentionality and conscious choice to counter the accusations of guilt and pollution that still cling to his name.

[30] See Owen (1968) 311: "We expect of Laius not ugly bloodthirstiness, but a tragic sense of shame and sorrow." See also Segal (1983a) 176-78.

In the *Phoenissae* the scepter is even more strongly the focus of the son's guilt for overthrowing the father and taking possession of his power. In the rhetoric of the unconscious, that guilt is now displaced metonymically from the father to the scepter of the father. Oedipus, deeply distraught by his memories of the past, imagines Laius calling him and raging against him, brandishing the bloody scepter (39-41):

> genitor vocat.
> sequor, sequor, iam parce—sanguineum gerens
> insigne regni Laius rapti furit.

> My father calls. I follow, I follow; hold off now—Laius rages, wielding the bloody emblem of his rule that I tore away.

Later, as Oedipus rehearses his crimes in his torments of remorse, the scepter again symbolizes both the nearer and the remoter usurpation of the father's phallic power: the son's fertile union with the mother in the bedchambers (*thalami*) and the possession of the royal power in the city. His guilt and anxiety toward the father once more crystallize around the scepter. He has thrown it away as the prize of a father's murder (275, echoing *Oed.* 634f.), but even so it returns to wreak its destructive vengeance on the guilty offspring, in this case Oedipus' own sons, Eteocles and Polynices (270-76):

> leve est paternum facinus; in thalamos meos
> deducta mater, ne parum sceleris foret,
> fecunda. nullum crimen hoc maius potest
> natura ferre . . .
>   abieci necis
> pretium paternae sceptrum et hoc iterum manus
> armavit alias . . .

> The crime against my father is slight: my mother was led into my bedchambers, lest there be too little crime, (to be) with child. Nature can bear no greater crime than this. . . .

The prize of murdering my father, the scepter, I cast away,
and this once more has armed the hands of others.

The scepter that should signify the paternal authority in
house and kingdom is here the sign of the worst crimes of nature (272f.), what a man unconsciously most desires and fears.
Though rejected as the "prize of a father's murder," the scepter
still continues as a source of violence. Quasi-personified, it "has
armed the hands" that in the next generation will further rend
the order of house and kingdom.

The *Medea*, finally, uses the scepter to focus the subversion of
the rational order by the bursting forth of suppressed female
rage and passion. In the first stage of her victory over Jason, father and husband both, Medea kills one of his sons and threatens to kill the other. Casting secrecy to the winds, she shows
herself from the palace. Jason calls upon the city's warriors and
their arms (980f.):

huc, huc fortis armiferi cohors
conferte tela, vertite ex imo domum.

Here, here, my mighty band, bearers of weapons, bring
your spears; overturn the house from its depths.

Medea replies triumphantly from the roof that she has now regained the scepter of her native land (982-84):

iam iam recepi sceptra germanum patrem,
spoliumque Colchi pecudis auratae tenent;
rediere regna, rapta virginitas redit.

Now, now I have regained scepter, brother, and father; and
the Colchians hold the prize of the golden ram. My
kingdom has come back to me, back to me my maidenhood
once torn away.

In repossessing the male scepter, Medea not only completes her
triumph over her husband, but also symbolically cancels out her
sexual subjection to the male by regaining her virginity (*rapta*

virginitas redit, 984).[31] She continues her subversion of masculine sexual power even more bitterly in the next lines as she associates this day of victory with her wedding day (985f.):

> o placida tandem numina, o festum diem,
> o nuptialem! vade, perfectum est scelus.

> O divinities appeased at last! O day of celebration, day of
> marriage! Come, the crime is completed.

This ironical marriage destroys both the social order and the
generative potency of the father. The wife holds the scepter, and
neither her body nor her offspring are his possessions. She does
nothing, it is true, against her family of origin, *her* father and
brother, whose kingdom she feels she is restoring (982, 984).
Her rebellion against the patriarchal power is focused entirely
on her husband, whereas in Phaedra's case the figure of Theseus
combines the roles of both father and husband, with the actual
father, King Minos, more prominent and more ominous in the
background.

Unlike Medea, however, Phaedra is not overtly challenging
the male-centered political order symbolized by the scepter. She
uses it, initially, only as a means to entice Hippolytus to love her
(617). Later she evokes it to reinforce her accusation of him to
Theseus (868). In both cases, she accepts and works within the
patriarchal order that the scepter embodies. Analogously, on
the level of the domestic order, she accepts the social conven-
tion of marriage as the framework for her love (597).

Yet Phaedra's subversion of the patriarchal order from within
is perhaps more insidious than Medea's head-on assault. In the
erotic uses to which Phaedra would put the royal scepter, as in
those to which she will put the sword and its emblem of paternal inheritance (896-900), she displaces political to sexual vio-

---

[31] Similarly in 1012f. Medea would tear out of her body the fetus that constitutes the "pledge" or "bond" of love with her husband (*pignus*). As in 984,
she would remove from her body the signs of sexual domination by the male,
while she also, paradoxically, uses her role and power as mother to take her revenge: see Segal (1983a) 178.

lence and thereby reveals the harshness and destructiveness of the father-figure of the realm.

The play is not political allegory; but one could easily extrapolate from the results of offending against the Athenian *sceptrum* to the results of offending against the imperial *maiestas*. The psychological and political implications of the punitive father-figure closely overlap. Offense to the ruler of house, city, and kingdom and insult to the symbol of his power bring swift, unreasoning, irresistible punishment. There is no appeal; the judge is remote from the defendant and invisible, and at a single command he calls forth a massive punitive machinery of limitless destructive energy.

EIGHT

Desire, Silence, and the Speech of the Sword

I

For Seneca's Phaedra, as for Euripides' and Racine's, the crossing of the barrier between silence and speech is the critical event. Once these words of desire are spoken, the relation between the speakers is irrevocably changed. Neither the lover who confesses the love nor the beloved who receives the message can ever be quite the same toward one another again. This climactic point of decisive speaking lies at the heart of dramatic representation: the art of converting the exchange of words and feelings into theatrical situation. Communication becomes surrounded with a suspenseful direction that draws us inevitably toward an overwhelming spectacle. In the ancient Greek theater such moments come at "the terrible" (*to deinon*) of hearing and speaking in Sophocles' *Oedipus Tyrannus* or in the single syllable, "ah," uttered by Dionysus in Euripides' *Bacchae* when he elicits from Pentheus the overt statement of his desire to "see."[1] What Roland Barthes calls "le *tenebroso* racinien," the revelation of desire from the muted and penumbral background of Racine's theater, has its origins in Seneca: "The erotic scene is theater within theater; it seeks to *render* the most vital but also the most fragile moment of the struggle, that in which the shadow is penetrated by a flash of brilliance. . . . It is this pure suspense, this fragile atom of duration in which the sun *makes us see* the night, without yet destroying it, that constitutes what one may call Racine's *tenebroso*."[2]

---

[1] Soph., *Oed. Tyr.* 1169; Eur., *Bacchae* 810.
[2] Roland Barthes, *Sur Racine* (Paris 1963) 32 (my translation). On the importance of speech and silence generally in relation to desire, see also Barthes' remarks, pp. 26ff., 115f.

Incestuous desire in particular is enacted onstage as the violent forcing of the barrier of silence that must surround desire within the family. The unrepressing of desire is enacted as a violence in language. In the theater, where reality is condensed (or transposed) into the symbolic microcosm of words, to speak is to act, and vice versa.[3]

In Euripides' *Hippolytus* the overt speaking of desire takes place only in the privacy of Phaedra's conversation with the Nurse, who is first the voice of her own reality-testing, then of her rationalizing.[4] The truth breaks into language, as in Seneca's play too, only in broken statements and covert allusions. In a dialogue that returns again and again to the contrasts of speech and silence, the Nurse mentions, almost in passing, "the horse-driving Amazon queen" and her "bastard son of noble thoughts, Hippolytus," a danger to the inheritance of her children (*Hipp.* 307-10). This first utterance by a mortal of the name "Hippolytus" wrings from Phaedra her cry, *oimoi*, that cuts abruptly into the meter, and her entreaty for silence (310-12). The crucial word comes forth only when speech is engaged in evasion rather than communication, for the two interlocutors, Phaedra and the Nurse, are here talking to one another on quite different tracks.

When the Nurse persists and succeeds in forcing Phaedra to break her silence (326-36), the truth of her desire can again emerge only through a path of indirection, by allusion rather than explicit statement (*Hipp.* 337-42):

PHAEDRA: Alas, poor mother, what a love you loved.
NURSE: Her love for the Bull, my child? Or what is it you are saying?
PHAEDRA: You too, unhappy sister, Dionysus' bride.
NURSE: Child, what is wrong? Do you defame your kin?

[3] On the importance of speech and silence in the Euripidean play, see Knox, 207, 212ff., 218f.; Segal (1965) 147f..
[4] Cf. *Hipp.* 353-62 and 433-524 respectively.

PHAEDRA: And third in misery, how I am destroyed.
NURSE: I am thunderstruck. To what point will the tale
advance?

Unfolding in the still inviolate, protective space of her house
and her domestic identity, Phaedra's desire is still distanced by
the remote past of her mother and sister. But it can emerge only
via this detour into the past; and it is the Nurse, not Phaedra
herself, who must pronounce the fateful name (*Hipp*. 350-52):

NURSE: What are you saying? Are you in love, my child?
With whom?
PHAEDRA: Whoever this one is, the Amazon's . . .
NURSE: You speak of Hippolytus?
PHAEDRA: From yourself you hear it, not from me.

In Seneca, however, Phaedra speaks her desire directly to
Hippolytus. In this different presentation of desire, the decision
to speak becomes even more fraught with erotic power, since
the speaking will be to the beloved himself and is, therefore, not
just an avowal of desire but a seductive act.[5] In this change too
the inhibiting or legitimating figures of the background move
closer to the forefront of the action and become more visibly
operative on both sides: Pasiphae, Ariadne, Minos, and Theseus for Phaedra; the Amazon mother, Diana, and also Theseus
for Hippolytus.

Seneca's recasting of the way in which the desire is avowed
follows Euripides' lost first Hippolytus play. This version enables Phaedra to dramatize the expression of her love as a truly
theatrical event. As she openly declares her secret to the object
of her love, she makes her language into the transitive vehicle of
desire, reaching out to encompass its object. The tableau on the

---

[5] In the terminology of Austin and Searle, the language shifts from an illocutionary to a perlocutionary function: see J. L. Austin, *How to Do Things with
Words* (Oxford 1962) and J. R. Searle, *Speech Acts* (Cambridge 1969), chaps. 2
and 3. "Illocutionary" refers to what we do "in saying"; "perlocutionary" to
what we do "by saying." For a lucid explanation, see Paul Ricoeur, "The Model
of the Text," *New Literary History* 5 (1973-74) 93f.

stage then leaps from the realm of ambiguous words to violent theatrical gestures with the sword. In the next scene Phaedra will make her speech persuasive by another powerful gesture with the sword. Finally, in her last appearance, she will make the sword the most powerful theatrical object in the play, plunging it into her body for her onstage suicide. In each case the rhetorical display of the sword accompanies the swelling exuberance of the language and upstages the suspenseful moment when words barely emerge, with painful difficulty, from their encompassing and repressing silence.

The interplay of speech and silence around the sword creates a dialectic not only between acting out and repression, but also between muffled verbal effects and grandiose, shocking gestures. Tense silences around ambiguous and hesitant confession alternate with vehement exaggerations and exclamations that seem at times to reach the point of hysteria. Seneca does not reflect so self-consciously as Euripides on the relation between the verbal and gestural components of his dramatic art,[6] but his rapid juxtaposition of the two types of effect is characteristic of the contrapuntal movements of his "baroque" style. In this play the jagged movements, uneven rising and falling, and steep contrasts pitch us suddenly from muted conspiracy to the extremes of violence.[7]

II

In the archetypal literary model of the suppression of sexual knowledge, Sophocles' *Oedipus Tyrannus*, Oedipus' non-speaking about the scars on his feet and Jocasta's silence about her exposed infant are the tacit conditions for the unfolding of the action on the stage. In Seneca's *Phaedra* there are comparable suppressed narratives; the blurred outlines of Theseus' union with Hippolytus' Amazon mother, her death at his hands, Hip-

---

[6] See Segal (1982a) 149-51; also Segal (1982) 296-98.
[7] For some aspects of this "baroque" artistry, see Segal (1984).

polytus' childhood, and Theseus' descent to the Underworld, with hints of his erotic motives.[8]

The love that Phaedra brings forth from concealment, once spoken, can never again be repressed. It can only be displaced onto Hippolytus, projected as his desire, not hers. This is the next step in the plot, the distortion and concealment of desire by words as a result of the Nurse's decision to veil crime by crime (*scelere velandum est scelus*, 721). What she "veils" is Phaedra's desire to set Hippolytus in the place of the father. From another point of view, she would create a Hippolytus who has the sexual drive and potency of the absent father. Her language thus speaks of a desire (or set of desires) of which Hippolytus has no conscious knowledge but which become the central concern of his life once they have been spoken in the language of the other. The crime of desire—a crime so terrible that Hippolytus must immediately elide it from speech—is to be "veiled," as the Nurse says, by another crime that substitutes for it. In the action of the play this process takes the form of replacing the phallus that Phaedra desires with the ambiguous substitute for the phallus that in fact negates Hippolytus' sexuality. This is the sword, the instrument that he uses to suppress desire, to counter its appearance, and to force it back into silence.

The asymmetry of desire between Hippolytus and Phaedra, however, necessarily produces an asymmetry in their verbal communication. It brings abrupt fluctuations between ambiguous silences and vehement denunciations, between crafty lie and desperate outcry, and between secretive hinting and hysterical shout. Their language, like their whole relationship, shifts between unspeakable desire and noisy verbal aggression, between language as seduction and language as weapon.

III

The erotic crises of the play develop as crises of duplicitous language and problematical communication. Only in the solo

[8] On Theseus and Antiope, see 227-32, 659f., 908-11, 926-28, 1164-67; on Theseus and Peirithous, see 244; on the alleged erotic motives for Theseus' descent, see 93-98, 627f.

lyrics of Hippolytus' opening song do we have a univocal language of single-spirited intentions. Yet that unity too rests on latent tensions.[9] The unity of self and speech, of will and communication, that finds its formal expression in the self-enclosed lyrical monologue is fragmented as the ensuing dramatic interactions create ever more complicated modes of discourse. Only in the monologues of Phaedra and Theseus in the closing scenes is this unity restored, but then it is too late.

Hippolytus first encounters Phaedra's desire in his dialogue with the Nurse. This scene expresses her desire obliquely, through an intermediary who uses hints and suggestions. Ostensibly a discourse of friendly advice by an older, maternal woman to an inexperienced youth, the scene in fact conceals a discourse of seduction. In the next scene Phaedra, having rejected the Nurse's attempt to place the Name of the Father between her desire and its incestuous object,[10] ambiguously pronounces Hippolytus the substitute for the father (617-21, 646ff.). The last crisis develops as a natural result of the preceding. The power of speech is now usurped by the sword (896). In all three scenes repressed desire emerges painfully out of hints and double meanings, with calamitous results.

Phaedra's attack on the father in the form of the quasi-incestuous desire for his son is also an attack on language in the realm of the father. The language that belongs to the father's effective authority in the "outside" is drawn into ambiguity, obliquity, and the unspeakable things of Phaedra's house.

As the city and public life are displaced from prominence in the first part of the play,[11] an analogous displacement occurs in language. The women of the house urge Hippolytus to greater concern with citizens, but they are not interested in the civic order. The words *citizens* and *Athens*, in fact, occur only in the mouths of the Nurse and Phaedra and aim at subverting regal

[9] See above, chap. 3 and 4.
[10] Cf. 154ff., 217ff., 242ff.
[11] Thus when the Nurse urges Hippolytus to inhabit the city and cultivate the citizens' gathering (*urbem frequenta, civium coetum cole*, 482), he replies with a sharp attack on the evils of city life (483ff.).

and paternal authority.[12] First Phaedra exhorts Hippolytus to usurp his father's power over the citizens ("strong with your father's rule, command the citizens," *cives paterno fortis imperio rege*, 621), where her motives are intensely personal. Later her guile and deceptive speech, the result of thwarted feminine desire, triumph over the king and his heir as she describes "the arrival of citizens" that made Hippolytus drop his sword (*civium accursum*, 897). The Nurse's cry to Athens in 725 invokes the civic realm for similarly private and covert ends. Only with Phaedra's answering appeal to Athens in her confession at the end (1191) is there a shift back to the moral and political order (inadequate though it is) of king and father.[13]

IV

At three critical points in the play full speech emerges slowly and painfully from a precarious dialogue. These are Phaedra's confession of love to Hippolytus, her reluctant (and mendacious) accusation of Hippolytus' alleged attack when Theseus returns, and the Messenger's difficulty in speaking when he reports Hippolytus' death. All three scenes are thematically and causally related in a widening circle of violence.

The first exchanges between Phaedra and Hippolytus are about speaking and not speaking, repression and freedom of speech. Terms for ears, words, permissible and impermissible utterance dominate the preliminaries of their encounter.[14]

---

[12] *Cives*: 482 (Nurse); 621 and 897 (Phaedra). Similarly, where "city" (*urbs*) is mentioned, the context is Hippolytus' attack on civic life (494 and 531; cf. 561) or his exile from the city (1000) or Phaedra's subversion of the regal and political authority by offering it illegitimately to the son (e.g., 619: *muliebre non est regna tutari urbium*, "It is not a woman's task to watch over the rule of cities," 619; cf. 621). The Nurse's command at Phaedra's collapse in 733, "Carry (her) to the city" (*perferte in urbem*), occurs in a context that might suggest the conveying of the female deception "to the city" as well, as "the marks of so great a crime" occur in the previous line (*facinoris tanti notae*, 732). The A-tradition, in fact, so understood the meaning, reading *notas . . . referte*: see Grimal ad 733. For another aspect of the motif of the city in the play, see Petrone (1984) 73ff.

[13] Cf. *adeste, Athenae* ("Be present, Athens") in 725 and *audite, Athenae* ("Hear me, Athens") in 1191.

[14] Cf. 593, 596, 600, 602, 606, 607, 608.

Nearly every word in her confession of love has a *double-entendre* (589-666). Her line, *curae leves loquuntur, ingentes stupent* ("Light cares speak, the heavy ones are dumb," 607), is a characteristically Senecan antithesis; but it effectively portrays the most powerful concerns of her emotional life as marked by a negative sign, the absence of voice. That very non-speaking appears as a form of action, indicated by the verb, *stupent*.[15]

Characteristic of the whole scene is Hippolytus' question, "Is your mind, desiring to speak forth something, unable to?" (*animusne cupiens aliquid effari nequit?*, 606). The line fuses Phaedra's desire for Hippolytus with her desire for speech. *Cupiens*, "desiring," is so placed as to suggest both possibilities ("desiring something" and "desiring to say something"). When Phaedra is ready to utter that desire, she must clear the ground by removing the chief verbal impediment, the "name of mother" (607-12):

> PHAEDRA: curae leves loquuntur, ingentes stupent.
> HIPP.: committe curas auribus, mater, meis.
> PHAEDRA: matris superbum est nomen et nimium potens;
> nostros humilius nomen affectus decet;
> me vel sororem, Hippolyte, vel famulam voca,
> famulamque potius; omne servitium feram.

> PHAEDRA: Light cares speak; the heavy ones are dumb.
> HIPP.: Entrust your cares, mother, to my ears.
> PHAEDRA: "Mother"—the name is proud and too powerful.
> A humbler name befits our affection.
> Call me sister, Hippolytus, or slave—
> Yes, better slave. Slavery in every form will I endure.

The contradictions in which the denial of the proud name of "mother" involves Phaedra are clear from line 610: she would refuse the name of "mother" because of an affection which de-

---

[15] On the blocking of speech, see also 602 and 637. Cf. also the motif of silence in Ovid, *Heroides* 4.7f., on which see Jacobson (1974) 148. Cf. also Dido's inability to speak in Virgil *Aen.* 4.76: *incipit effari mediaque in voce resistit* ("She begins to speak but in the midst of her voice stops short").

serves a lesser name. Yet that affection, hitherto unspeakable, will in fact claim as great a force as that of a mother, as Phaedra's willingness to endure any servitude (612) and the later course of the action will show.

As that proud and potent name gives way to the humility of Phaedra's subservience to desire ("I will bear every slavery," 612), she moves to the name of "sister" (611), hardly an improvement as far as her project is concerned, and then to "slave" (612). The language of domestic order, from mother to sister to the household servant (*famula*, 612), yields to the elegiac theme of the *servitium amoris* implied in 612, "I will bear every servitude." This amorous *topos* has no place in the well-ordered household. Phaedra must break down the name of "mother" and replace it with the language of erotic passion. The first step in her seduction, then, is a linguistic transformation. This in turn displays her passion in contrasting registers of language. She speaks with the authority of the Roman *matrona* in her *domus*, but she also uses the words that one would expect to find in the demi-monde of Roman elegy.

As Phaedra moves closer to the confession of her desire, her language focuses more sharply on speech and silence: "Did I say enough . . . Hear the prayers of my silent mind . . . I regret speech and silence both" (635-37).[16] "Speak openly," Hippolytus urges her, puzzled at her "ambiguous words" (640f.). But the terrible words come out accompanied by the visible gestures that make the force of desire unmistakable: she falls at his feet, an abject suppliant and an avowed lover (*supplex*, 666; *amantis*, 671). She soon repeats that gesture, with even greater desperation and greater recognition of the hopeless distance between her subjection and his pride: *iterum, superbe, genibus advolvor tuis* ("Once again, proud man, I grovel at your feet," 703). For Hippolytus both the words and the gesture are crimes that "the great ruler of the gods" will perceive and swiftly punish *magne*

---

[16] With Grimal (1965) ad 635, I prefer to follow the reading of E, *satisne dixi*, to A's *satisne dixit*. The point is Phaedra's speaking, as 637 shows, not Hippolytus'.

regnator deum, / *tam lentus audis scelera? tam lentus vides?* ("Great ruler of the gods, are you so slow to *hear* such crimes, so slow to *see* them?" 672f.).

Language now enacts the ambiguities of desire: it holds the delicate balance between the appearance of propriety and the reality of illicit lust. When Phaedra refers to her love for Theseus when he was a youth (*quondam puer,* 647), she simultaneously declares emotional allegiance to her husband and alludes to the incestuous nature of the love that she is on the verge of declaring. By using the proper names, "Hippolytus," "Theseus," in the same verse, Phaedra verbally as well as emotionally runs the son and the father together: *Hippolyte, sic est: Thesei vultus amo.* . . . ("Hippolytus, thus it is: it is Theseus' face I love," 646).[17]

The juxtaposition of names corresponds to the juxtaposition of faces, for with deliberate ambiguity she declares her love for Hippolytus as love "for Theseus' features of old, those he bore long ago, as a boy" (646f.). The tension in her language parallels the tension in her thoughts. She shifts between juxtaposition and substitution, between running on from Hippolytus to Theseus and putting Hippolytus in the place of Theseus (*Hippolyte . . . Thesei,* 646), between a historical account of the past and the intense concerns of an all-absorbing present.[18] At the end of this crucial speech, just before the climactic gesture of throwing herself on her knees, she makes explicit her identification with Ariadne and once again joins father and son in a single verse (665f.):

domus sorores una corripuit duas:
te genitor, at me natus.

One house carried off two sisters, you, the father; me, the son.

---

[17] The name gets special emphasis as the first of Phaedra's three direct addresses to Hippolytus in the vocative in this scene.

[18] This sense of the past is expressed emphatically in the words *priores* and *quondam,* 647, and *tum,* 651. From another perspective the passage shows the same tendency to absorb the historical into the personal and to project personal history into the past that we have seen in the case of Hippolytus' Golden Age: see above, chap. 4.

In the word order of *domus sorores una* and the enframing allit-
eration of *domos . . . duas*, the one house grammatically enfolds
the two sisters in a common doom. The parallelism of the two
clauses of the next line has the same effect.

V

The scene of Theseus' return is sequential in time but also
symmetrical in structure to the scene between Phaedra and Hippolytus. Here Phaedra is again the object of entreaties to speak
(compare 858f. with 607 and 639). In the former scene she violates the taboo imposed by the "proud name of mother" and
entrusts to the ears of a son words they should not hear. In the
latter she would respect the taboos around a husband's hearing
and keep from a husband's ears words about the wife that he
should not receive (874): *aures pudica coniugis solas timet* ("A
chaste wife fears only her spouse's ears"). But this ambiguously
"chaste wife" really does intend to speak. The whole point of
Phaedra's interview with Hippolytus lay in reaching through silence to speech. The whole point of her interview with Theseus
lies in keeping silence: *si causa leti dicitur, fructus perit*, she tells
him ("If the reason for [my] death is told, its fruit [reward, ben-
efit] perishes," 872).[19] But in both scenes the silence imposed
by the incest taboo ("name of mother," "husband") masks a
speech that will come forth and is determined to come forth.

The scene between Hippolytus and Phaedra began with her
ambiguous hesitation to allow "passage" to her words of desire:
*sed ora coeptis transitum verbis negant: / vis magna vocem mittit et
maior tenet* ("But my mouth denies a passage to the words that
have been begun; a great force sends forth my voice, and a
greater holds it back," 602f.). At Theseus' arrival the situation
is repeated, but now blockage of speech is transposed to
blocked entrance. Locking herself up in her palace, Phaedra
"does not open to any one" (*haut pandit ulli*, 860). The sequence, "speak *openly*" (*aperte*, 859) and "she does not *open* to
anyone" (860) contains the analogy between speaking and en-

---

[19] On the ambiguities of this line, see Grimal (1965) ad loc.

tering. Theseus has to give commands to unlock the closed gates of the king's abode (*reserate clausos regii postes laris*, 863).[20] The scene that will enact the veiling/unveiling of desire through the display of the sword begins, appropriately, with an implicit parallelism between opening the secrets of chamber, speech, and body.

Phaedra's meeting with the father has both verbal and thematic parallels with the meeting with the son. Theseus addresses Phaedra's surrogate, the Nurse, as follows (858f.):

perplexa magnum verba nescio quid tegunt.
effare aperte quis gravet mentem dolor.

Your tangled web of words conceals some great thing.
Speak out openly what grief weighs down your mind.

He is echoing Hippolytus' address to Phaedra in the previous scene:

animusne cupiens aliquid effari nequit. (606)

"Can your mind, desiring to speak something, not speak it forth?

ambigua voce verba perplexa iacis.
effare aperte. (639f.)

You utter words of double meaning with tangled sense.
Speak out openly.

In the later scene, however, the emotion that lies behind reluctant speech is no longer love (*amor*), but grief (*dolor*): "Speak out openly what grief (*dolor*) weighs down your mind" (859).

---

[20] The attribution of 863 is divided in the mss.: A gives the line to Theseus, E to the Nurse. Grimal (1965) argues in favor of Theseus, but other editors follow A: so Giardina, Herrmann (1925), Miller, Lawall. Contrast the far gentler use of the motif of gates at Theseus' entrance in Eur., *Hipp.* 792f., where Theseus says, οὐ γάρ τί μ᾽ ὡς θεωρὸν ἀξιοῖ δόμος / πύλας ἀνοίξας εὐφρόνως προσεννέπειν ("The house, opening its gates, does not deem it fit to address me happily on my return"). Here, however, the personification of the house adds a vivid emphasis to this point of crucial entrance. Theseus' closely parallel command in 1275, *patefacite acerbam caede funesta domum* ("Throw open the house bitter with funereal slaughter") also helps support the attribution of 863 to him.

When Phaedra breaks her silence before Theseus, she does not simply blurt out, "Hippolytus." Instead, like her Euripidean prototype, she places him at the end of a chain of signifiers from which his name is actually elided, to be replaced by the more telling signifier of desire, the sword.[21] When she tells Theseus that she has been violated, he responds immediately: "Who, utter it, was the destroyer of our honor?" (*quis, ede, nostri decoris fuit*, 894). Broken question and answer follow (895-97):

PHAEDRA: quem reris minime.
THESEUS: quis sit audire expeto.
PHAEDRA: hic dicet ensis quem tumultu territus
        liquit stuprator civium accursum timens.

PHAEDRA: Whom you least would think.
THESEUS: Who it is I demand to hear.
PHAEDRA: This sword will tell, which my ravisher
        abandoned, frightened by the noise, fearing the approach
of citizens.

Her mode of revealing her secret has two effects. First, it creates the space in which Theseus' unconscious fears can be aroused to the fullest in the suspense and the invitation to reflect offered by her words, "Whom you least would think." It enlists him in the process of discovery and makes him participate directly in the horror of uncovering the "truth." Second, her personification of the sword as the "speaker" brings closer to the surface its hidden meaning as the signifier of desire.[22] The sword will all too eloquently speak to Theseus of desire, but it is the imaginary desire of Hippolytus that Phaedra has

---

[21] Cf. Eur., *Hipp.* 337ff., cited above, sec. I.
[22] For other aspects of the ambiguity of Phaedra's language in 891ff. and the withholding of Hippolytus' name, see Seidensticker (1969), 148f., who remarks, "Theseus müssen die dunklen und halben Antworten Phaidras in immer grössere Unruhe und Erregung versetzen. Psychologisch wird auf diese Weise die Tatsache, dass er im Augenblick der ungeheuerlichen Enthüllung nicht eine Sekunde zweifelt, sondern sofort in die Verfluchung des Sohnes ausbricht, gut vorbereitet" (148).

(re)created in her fantasies and her falsehoods. Her deliberate indirectness about the name which Theseus most fears to hear creates the active field in which his (and, by extension, our) unconscious fears and fantasies can fill in the details: the son at home, old enough and mature enough to wear a sword; the wife, still young and attractive, in the house, undefended by the father and sexually available.[23] Her narrative, bare and elliptical as it is, completes the field of possible imaginings by sketching in the ravisher's fear of using the sword, "frightened by the noise, fearing the approach of citizens" (896f.).[24] This is a fear that Theseus "knows" as appropriate to the son who has lived under his own authority in this house.

VI

By refusing to speak and by closing the doors of her chambers (860ff.), Phaedra denies Theseus access to the secrets that are most intimately his own. Yet in the very act of closing these apertures she creates an ambiguously seductive discourse which invites him, indirectly, to unbar her gates and lay bare her secrets. Her language here functions as a kind of photographic negative of normal speech. The most powerful word, the name of the son, is excluded from speech; and that verbal exclusion parallels the exclusion of the actual son from those interior chambers which only the father may enter. The sword highlights Phaedra's ambiguous "won't tell" by shunting the revelation of her message on to a roundabout track of secondary signifiers, including the very reluctance to speak.

[23] Phaedra is to be thought of as probably much younger than Theseus and perhaps not so far from the age of Hippolytus: see Lattimore (1962) 7. Phaedra's talk of Theseus' youthful countenance when he vanquished the Minotaur (646) may also suggest the age differential between them: see Friedrich (1953) 131. Psychologically, her age corresponds to the desires and fears that she arouses in the two male figures of her tragedy.

[24] At the same time this evocation of a public voice sets off the private world of her fantasies, desires, and anxieties. Heldmann (1968), 106, points out the un-Greek use of the address to Athens (cf. 725, 901, 1191), a group not really existing as a stage presence. From the point of view of Hippolytus, is the approach of citizens supposed to appear as especially fearful to one who has spent his life in the woods and relinquished the regal and urban pursuits of his father?

When Phaedra allows the sword to "speak" to Theseus (896ff.), its role replicates the movement of the plot in general. It marks the substitution of words (Phaedra's) for acts (Hippolytus'). Itself a substitute for the phallus, it replaces repressed incestuous desires with a symbol of their fantasied enactment. The sword's "speech," though addressed directly to Theseus, who is present on the stage, is also a reply to the absent Hippolytus: it remakes his speech about the sword (706ff.) as her fantasy of a desirous Hippolytus.

The alternation of speech and silence throughout this scene sets into relief the paradoxical "speaking" of the sword. The "tearful groaning" of the servants (*fremitus flebilis*) literally "smites" Theseus' ears as he enters the house after his long absence (*quis fremitus aures flebilis pepulit meas?* 850). This outcry, in turn, contrasts with the determined silence of Phaedra later (*silere pergit*, 882). Theseus finds the Nurse's explanations full of ambiguous words that conceal something big (*magnum nescio quid tegunt*, 858).

The first real exchange between Theseus and Phaedra concerns the privacy and concealment of what they will say (873-76):

THESEUS: Nemo istud alius, me quidem excepto, audiet.
PHAEDRA: aures pudica coniugis solas timet.
THESEUS: effare: fido pectore arcana occulam.
PHAEDRA: alium silere quod voles, primus sile.

THESEUS: No one else, myself excepted, will hear this.
PHAEDRA: A chaste woman fears only the ears of her
    husband.
THESEUS: Speak out: I will conceal the secret things in a
    trusted breast.
PHAEDRA: What you want another to keep in silence, keep
    silent first yourself.

This scene not only interweaves familial, sexual, and linguistic codes in the play's discourse, but also reveals language itself as a mode of sexuality. Theseus insistently penetrates Phaedra's silence to expose her *arcana*. Their further dialogue attempts to recreate the initial agreement between man and wife to hold certain things as secrets between them (873ff.). Theseus would reclaim those secrets by a forceful throwing open of gates (863). It is indicative of Theseus' relation with Phaedra, and perhaps of her marital unhappiness, that his triumph comes through commands and force rather than persuasion or seduction (882-85). At just this point the marital exchange of the secret things that husband and wife share (873-76) breaks down in Phaedra's determination to keep silence. Theseus frustratedly remarks, "She persists in silence" (*silere pergit*, 883).

The sexual significance of the gates, familiar in classical literature (e.g. Aristophanes' *Lysistrata*), has resonances in other versions of the myth. In the summary of Pseudo-Apollodorus, for instance, Phaedra uses as evidence of Hippolytus' violence (cf. *Phaedra* 890-92) the broken door of her chamber and her torn clothing: "Phaedra, fearing that (Hippolytus) would accuse her to his father, split the door of her bedchamber and tore her clothes and made her false accusation of Hippolytus' violence."[25] Seneca has shifted his emphasis from the visual detail of the broken door to the more complex signs of the son's presence in the forbidden interior—the sword and the themes of speech and silence that cluster around it.

Phaedra's closing of the gates upon Theseus is parallel with her desire earlier to keep him in the Underworld (cf. 218-24). She refuses to accept the return of the father, both because she loves Hippolytus and because she fears punishment for that love. Her resistance to Theseus' return earlier took the form of insisting that the gates of Hades are closed upon him. The Nurse, the voice of Phaedra's reality-principle at this moment, emphasizes Theseus' power as one who breaks his way through

---

[25] Ps.-Apollodorus, *Epitome* 1.18. Cf. also Soph., *Oed. Tyr.* 1261ff. (Oedipus breaking down the doors to Jocasta's bedchamber). See Fauth (1958) 558f.; Friedrich (1953) 132; Barrett (1964) 38; Zintzen (1960) 103ff. On doors and female sexuality, see Adams (1982) 89. Cf. the interlocking of the themes of gates and speech in Eur. *Hipp.* 807f. and 882f. Seneca's Theseus, of course, is speaking not to the servants of his dead wife, but to Phaedra herself, the *socia thalami* (865).

closed gates. "Trust not in Dis," she warns, "even though he has closed up his kingdom (*clauserit regnum*) and though the Stygian hound (Cerberus) keeps watch at the fearful gates" (*diras . . . observet fores*). Phaedra later acts out her fantasy of keeping Theseus in the Underworld: she closes up the gates. But they are no barrier to the father, whose single command throws them open (864). He is ready to use violence (*vis*, 884; cf. 892) to break into her hidden places and force her secrets (*secreta*, 885).

"Only Theseus," the Nurse predicted, "always finds the paths that have been denied him" (*solus negatus invenit Theseus vias*, 222-24). In her first speech, however, Phaedra herself was the one to point out Theseus' ability to make his way through the deep shadows of the lake that offers no path (*per altas invii retro lacus / vadit tenebras*, 93f.). This ability to achieve passage is part of the aggressive and destructive sexuality of Theseus that Phaedra would deny by keeping him "closed up" beneath the earth. In his return the aggressive force preponderates over the erotic. Responding to Phaedra's accusation, he displays a murderous energy of passage: his curse of Hippolytus repeats the imagery of penetrating closed places and cutting through pathless wastes (938-40):

> I will press you [Hippolytus] down though you flee persistently through every *hiding place*; I shall *make my way* through places distant, *closed*, hidden away, remote, *pathless*. No place *will be an obstacle*. You know *the place from which I return*.[26]

VII

Theseus' violent re-entrance to the house is a symbolical condensation of his relationship with Phaedra. In her opening speech of the play she had stated her hostility to him as one who

---

[26] For 938 note how "pressing down" is associated with the punitive authority of the father figure in the Nurse's reference to Minos in 149, "he who presses down the seas in his broad reign." The oppressive force that the father-figure there exercised on Phaedra shifts to Hippolytus here in 938. See above, chap. 2, sec. III; also below, chap. 9, note 20.

has kept her closed within, as a hostage (89ff.). His violence against the Nurse to compel speech later is a form of violence against Phaedra; and this violence has already weakened his claim to a "trusty breast" which could "conceal secret things."

As in Racine's *Phèdre*, the Nurse symbolizes not only Phaedra's reality principle but also her instinct for survival.[27] It was the Nurse who gave her the means of survival by converting Hippolytus' horrified flight into evidence for rape (725-32). Threatening the Nurse here, Theseus sets into motion that survival mechanism which had originated with her, not with Phaedra. Until line 885, when Phaedra makes the fateful declaration, "I myself will speak; wait!" we do not know for sure whether she intends to die in noble silence or adopt the Nurse's stratagem of incriminating Hippolytus (726ff.).[28] Theseus' mode of action pushes her to the fateful decision.

The speech that Theseus finally elicits from Phaedra is far from the directness that was promised in 885. She "turns away her face" and "with her robe held up before her covers up the tears that arise suddenly on her cheeks" (*lacrimas genis / subito coortas veste praetenta optegis*, 886f.). Speech is still surrounded by concealment (*optegis*; cf. 858, 860, 875). The gesture accompanies the sword as the visible embodiment, on the stage, of the concealment implicit in her speaking. It could also suggest a last hesitation, even a moment of tacit self-recrimination or self-condemnation, a guilty half-recognition of what she is doing before the irrevocable plunge into evil.[29] But Phaedra is not yet ready for open defiance of Theseus, and she proceeds with the lie.

Phaedra claims that the third party of this "family romance," who is necessarily excluded from the secrets between his mother

[27] See Orlando (1978) 34.
[28] Grimal (1965) ad loc. notes the ambiguity of *quod vivo* in 880: (a) I regret life because I didn't carry out my earlier resolve to die before confessing my love to Hippolytus; and (b) I regret being alive because I survive the stain on my chastity as a wife. On Phaedra's death-wish, see above, Introduction, sec. II, ad fin., with notes 27 and 28.
[29] In this sense, *quod vivo* in 880 contains an edge of bitterness, despair, and hopelessness in her guilt, the first of the two meanings suggested in the previous note.

and father, has penetrated to places he should not enter. By invoking the remote fathers of her house—Jupiter who dwells in the heavens and Sol who shines in the sky (888-90)—she summons patriarchal authority for her false accusation. The presence of the sword in her chambers, in the very robes of Phaedra, is not merely evidence of the offense but the symbolical reenactment of the offense. For all the talk of the openness of speech, the message continues to operate more powerfully, still, through what is hidden than what is revealed.

At the crucial moment the emphasis shifts from speech to vision: communication again comes to depend less on the exact significance of words than on the images which they evoke. This stage-prop now becomes the most powerful "speaker" of the scene. It also becomes the emblem of the power of words ("signs" interpreted through words) to create a scene of decisive emotional impact.

Phaedra lets the sword's "speech" shape its visual tableau (896f.):

hic dicet ensis quem tumultu territus
liquit stuprator civium accursum timens.

This sword will tell, this one which the ravisher, frightened by the noise, abandoned, fearing the approach of citizens.

Her words echo the Nurse's "description" of the alleged attack (728-30):

en praeceps abit
ensemque *trepida* liquit attonitus *fuga*
pignus tenemus sceleris.

Look, he goes off headlong and abandoned the sword, thunderstuck in trembling flight. We have the evidence of the crime.

And speaking to Theseus a few lines later, Phaedra echoes even more of the Nurse's words as she adds another explicitly visual component of the scene (902f.):

   hi *trepidum fuga*
videre famuli concitum celeri pede.

These servants *saw* him, trembling in flight, agitated with rapid foot.

Through these echoes she takes over for herself the Nurse's re-construction of the scene. The Nurse has put the words in Phae-dra's mouth; but Phaedra puts images before Theseus' eyes. Her visual detail of the servants seeing Hippolytus (*videre*) was not part of the Nurse's description of the scene in 725-30.

For Theseus the visual effect suddenly predominates over the verbal: he beholds or sees the crime or monstrosity (*quod faci-nus, heu me, cerno? quod monstrum intuor*, 898). His reaction to a metaphorical monster precedes his visual perception of the sword itself as a physical object: only in his next line does he mention its hilt, with the glitter of ivory (*refulget*, 900).

For all the vividness of its message (*dicet*, 896), the sword conceals crucial lacunas in time: "The sword will tell, the sword that he, frightened by the noise, / the ravisher, abandoned, fear-ing the approach of citizens" (896f.). The verbs move from fu-ture to past ("will tell," "abandoned"), from passive to active participles of fear ("frightened . . . fearing," *territus . . . timens*), from the metaphorical action of the "telling" to the all too literal action of the sword implied in *stuprator* ("ravisher"). This crim-inal act appears only negatively, not only in Phaedra's silence but also in her refusal and resistance: "My spirit did not yield to the sword and threats" (*ferro ac minis / non cessit animus*, 891f.). The rapid sequence of images and events lend to her words the credibility of circumstantial detail, but it is only her words that give "reality" to the sword's speech.

The specific manner of Theseus' recognition of Hippolytus in the sword deserves further attention (898-901):

   quod facinus, heu me, cerno? quod monstrum intuor?
   regale parvis asperum signis ebur

capulo refulget, generis Actaei decus.[30]
Sed ipse quonam evasit?

What crime, alas for me, do I discern? What monstrosity do
   I behold?
The royal ivory, rough with small figures,
Shines on the hilt, glory of the Athenian race.
But the man himself, where has he gone?

The "small figures" (*parva signa*, also "small signs") stand out in
the tactile quality of their "roughness."[31] The finely carved or
embossed surface of rich miniature carving or intaglio reinforces the visual play of light and shadow implied in *refulget* (a
stronger verb than *fulget*, which Seneca might have used).

   Seneca has added these tactile and visual elements to the
purely intellectual apprehension of the hilt's meaning in Aegeus' recognition of Theseus in Ovid's *Metamorphoses*. Here, as
a result of Medea's trickery, Aegeus hands Theseus a cup of poisoned wine but in the nick of time recognizes him by the sword
that he carries (7.419-23):

>   ea coniugis astu
> ipse parens Aegeus nato porrexit ut hosti.
> sumpserat ignara Theseus data pocula dextra,
> cum pater in capulo gladii cognovit eburno
> signa sui generis facinusque excussit ab ore.

Through the craft of his wife the father himself, Aegeus,
offered that (poison) to his son as if to an enemy. Theseus
had taken the proffered cup with ignorant right hand, when
the father recognized the marks of his family on the sword's
ivory hilt and dashed the crime [of poisoning by Medea]
from his hand.

---

[30] In 900 I follow the reading of E, with Grimal (1965) ad loc., *generis Actaei decus* rather than A's *gentis Actaeae decus*, preferred by Giardina. The variant does not substantially alter the meaning of the passage.

[31] Grimal (1965) cites Virgil, *Aen.* 9.263f., *aspera signis pocula*, in turn a possible reminiscence of Pindar, *Isth.* 6.40. One thinks too of the embossed cups of
Theocr., *Idyll* 1 and Virgil, *Ecl.* 3.

Seneca has elaborated Ovid's bare verb *cognovit* with the details of light and touch, and he adds the qualifying *parva*, "small," to Ovid's *signa*. He thereby stresses the dramatic concreteness and the tactile qualities of the object that effects the recognition, and he intensifies the almost tangible horror of receiving the fateful *signa*.[32] This intensification of the Ovidian recognition is also clear from the highly emotional statement of perception in Theseus' previous line, *quod facinus, heu me, cerno? quod monstrum intuor.*

In Ovid's scene recognition by the sword confirms a son in his rightful place in a father's house, establishes proper succession to the throne, and foils the machinations of an evil stepmother. This stepmother is in fact the archetypally evil *noverca* of our play, for in his first meeting with Phaedra's emissary Hippolytus twice calls Medea "spouse of Aegeus" (*coniunx Aegei*, 558, 563f.). In Seneca the (step)mother, instead of being the agent of wrongdoing, is, ostensibly at least, the victim of wrongdoing (891-93) and, in the eyes of the father, the victim of the worst possible wrongdoing that the son could commit. In Ovid the sword prevents the *facinus* ("crime") that the father is about to inflict on the son (7.423). In Seneca the sword itself embodies the crime of the son against the father: *quod facinus, heu me, cerno?* ("What crime, alas for me, do I discern," 898).

The small figures or signs on the hilt are presumably too small to make an impression in a stage performance or to be significant to anyone not sensitive to their meaning. But Theseus has no difficulty in "reading" their message. With its small signs, the sword speaks to the father of a name that should be a silence, a presence that should be an absence behind the gates of those interior chambers that he shares with Phaedra as the *arcana* or *secreta* between husband and wife.

---

[32] Recognition by the sword is also emphasized by Plutarch's account (*Theseus* 12, possibly drawing on Euripides' *Aegeus*) with which Ovid closely agrees; but Plutarch makes no mention of the hilt or any identifying marks (12.4). Similarly the scholion to *Iliad* 11.741, which may also be summarizing the *Aegeus*, refers only to the "sword and shoes" by which Aegeus knows his son.

All of the physical details surrounding the sword, including the public outcry to Athens (725f.) and the noisy arrival of citizens (896f.), are less important than the private attempt to exchange secrets and the miniature dimension of the small figures on the hilt. These, mere symbols, have a far greater impact than the citizens or servants who are present large as life on the stage. The real power of communication now belongs to the image-world of the unconscious, and it is this realm that is evoked by the "monsters" on the hilt (898).

These small signs, like the letters of a verbal text, tell a hidden story about sons and fathers, patrimony and succession, (step)mothers and sons. The decorative elaboration of the familial, political, and social order in the figures that should be the "glory of the Athenian race" (900) becomes the vehicle for the fears and fantasies of the unconscious surfacing through the "won't tell" of what Phaedra's message really has to say.

When Phaedra evokes this scene, no bearer of the sword is mentioned. She carefully omits any overt mention of a second person brandishing the sword or uttering the threats. The only verb with a personal subject is the vital *restiti:* "Tried, I resisted prayers" (*temptata precibus restiti*, 891). This is her most direct lie, and it is a statement about herself, not about Hippolytus. For the rest, she avoids personal statements and speaks only of her mind, her body; the stain of her modesty that her blood will wash away (*ferro ac minis / non cessit animus; vim tamen corpus tulit. / labem hanc pudoris eluet noster cruor*, 891-93). The personal agent crystallizes into the unnamed ravisher (*stuprator*) only after the "speech" of the sword (897f.).[33]

The sword's revealing of its truth contains a number of curious inconsistencies. The sword is one of three proofs of the veracity of Phaedra's tale. The first is the Nurse's cry, "Come hither, Athens; bring help, you trusty band of slaves" (725); the second is the sword itself; and the third is Phaedra's dishevelled hair (730-32). As to the last, the Nurse had providently advised, "Let her pulled hair and torn coiffure remain as they are,

---

[33] On the suppression of the name of Hippolytus, see Friedrich (1953) 133.

the marks of so great a crime" (*crinis tractus et lacerae comae / ut sunt remaneant, facinoris tanti notae*, 731f.). The lines refer to the brutal gesture of Hippolytus who twisted her hair (*crine contorto*) as he bent back her head to cut her throat in a blood-sacrifice to his virginal goddess (706f.). This was the moment when the sword made its appearance: *stringatur ensis*, "Let the sword be unsheathed," he cried (706). Thus the Nurse's detail of the hair takes us back to the sword and reminds us of Hippolytus' true crime (what the sword replaces) beneath the crime that the Nurse is fabricating.

Some hundred lines later the chorus makes a point of the dishevelled hair, along with the tears, as proof of the accusation that is being prepared against "the guiltless youth" (825). "Behold the crimes!" they exclaim; "with her torn hair she seeks (to win) credence; she disturbs all the glory of her head; she wets her cheeks; guile is drawn up with every artful deceit of woman" (826-28). When Theseus finally sees Phaedra, he notices her tears (886), but says nothing of the hair, even though its disorder has been twice strongly emphasized and the cause of the disorder has been vividly enacted on the stage (706f.).

The omission is not just masculine (or marital) inattention to female dress, nor the result of Seneca's carelessness.[34] It is, rather, part of the shift of emphasis characteristic of Senecan drama from circumstantial detail and legalistic reasoning (of the sort beloved by Euripides) to the symbolic and psychological dimensions of action and language. For all the emphasis on the ocular evidence rendered by the sword, the act of which it speaks remains hidden.[35] The metaphorical monster glimpsed through the play of signifiers on the hilt, however, is answered by the overpowering vision of the monster from the sea (1016, 1034, 1046).

VIII

The description of this monster in the Messenger's narrative is the play's third occasion of speech after ominous silence. The

[34] So essentially Barrett (1964), p. 39 with note 1.
[35] For the visual evidence of the sword, see 725ff., 826-28, 896f., 901f.

Messenger enters lamenting his harsh and bitter fate in bearing
such grim news (991f.). Theseus encourages him (993f.), but
the Messenger still cannot speak: "My tongue refuses voice to
the grievous pain" (995; cf. Phaedra in 593, 602, 637). Theseus
must again urge him on.[36] In a single line the Messenger blurts
out the essential fact: "Hippolytus—alas for me—lies in tearful
death" (*Hippolytus, heu me, flebili leto occubat*, 997). Even this
statement emerges only in broken discourse: the pathetic inter-
jection of *heu me* comes abruptly between subject and predicate.
Theseus, less moved than the Messenger, must again encourage
speech: *mortis effare ordinem* ("Tell the order of his death,"
999). This last request, Theseus' third (cf. *fortiter fari*, 993; *pro-
loquere*, 996), finally launches the Messenger on his long narrative.

This delay in speaking is parallel to the slow and gradual
process by which the creature actually rises from the ocean.[37]
The shift into the nightmare world called forth by the father's
terrible curse breaks into language only after overcoming resistance, only under the sign of a "won't tell." Once this barrier is
pushed aside, speech rushes forth in full spate, and the Messenger multiplies the gruesome details.

In a dramatic performance a long narrative speech has a special force because the on-going stage action, the truly dramatic
representation, halts and becomes static.[38] The major protagonist becomes a listener, but a listener whose involvement (inter-
ference) in the story is itself of the greatest significance for the
meaning of the narrative.

When the Messenger's tale is over, Theseus voices his reactions: he feels a mixture of satisfaction and grief, and he acknowledges the continuing strength of the tie of blood despite
his sense of justice (1114-22). Thus the silence of Theseus dur-

[36] Contrast Eur., *Hipp.* 1162, where the news of Hippolytus' disaster is given
at once, with no such hesitation. See Liebermann (1974) 15f., 26, and Zintzen
(1960) 70.
[37] Cf. 1007ff., 1025ff., 1031ff., 1036ff., 1046ff. For analysis of the scene and
its step-like presentation of the events, see Segal (1984) 321ff.
[38] On this effect of narrative in drama, see Segal (1982) 334.

ing the narrative is a speaking silence, heavy with meaning. We the audience listen with a double hearing: we hear the words of the Messenger, the telling of a story in involving, circumstantial detail. But we also "hear" the meaningful silence of Theseus.

The death of Hippolytus itself explodes from a tension between speech and silence. When Theseus uttered his curse, he complained that the waves "are still silent" (*cur adhuc undae silent?* 954). Within the Messenger's account, Hippolytus, as he departed, was unable to address his father in person (cf. 1005). Just as he had nothing to say about Theseus when Phaedra overtly declared her passion, so here his discourse is all with himself (*multa secum effatus*, 1004). He can curse his fatherland, but he cannot speak to his father (1004-6):

> tum multa secum effatus et patrium solum
> abominatus, saepe genitorem ciet
> acerque habenis lora permissis quatit.

> Then speaking much with himself and cursing the soil of his fatherland, he calls upon his father often; and bitterly, letting loose the reins, he shakes the straps.

Unlike the Euripidean Hippolytus, this figure's sole communication with his father is conveyed in three words, *saepe genitorem ciet* ("he calls often on his father" or "he often excites—stirs up—his father"). The ambiguity of this little phrase between asking for help and arousing anger is a microcosm of the ambiguity that surrounds the father-figure in the play.[39]

[39] The basic meaning of *saepe genitorem ciet* in 1005 is "He calls on his father for aid" (i.e., ignorant of the fact that it is his father who has caused his danger by the curse): see Grimal (1965) ad loc. The word *cieo* can also mean "stirs up" in anger. Lawall and Kunkel (1982) on 1005 comment, "Hippolytus would in fact have been calling upon Theseus for very different reasons from those which Theseus, believing Hippolytus to have raped Phaedra, would imagine." There is thus a triple ambiguity: (1) cursing Athens out of a sense of injustice and calling on Theseus for help (Hippolytus' supposed meaning); (2) cursing Athens and calling on Theseus in criminal anger and wicked hatred (what Theseus might take Hippolytus' outcry to mean); (3) "stirring up" Theseus to the paternal wrath that produces the monster from the sea (1007). The close juxtaposition of cursing the fatherland and stirring up Theseus (*patrium . . . abominatus . . . genitorem ciet*) might also suggest the son's latent anger at the father.

By eliminating Euripides' direct verbal exchange between Theseus and Hippolytus, Seneca establishes a close causal relation between Phaedra's sexual approach and Hippolytus' flight. This condensation of the action is in keeping with Seneca's refocusing of the Euripidean action from social and political institutions to individual psychology. His Hippolytus flees not as a direct result of his father's decree of exile, as in Euripides, but out of horror at Phaedra's advances.[40] His flight appears only secondarily as political exile from the *urbs* (1000, 1004). Primarily it is an emotional flight from women, and it harks back to his misogynistic flight in his statement of universal detestation earlier (*fugio*, "I flee them all," 566). First the impact of Phaedra's desire and later her and the Nurse's lies transform this flight from female sexuality into flight from the scene of rape (cf. *trepida attonitus fuga*, "thunderstruck with trembling flight," 729; *trepidum fuga*, "trembling in flight," 901).

Even the political overtones of exile from the city in 1000-1006 pass quickly into the nightmarish images of the monster's attack: "when all at once the vast sea thundered from the deep and grew forth to the stars" (1007f.). In the rhetorical exaggerations of Senecan description, the terrifying father-imago arises from the sea as a series of bizarre, distorted, phallic shapes. The sea itself, "turgid with its monster, rushes into the earth" (*tumidumque monstro pelagus in terras ruit*, 1016). The language of phallic erection recurs throughout the Messenger's account.[41]

After the thunderous roar of the sea (1007f.), the whole ocean bellows (*totum en mare immugit*, 1025f.); all the rocks by the shore roar, and great masses of water are thrown about as if a great whale were surfacing (1026-32). The creature tossed up

[40] Eur., *Hipp*. 1084-89; cf. also 893-98, 973-75, 1065-69. Seneca's Theseus also exiles his son (929ff.), and his word, *profugus* (929), is taken up by the Messenger in the first line of his story of Hippolytus' fate (*ut profugus urbem liquit infesto gradu*, 1000); but Seneca's handling of the events blurs the causal connection between paternal decree and son's flight that is so strong in Euripides. See Grimal (1965) ad 1000.

[41] Cf. 1016, 1020f., 1025, 1028, 1037f., 1042, 1046f.; on the last passage Gallardo (1973), 78, observes that this is the only time that *pone* occurs in Seneca's tragedies.

from the swelling waves is actually called a bull only once (1036; cf. 1067). Seneca's creature, unlike the clearly defined taurine beast of Euripides, can be envisioned only through a play of figures. It is likened to a whale (*physeter*, 1030) or a monster from the furthest ocean that swallows up or smashes ships (*talis extremo mari / pistrix citatas sorbet aut frangit rates*, 1049f.) Elsewhere it is "a fearful horned (beast) of the sea" (*corniger ponti horridus*, 1081) or just "that mass" *illa moles*, 1059). All these descriptions imply creatures that lie beyond the range of normal experience and that would be seen, if at all, only rarely and fleetingly. The metamorphic fluidity that surrounds its emergence from the sea gives even its formidable solidity (*moles*) an uncanny, nightmarish unreality (1031-49).[42]

These nightmare images may be described in Freudian terms as the result of the "inversion of the libido": "The part of the libido which is unconscious and turned away from reality . . . is by so much increased. The libido . . . has found its way back into regression and has reanimated the infantile imagos."[43] The thick rhetorical description solidifies the repressed terrors of Hippolytus as his psychic, and soon physical, coherence breaks up before us. Unable to communicate with the human reality of his father, Hippolytus encounters him only through the monstrous shapes that Phaedra's language in the play causes to surface from the subterranean places of earth or sea. The infantile imago surfaces as a gigantic phallus, an apparition of the father's anger in the form of a dreadful castrating weapon that completely overwhelms and destroys the helpless child.[44]

This fearful creature belongs to the repressed, unconscious

---

[42] For Seneca's elaboration of Euripides' description of the bull, see Giomini (1955) 92-97 (Seneca wishes to "increase the sense of the mysteries and the undefinable, to render more tense the expectation of the spectator, . . . and to sharpen the accent of the tragic and the terrible"); also Liebermann (1974) 39f.; Garton (1972) 200, who stresses the addition of the colors in Seneca. The echo in 1046-48 of the monstrous serpent of Virgil, *Aen.* 2.208 adds to the mood of remoteness, mystery, and malevolence in the divine (and paternal) agency.

[43] S. Freud, "The Dynamics of Transference," *Collected Papers*, ed. and trans. J. Riviere and J. Strachey (New York 1959) 3.315.

[44] See Lewis (1974) 108, apropos of *Aeneid* 2.

part of Hippolytus himself. It follows him as his close companion (*sequitur adsiduus comes*, 1077), a bestial double that he cannot openly acknowledge. It is the obverse of the luminous Hippolytus who, pathetically, closes the scene: "he who was just
now the brilliant *companion* of his father's rule and shone like
the stars, his certain heir" (*qui modo paterni clarus imperii* comes
/ *et certus heres siderum fulsit modo*, 1111f.). That other "companion," some thirty lines before (*adsiduus comes*, 1077), is not a celestial image of succession to paternal property in a rational
world-order (*certus heres*), but a terrible, all-destructive shape
that dogs his every step.

The roar of the sea is among the worst of the monster's terrors (1007; cf. 1026). Hippolytus' voice cannot check the
horses (1055f.). His little speech of confidence and defiance,
given in direct discourse, contains the only actual words of his
that we are allowed to hear. They are his last quoted words in
the play (1066f.), and they are pathetic in their inaccuracy and
misjudgment of the situation. He "thunders something great"
(*magnum intonat*, 1065), but his human voice is no match for
the monstrous "thunder" of his vast opponent.[45]

Over against all this elemental noise, the silence between father and son is, one might say, deafening. The "speaking" of the
sword takes the place of what they might have said to one another and what they in fact do say to one another in Euripides'
Hippolytus (992-1089).

The sword "names" Hippolytus less as a person than as a
body, as the signifier of the desires that Phaedra has brought out
into the open, unrepressed. In standing for both the name and
the specific function of Hippolytus in the narrative "slot" that
he is being made to fill, the sword replaces the son with the signifier of the phallus of the son. It functions in a terrifying metonymy, as the evocation of the son's presence in the places
most forbidden by the father. Its very physicality is the critical
point, both as a device of the theater—an object tangible and

---

[45] Cf. 1007, 1009-14, 1025-34; also 1050.

visible on the stage—and as a symbolic substitute for a corporeal contact that must be repressed into the unsayable. For this
reason too there is no open discourse possible between Theseus
and Hippolytus, only the chain of signifiers of desires and of
anxieties about those desires.

NINE

Father, Underworld, and Retribution: Phaedra and Theseus

I

Frequently in ancient literature the father's descent to the Underworld is the occasion for the release of repressed desires.[1] A fit of homicidal madness follows upon Hercules' return from Hades in Seneca's *Hercules Furens* and in its Euripidean original. Complementary to this motif is the chaos that results when the father-figure is absent. The absence of Father Zeus during the sleep that follows his seduction by Hera in *Iliad* 14 contributes to the disorder that culminates in the death of Patroclus and so, indirectly, causes the death of the chief hero, Achilles. In the *Aeneid*, although Jupiter is not actually absent, the invocation of his authority puts an end to the rampage of the underworld Fury, Allecto: "It would no longer be the wish of the Father, ruler of highest Olympus," Juno tells Allecto, "that you should wander with greater licence above the aether's winds" (*Aen.* 7.557f.). On a somewhat different plane, the hero's liberation from the death-like captivity on Calypso's island in the *Odyssey*, like Aeneas' rescue from the storm at the opening of the *Aeneid*, takes place under the sign of the Father.[2] Athena, taking advantage of the absence of the wrathful father-figure, Poseidon, enlists the support of Father Zeus (*Od.* 1.19ff. and 45ff.).[3]

---

[1] See Henry-Walker (1965) and Shelton (1978) passim; cf. Eur., *H. F.* 965ff.

[2] Virgil's Neptune, unlike Homer's Poseidon, is here a kindly *genitor* (*Aen.* 1.155) and a restorer of order after the disruptions brought by Juno's wrath. Father Jupiter's placating speech to Venus follows soon after (*Aen.* 1.223ff.)

[3] Recently Jenny Strauss Clay, *The Wrath of Athena* (Princeton 1983), though stressing the importance of Athena's wrath against Odysseus in delaying his return (see especially pp. 41-53), also points out the importance of the anger of divine father-figures like Zeus, Poseidon, and Helios (p. 47). Not to minimize the role of Athena (of all female goddesses, incidentally, the one most closely identified with the rule of the father), it is worth pointing out that union or reconciliation with the father, in a situation that stresses the "son's" superi-

In the *Phaedra* the regressive play of father-figures undoes the work of creating the father as the longed-for yet dreaded representative of order and lawfulness. To what extent such a world can rehabilitate the figure of the father as a valid correlative for the order of law is one of the questions that we shall have to address later.[4]

Seneca's play combines the absence of the father with his underworld descent. It also overdetermines the release of sexual inhibition that takes place in the father's absence. Theseus' journey not only permits Phaedra's expression of her passion, but its purpose is a sexual exploit of his own. This sexual motivation is a departure from Euripides' extant *Hippolytus*, where the father's absence is due to the pollution that results from shedding kindred blood (*Hipp.* 34f.)—an ominous indication of his capacity for murderous violence against members of his own house.[5]

In her first speech Phaedra accuses Theseus in the Underworld of just those acts of licence that will later be thrown back at her: *furor* (96), lack of *pudor* (97), crimes of lust and illicit sexual union (*stupra et illicitos toros*, 97). She thus projects her own forbidden desires upon the absent master of the house.[6] Later

---

ority, is a climactic point in both epics: Achilles' ransom of Hector's body to Priam in *Iliad* 24 and Odysseus' recognition by Laertes, the last of his family recognitions, in *Odyssey* 24. One may add the multiple restorations of paternal authority at the end of the *Odyssey*: Laertes' joy in the three male generations fighting together against the enemies of the house (24.514f.) and Zeus' intervention with the thunderbolt for a closure in favor of the patriarchal order (24.539-44).

[4] See secs. IV and V below.

[5] On the *miasma* of Theseus in *Hipp.* 34f. and its connection with the larger theme of purity centered on Hippolytus, see Segal (1970) 296f. Seneca may be following an alternative version of the myth that attributes Theseus' absence to a descent to the Underworld, possibly used by Sophocles in his lost *Phaedra*. Yet it remains significant that Seneca chose the erotic motivation for the descent over the juridical one in Euripides' *Hippolytus Crowned*. The sexual motivation of Theseus' absence occurs also in Ovid, *Her.* 4.59 and 109-12, and is not certainly attested before Ovid: see Giomini (1955) 33; Paratore (1952), p. 203 with note 10, and p. 229; Lefèvre (1972) 354-56; Jacobson (1974), p. 155 with note 32.

[6] See Giomini (1955) 33; Vretska (1968) 163; Heldmann (1974), p. 93 with note 251.

she explicitly connects the vehemence of this criminal love to the certainty of Theseus' imprisonment in Hades (218-21). When she is on the verge of declaring her love to Hippolytus, Theseus' alleged sexual crimes in Hades give her the boldness that she needs to continue (625-28):

> regni tenacis dominus et tacitae Stygis
> nullam relictos fecit ad superos viam:
> thalami remittet ille raptorem sui?
> nisi forte amori placidus et Pluton sedet.

> The lord of the grasping realm and of silent Styx has made no path toward those left behind in the upper world. Will he then let go the ravisher of his own bedchamber? No, not unless Pluto too sits there complaisant to (such) love.

At the end of that disastrous interview the Nurse will transfer to Hippolytus Phaedra's words about Theseus (*thalami raptor*, 627; *nefandi raptor Hippolytus stupri*, "Hippolytus, ravisher of a criminal lust," 726). She thus prepares the way for the release of the "underworld" elements in Theseus too whereby he will project upon his son his own sexual transgressions in the realm below.

In the absence or debility of the father (cf. 840ff.), Phaedra can release the repressed female desire of her past. For her the return of the repressed takes the form of a regression to the monstrous lust of her mother, Pasiphae, with whom she identifies in her first speech ("Mother, I pity you," 115; cf. 142ff., 169ff., 688ff.). For Hippolytus the return of the repressed takes the form, rather, of the Evil Mother, licentious and sexually aggressive; and for Theseus it takes the form, as we have seen, of the wrathful father who tears the son apart for his Oedipal offense.

It is an aspect of Hippolytus' submission to the authority of the father that he never questions the certainty of Theseus' return. When the Nurse approaches him with downcast looks, he asks about his father with a confidence that nothing in the present circumstances has justified: *sospes est certe parens* . . . ("My father is surely safe and sound," 433). At Phaedra's appeal that he pity a widow, he averts the omen with the "highest god," the strongest Name of the Father(*summus hoc omen deus / avertat*, 623f.). He continues in the same verse with an echo of the previous certainty of his father's arrival forthwith (*aderit sospes actutum parens*, 624; cf. 433). When Phaedra counters this confidence by repeating her point about the tenacity of the gods below (625-29; cf. 219-21), she is reasserting that submersion of the father-figure in the Underworld, and recalling that "greatest Kingdom of Love," of which she is in fact a humbled subject (218). Promising in reply "to fill a parent's place" or "his parent's place" (633), Hippolytus may be saying more than he consciously knows; but he remains unshaken in his conscious belief that "the just gods above will lead (Theseus) back" (629). Yet, as we have noted, when Phaedra's proposition is out in the open, Hippolytus has not a word to say about Theseus, although he twice invokes powerful and remote symbolic fathers (671ff., 717f.).

II

Phaedra's wish to suppress the father and replace him with the son cannot change the inexorable reality of his return. When he surfaces from the depths where Phaedra, in her *furor*, had kept him, he has the triple aspect of Neptune's deep sea (1159), the monstrous bull with its phallic destructiveness (1015ff., 1035ff.), and Theseus himself. The father she now invokes (1164) is the father-imago, whom she calls simply "father" (*genitor, pater, parens*; cf. 1191, 1194, 1199). She reveals a figure of underworld darkness and violence (1164ff., 1199f.), a monstrous double of the patriarchal ruler.

Her last direct address to Hippolytus in the vocative, now for the fourth time in the play (1168), no longer confuses father and son in a desperate criminal love.[7] She clearly discerns the

---

[7] Cf. 611, 646, 666, 710; also 171f.

father's harshness (1164) and its destructive effects in the family
(*natus et genitor nece / reditus tuos luere*, "Son and father paid for
your returns with death," 1165f.).[8] Yet she does not make him
the sole instrument of Hippolytus' death, but acknowledges her
own role in the horrible mutilation before her. Instead of fan-
cying Hippolytus' face as a reflection of the boyish Theseus
(646ff.), she awakens to the brutal reality of what she has done
(1168f.): "Hippolytus, are such the features of your face I see,
and did I make them so?" (*talesque feci*).

With the return of the father Phaedra makes the sword a signifier not of desire but of the Law. She grasps it as her present
means of communicating truth, not falsehood, between herself
and Hippolytus; and she speaks of crime and punishment, not
love and desire (1175-78):

> ades parumper verbaque exaudi mea,
> nil turpe loquimur: hac manu poenas tibi
> solvam et nefando pectori ferrum inseram,
> animaque Phaedram pariter ac scelere exuam.

> Be present a little while and hear my words.
> I speak nothing base: with this hand I shall pay to you
> my penalty and plunge the sword into an evil breast,
> and so with equal stroke remove Phaedra from life and from
> crime.

"I speak nothing base" (*nil turpe loquimur*): the sword in a sense
still does the significant "speaking" among the three major characters; but now the syntax carefully distinguishes between the
figurative and the literal speaker. Instead of lies about Hippolytus, she addresses to him the words that are truly her own: *ver-
baque exaudi mea*, "Hear my words."[9] Instead of guilty silence
and the deceptive "speaking" of the sword, she recalls those

---

[8] With the collocation of "son" and "father" (Theseus and Aegeus) in 1165
contrast the close juxtaposition of "Theseus" and "Hippolytus" in the *furor* of
646; cf. also 1164 and 1168. Note also the alliterative play on *pater . . . punisti*
in 1194.
[9] Note the force of the preposition in *ex-audi* in 1175.

other authentic words, passionately spoken in the fateful avowal of love: *tacitae mentis exaudi preces*— / *libet loqui pigetque* ("Hear the prayers of a silent mind—to speak is my joy and my sorrow," 636f.). Echoing 636 in her last speech (*verba exaudi mea* 1175), she has moved beyond the ambiguities of a speech that shame kept concealed in silence.

"Speak," Theseus had urged her; "I shall hide your secrets in a trusty breast" (*fido pectore arcana occulam*, 875). Unveiling the truth, she will now "drive the sword into (her) evil breast" (*nefando pectori*, 1177). The nobility of her act qualifies the evil (*nefandus*, 1177) in herself that she thus punishes.[10]

In her first interview with Theseus, Phaedra allowed the sword to give an ambiguous reply to his question, "What crime is to be atoned for by (your) death?" (*quod sit luendum morte delictum indica*, 878). Theseus had made the son atone (*luere*, 1166). Now Phaedra, claiming the crime and the death, brings both together in the sword. She makes requital not to Theseus, but to her own victim, Hippolytus, to whom she "pays the penalty with this hand" (*hac manu poenas tibi solvam*, 1176f.). Theseus, calling curses down on his son, had threatened terrible "penalties" for his crimes: *sceleribus poenas dabit*, (937). The erotic connotations of the earlier scene with the sword (710-12) change to the legal and moral overtones of *poenas solvere* and *scelus* (1176-78; also *nefandus*, 1177). Phaedra now moves back to the regal and masculine sphere, to Theseus' language of crime and punishment, but she speaks of retribution and moral responsibility with less anger and more truth than he had.

Phaedra's emphatic "with this hand," *hac manu* (1176), keeps distinct the categories of word and action, figurative and literal, that she had blurred before. She reverses the "base speech" (cf. 1176) that had transformed the sword from repulsion of desire in Hippolytus' "hands" to the pursuit of desire in hers (cf. *hac manu*, 1176 and *manibus tuis*, 712).

---

[10] On the importance of the term *nefas* in Senecan tragedy generally, including *Phaedra*, see Opelt in Lefèvre (1972) 94ff.

Her next lines express another reversal of erotic fantasies
(1179f.):

et te per undas perque Tartareos lacus,
per Styga, per amnes igneos amens sequar.

And I shall follow you madly through the waves and lakes of
   Tartarus,
Through the Styx, through the streams of fire.

The lines echo four earlier passages in which Phaedra, in the full
fury of her passion, would pursue Hippolytus over mountains
and groves and through streams, snow, and fire.[11] This final
pursuit, however, is no longer through the virginal forest world
of her earlier desires (cf. 235, "I am resolved to follow him
through the tall groves and through the mountains") but to a
place of violence and death.[12] The paronomasia of 1180, *amnes*
. . . *amens*, deepens the mood of suicidal despair by associating
the madness with the streams of subterranean fire. The rivers of
this landscape are not those of his mountain haunts but the rivers of the Underworld (1179f.). Analogously, giving her breast
to the sword (616) is no longer just a verbal action (1176).

In her tragic fusion of love and death Phaedra is now ready
to retrace Theseus' descent to the infernal lakes. In her first
speech she had imagined his passage "through the deep darkness of the pathless lake" to abduct Persephone (93f.). Like
Theseus, she makes a journey for erotic motives to the Underworld, but her madness (*amens*, 1180) is now of despair rather

---

[11] "It is my resolve to follow him as he clings to the snowy hills and treads the
harsh road with nimble foot, to follow him through the deep groves and
through the mountains" (233-35). "Even if he flees through the seas themselves, I shall pursue" (242). "Not even if you order me to go through the deep
snows would I hesitate to walk on the Pindus' frozen ridges; or if through fire
and hostile ranks, I would not hesitate to offer my breast to the readied swords"
(613-16). "Even through fire would I follow you, through the raging sea, and
over rocks and streams that the rushing water carries along; wherever you take
your way, there in my madness I shall be driven" (700-702).

[12] On the motif of Phaedra's pursuit, see above, chap. 2, sec. V, ad fin.

than desire; and she can expect no Herculean rescue back to the
light of day.

Echoing Phaedra's words about the fiery waters of Hades
(1179f.), Theseus too would descend to Hades' stream of fire in
remorse and self-punishment (1226-28):

graviora vidi, quae pati clausos iubet
Phlegethon nocentes *igneo cingens vado*;
quae poena memet maneat et sedes, scio.

I have seen the heavier (torments) that Phlegethon orders
the guilty, enclosed by its stream of fire, to undergo. What
punishment and what place awaits me I know.

These lines bring the theme of erotic descent full circle (cf. 93f.)
and complete the transformation of the motives for the underworld journey from lust to remorse. In both 1179f. and 1226-
28 the release of sexual desire symbolized by descent to Hades'
fires and darkness takes on a deeper psychological meaning: the
threatening features of the underworld landscape symbolize
also the inner torments of guilt. The punishment is inherent in
the crime itself; and both judge and torturer are within.[13]

The imagery of fire also shifts from passion to guilt. The final
blaze is the "single torch" that consumes Phaedra and Hippolytus in the funerary fires, the end of her tragic union of love and
death (1213-16).[14] At the same time the motif of the descent
transfers to her the heroic spirit of the mythical catabasis. Her
journey to the Underworld has a nobler aim and a truer heroism
than that of the man whom she first addressed as *magnanimus*
("great-spirited," "noble," 869).

The end belongs to Phaedra, and it belongs also to the darkness of the Underworld. In her very last words of the play (if

---

[13] Seneca's imagery implies what is an explicit tenet of the ancient philosophical tradition, e.g., Lucretius 3.978-1023 ("Everything that is reported to be in
deep Acheron is in life for us," 978f.).
[14] On the motif of the torch, see above, chap. 2, note 38.

1199f. are in fact spoken by her), she again consigns Theseus to
Hades: (1199f.):

quid facere rapto debeas nato parens,
disce a noverca: condere Acherontis plagis.

What you should do, a parent whose son is carried off,
learn from the stepmother: hide yourself in Acheron's
fields.[15]

What she had made the condition of her love in her fantasy of
the father's perpetual absence (218-25) is now solely a place of
death. The phrase *rapto nato*, "with your child carried off," in
1199 recalls Theseus' share in the blame for Hippolytus' death.
It also exchanges the absence of the father at the beginning for
the absence of the son here. By sending Theseus back to the
chthonic darkness from which he entered the play ("night's
eternal field," 835), she deepens the ominous chthonic atmosphere around the father's return.

III

Theseus enters with evident relief at his "escape at last from
the realm of night eternal and the pole which casts the shadows
of its vast prison over the dead" (*tandem profugi noctis aeternae*

---

[15] The mss. are divided in the attribution of 1199f., A giving them to Phaedra, E to Theseus. Of recent editors Grimal, Giardina, and Lawall follow E,
Miller and Herrmann follow A. The lines seem to me more effective if spoken
by Phaedra, with Theseus' entrance marked by the change of meter in 1201. As
Fortey and Glucker (1975), 714, point out, it is "practically impossible to imagine" that Theseus would address himself in the second person here and then
change to the first-person address in the next lines (in fact, there would be a
change to the third-person reference to himself in 1203, *impium rapite*, and then
to the first in 1206, *meque ovantem scelere*). If spoken by Theseus, the lines
would suggest a possible tone of admiration toward Phaedra that is out of keeping with his harshness toward her in 1279f. If spoken by Phaedra, the lines are
totally consistent with her bitterness toward Theseus. Fortey and Glucker consider Phaedra's speaking the lines "anticlimactic" (714) and assign them to the
chorus. We need, however, to keep in mind the play's concentration on her
emotional situation in its movement toward the close. In either case Theseus is
to be "hidden" in Hades.

plagam / vastoque manes carcere umbrantem polum, 835f.). He acknowledges the "weary state" of his "manly strength" of old (*sed fessa virtus robore antiquo caret*, 846) and finds his steps still "trembling" or "tottering" after the hard climb (*trepidantque gressus*, 847). The exclamation *heu*, the polysyllables, and the multiple elisions of his next lines convey the painful effort of the ascent (847f.):

> heu, labor quantus fuit
> Phlegethonte ab imo petere longinquum aethera.

Alas, how great was the toil to seek the distant sky from deepest Phlegethon.[16]

Down below, he was utterly helpless: not his own strength but that of Hercules freed him from his underworld imprisonment (843f., 848f.).

Theseus' return follows directly upon the allusions to Hippolytus' youthful vulnerability in the choral song of 726-823. The scene juxtaposes innocence and experience, celestial light and subterranean shadow, the fresh hopefulness of youth and the weariness of maturity, worn by trials and suffering. Whereas Hippolytus fled the scene of sexual temptation more swiftly than the wind or a comet (736-40), Theseus' *virtus* is "tired" and "lacks its old vigor" (846) as he complains of the toilsome upward journey (847f.). Whereas Hippolytus has fled toward the sylvan realm that is his refuge from emotional reality (cf. 718), Theseus brings us back to Phaedra's sex-tormented house. The chorus's allusion to Peirithous in 831, just before his entrance, also keeps before us the sexual motivation behind his journey (cf. 91-98, 244, 625-28).

When Theseus begins his last long speech with an address to the jaws of pale Avernus, Taenarus' caverns, and Lethe's sluggish lakes (1201f.), he is reversing the direction of his first stage

---

[16] Note too the contrast between the resolutions of *Phlegethonte* and *petere* and the spondaic feet on either side.

utterance (835f.), where he gloried in escape from those infernal regions. Now he prays to be hidden and submerged, pressed down in Hades (*impium abdite atque mersum premite perpetuum malis*, "hide me, the evil-doer, and press me down, submerged in woes eternal," 1203). Deprived of both son and wife, made both widower and childless (*caelebs et orbus*, 1215), Theseus finds his return from the realm of death cancelled out by more killing (1213-16). As in the story of Hippolytus/Phaethon, a joyful movement toward the sky (*patuit ad caelum via*, 1213) becomes a saddened mortal fall to earth, back to Hades.

In accusing Hippolytus to Theseus, Phaedra appealed to the celestial Names of the Father, Jupiter and Sol (888-90). But when she accepts responsibility for her passion, she invokes the Father in his monstrous affinities: the "savage ruler of the deep sea," the instrument of Theseus' vengeance (1159-63). Open sky and celestial light in her false testimony of 888-90 give way to subterranean depths (*profundi freti*, 1159), concealment, and enclosure (cf. *intimo sinu*, 1161, *tegit*, 1163). She never again addresses the gods of the upper world. Theseus' anger figuratively brings darkness to the sky (cf. 946f., 955-58). The underground imagery now overwhelms Phaedra's celestial attributes of patriarchal authority.[17] The modification of the sky imagery in Euripides once more transforms theological concerns into psychological forces.

An authoritative father-figure begins to arise only when both sword and language speak their true contents (cf. 1176, "I speak nothing base"). Even so, the pity and remorse of the bereft father remain intertwined with the harshness of the unforgiving and uncomprehending husband.[18] Correspondingly, Phaedra's public address to Athens here (*audite, Athenae*, 1191) suggests the possible rehabilitation of the sphere of political ac-

---

[17] Compare 889-90 with 1159ff. and 1199f.; also 938-41, 1090-92, 1112, 1174f. On Euripides' celestial imagery, see Segal (1979) 152f., 156; cf. above, chap. 2, sec. VIII.

[18] For Theseus' remorse cf. his orders in 1247-50, 1254f., 1275-79. At the very end his command to search for Hippolytus' limbs and his curse on Phaedra come in the same verse, with an expressive enjambement of *inquirite* (1279).

tion that belongs to the father, but in the same breath she declares this father "worse than the murderous stepmother."[19]

When the sword reaches the destination that Phaedra's lie had claimed for it, Theseus, in the play's concluding speech, can acknowledge that part of himself that failed to ascend from the underworld darkness. He asks Hercules, his rescuer from Hades in 843-45 and 849, to take back his gift of light. In an oxymoron expressive of the psychological paradoxes operative here, he calls this light "dark" (*donator atrae lucis*, "giver of dark light," 1217). Like Phaedra too, he calls to the depths of the sea and asks that they now overwhelm him as they did Hippolytus (1204-6):

> nunc adeste, saeva ponti monstra, nunc vastum mare,
> ultimum quodcumque Proteus aequorum abscondit sinu,
> meque ovantem scelere tanto rapite in altos gurgites . . .

> Now be present here, you savage monsters of the ocean and you too, vast sea, and whatever remotest (creature) Proteus hides away in his bosom, and carry off to the deep swirling flood me who rejoiced at so great a crime.

He echoes the language of monstrosity called forth earlier by Phaedra's passion and, like her, asks the sea's depths to overwhelm him.[20] But he can now discern in himself the force that pulled the anger of the divine father into his own anger: "You, father, always too easily in agreement with my anger" (*tuque semper, genitor, irae facilis meae*, 1207). He can also acknowledge his own role as the cruel punitive father, *vindex severus*, "the harsh avenger" (1210). As he puts it a little later, "Lest I be guilty only once or alone, a father about to dare an outrageous

---

[19] Contrast the Nurse's cry to Athens in a speech of deception, 725, and see above, chap. 8, sec. III, with note 13.

[20] Cf. 1204-6 and Phaedra in 1159-63. Note too the echo of the motif of "pressing down" (*premite*) between Theseus's remorse here in 1203 (*mersum premite*, sc. *me*) and his threat to Hippolytus in 938, *profugum per omnes pertinax latebras premam* ("In your flight I shall press you down steadfastly in all your hiding places"). Cf. the "pressing" image also for Father Minos in 149, and above, chap. 2, sec. III, and chap. 8, sec. VI, ad fin., with note 26.

crime I called on a father" (*facinus ausurus parens / patrem advo-cavi*, 1251f.). In wishing to join the famous sinners in Hades, he at last recognizes the hell in his own soul (1226-37).

Theseus would make a second journey to the Underworld, not to carry off a prize of lust, but in purity, for chaste motives: "Do not fear, you who rule the shades; in purity we come" (*ne metue qui Manes regis*; / *casti venimus*, 1240f.). In Phaedra's nec-essary relegation of the father to the lower world, his goal there was "acts of lust and illicit beds" (*stupra et illicitos toros*), and he brooked neither fear nor shame as a check (96-98). Now The-seus too, like Phaedra, integrates the subterranean capacity for destruction into a fuller vision of the self: "I recognize my crime" (*crimen agnosco meum*, 1249; cf. 1260 and 113). He makes this descent not at another's bidding nor as the "compan-ion in love-madness" of Peirithous (*furoris socius*), as Phaedra had seen him (96; cf. 244), but on his own initiative, in sorrow and remorse, and alone. This is the father who, at the news of Hippolytus' death, felt the bond of blood as a powerful tie of nature (1114-16): "O Nature, too powerful, with how great a bond of blood do you hold parents." This is the father too who, despite his anger and sternness of revenge, wept at his own pun-ishment of his son (1118-21) and felt himself caught in the puz-zling paradox of grief "not because I killed him, but because I have lost him" (*quod interemi non, quod amisi fleo*, 1122). "In his guilt I wished to kill him; lost, I bewail him," he said just before (1117).[21]

Theseus' remorse, however, like Phaedra's comes too late. "Father," *pater* or *genitor*, in his closing lines stands next to the havoc unleashed by the wrathful father-figure. His expressions of guilt repeatedly stress the destructive turn of his paternal role:

---

[21] Cf. also the mixed feelings of the Euripidean Theseus, *Hipp.* 1257-60. The Euripidean Theseus is still full of bitter anger (he asks if his son was killed by someone else whose wife he tried to ravish, 1164f.); and the emphasis on the proof of Poseidon's paternity through the potency of the curses (1169f.) is not taken up by Seneca.

munere en patrio fruor. (1252)
Look, I enjoy a gift of my father.

dum membra nato genitor adnumerat suo (1264)
While the father counts up the limbs for his son . . .

sic ad parentem natus ex voto redit? (1272)
Does the son return thus to the parent in accordance with
his prayer?

en haec suprema dona genitoris cape,
saepe efferendus (1273f)
Here, receive the ultimate gifts of a father, you who
are often to be carried out to burial.

The sadness of this ultimate gift of the father to his dead son
contrasts with the destructive gift of the father (*munere patrio*,
1252) given by the divine parent, Neptune, to Theseus (cf.
1207).[22] As in Euripides' play, the bonds between the mortal
and the divine parent are attenuated as those between the mortal kin gain in importance.[23] The gift of the divine father proves,
finally, a cruel blessing (*numinum o saevus favor*, 1271).

Yet even this last gift of a mortal parent, the rites of burial, is
marked by an absence: the missing parts of the body, the result
of the mutilation caused by the monster. In lines typical of Seneca's attention to physical violence, Theseus cries, "I am doubt-
ful what part of you this is. A part of you surely it is. Here, here,
place it, not in its own but in an empty place" (1267f.).[24] The

---

[22] Note also the chorus's appeal to Theseus as father (*genitor*) to put the mangled limbs in order, 1256f.

[23] Cf. the embrace between father and son in Eur., *Hipp.* 1431ff.; see Knox
(1979) 228.

[24] For the emphasis on physical violence, see Regenbogen (1930) 208ff. To
H. E. Butler, *Post-Augustan Poetry* (Oxford 1909) 69f., the mutilation of the
body is the "climax" of absurdity in the "ghastly and exaggerated account of the
death of Hippolytus." The unsatisfactoriness of the rite as closure is sensed also
by Giomini (1955), 108, who views the grim details of the missing pieces of
flesh as a deflection of attention from the human suffering of Theseus to the unreality and exaggerated theatricality of the scene. For the problem of sources
(especially Seneca's use of Euripides' *Bacchae*), see Zintzen (1960) 122 and
Runchina (1966) 22-25.

body of the son, mutilated and castrated by the wrathful father thrown up from Theseus' own depths, remains an emptiness that cannot be filled. This empty place (*vacuus locus*, 1268) is the physical correlative of the empty place left in the house, a house left as broken and mutilated as Theseus' own life now (1253): "Childlessness, sad evil of my broken years" (*O triste fractis orbitas annis malum*, 1253).[25] All that he can embrace or cherish (*complectere, fove*) are these shattered limbs (*artus*, 1254f.).

Even the rite that might provide closure has the attendant emptiness of something that must be continually reenacted in the emotional life of the father henceforth: "O you who must be often carried forth to burial," Theseus says in the last words he addresses to Hippolytus (*saepe efferendus*, 1274).[26] "Meanwhile," he goes on, "let the fires carry off these remains" (*interim haec ignes ferant*). The word "meanwhile," *interim*, calls attention to the incompleteness of the rite: the obsequies, because of the dispersion of Hippolytus' remains, have a provisional status. Turning to his followers, Theseus then instructs them to find the missing pieces scattered over the fields (*et vos per agros corporis partes vagas / inquirite*, 1278f.).

The vision of tragedy, including Senecan tragedy, is unforgiving; and Theseus has failed both as a father and as a spouse. Phaedra's last act is to abandon forever the "bedchamber of a husband, made unholy by so great a crime" (*coniugis thalamos . . . tanto impiatos facinore*, 1185f.). She joins herself to Hippolytus in a death that has the overtones not only of a *Liebestod* but also of a marriage. The attribute of "holiness" that she would preserve for her marriage bed by returning there as if guiltless (cf. *vindicato sancta toro*, 1187) she now assigns to Hippolytus,

---

[25] In 1253, which is a "golden line" (*o triste fractis orbitas annis malum*), the placing of the abstract noun *orbitas* symmetrically between the more concrete words, especially after "sad" and "broken," conveys something of this feeling of Hippolytus as an absence.

[26] *Saepe efferendus* is generally taken in the sense "needing to be buried seriatim" ("à plusieurs reprises," says Grimal, 1965, ad loc.); it can, however, also carry the nuance I have given it, "having to be buried frequently," in the sense of Theseus' re-experiencing of the grief of loss in the future, an interpretation supported by 1250-53, especially 1253.

for she will pour forth her blood, drawn with his sword, to him as *sanctus* (1198): "This blood pays its debt to the shades of a man of holy purity" (*cruorque sancto solvit inferias viro*). Instead of the fantasied union of bodies (cf. *corpus* in 892), she finally seeks a tragic union of souls and of destinies (1183f.).

non licuit animos iungere, at certe licet
iunxisse fata.

It was not granted us to join our minds; but surely the joining of our fates is granted us.

In her lie about the violation of her body (*vim corpus tulit*, 892) she had attacked, in self-defense, Hippolytus' harsh ideal of his chaste body (*castum corpus*, 704). In accusing him, she had assumed the title of "chaste wife" (874): *aures pudica coniugis solas timet*, "A chaste woman fears only the ears of a husband." At the end she shifts the term for "chaste" from herself to Hippolytus. She thus moves from falsehood to truth, and also from fear (*timet* in 874) to courage. By freeing herself of this fear of Theseus as a repressive and terrifying figure, she can claim a kind of chastity for herself. 'Die," she says to herself, "if you are chaste, for your husband; if unchaste, for love" (*morere si casta es, viro*; / *si incesta, amori*, 1184f.).[27] Yet in her tragic world this chastity, like that of Hippolytus, is rendered ambiguous by the *Liebestod* which has "joined" the two victims in their doomed "destinies" (*iunxisse fata*, 1184).

Through her death and confession, Phaedra restores to Hippolytus the chaste body that Theseus had bitterly ridiculed. The Amazon women "prostitute the body, long chaste, in promiscuity" (*castum diu | vulgare populis corpus*), he had said scornfully of Hippolytus' mother in 910f. But Phaedra's effect on his life was to destroy that ideal and leave his vaunted chaste body a lifeless object, only a *corpus*, and barely even that (1086, 1110, 1158, 1265; cf. 704 and 910f.).

[27] Cf. the motif of renewed virginity in *Medea* 984, discussed in chap. 7, sec. VI.

In joining herself to Hippolytus in one sense, she creates an impassable barrier between them in another, as she defines him now as forever unreachable, chaste (*pudicus*, 1196), a man "holy" in his purity (*sancto . . . viro*, 1198). She thereby perpetuates the fantasy-element that surrounds this love, for there is little that we have seen in Hippolytus that justifies the appellation *sanctus*. But now guilt fuses with love and adds its overlay to the complex fusion of real and imagined. Instead of "enjoying (her) husband's bed" as one who is herself *sancta*, speciously "pure," in holy union (1187), she bestows that quality of *sanctitas* upon Hippolytus (1198). She thereby undoes her murderous lie and triumphs over the apparently invincible "sacred fire," the supernatural power of love (*sacer est ignis*, "it is a holy flame," 330).[28] But she is also continuing her bondage to the impossible fantasy that was an essential constituent of that love, the very unattainability that made it so fascinating and irresistible. Hippolytus may be *castus* and *pudicus* ("chaste" and "pure"), as she calls him in this scene; but he is not entirely *insons* ("innocent," "harmless," 1195f.), and it is certainly questionable if he is *sanctus* (1198). For all that she has lifted this love to a new level in her own spiritual and moral life, she is still subject to the false idealization of its object. The very qualities that she extols in Hippolytus—chastity, purity, holiness—are the ones that leave no place for her in his life or his scale of values. Those are the values that in fact make him incapable of compassion for or understanding of her condition.

Her final words about Hippolytus compound her tragedy by suggesting that she has surrendered, at the last, to his own image of himself as pure and innocent (cf. *pudicus, insons*, 1196). She persists in her fantasies about Hippolytus, if not about Theseus. It is a cruel irony too that she has now, in a way, a better claim to *pudor* than either the self-righteous, sexually repressed

[28] Compare also Phaedra's feeling of her impurity in the prologue, when she can no longer "brandish the torches that share the secrets of the silent rites" of the Eleusinian mysteries (*tacitis conscias sacris faces*, 107).

worshiper of a *diva virago* or the philandering, irascible adventurer who rules her house.

Theseus' near-closing command, "Throw open a house bitter with funereal death" (*patefacite acerbum caede funesta domum*, 1275), echoes the earlier opening up of the house that revealed Phaedra's love-sickness (384-86). Theseus had those gates thrown open at his return from Hades (863), but that expression of order and control is premature. When he commands entrance to the closed portals (*clausos postes*, 863) that lead into Phaedra's chambers, he lets the light of reality and the public world in upon the sheltered fantasies of her hidden thoughts. But he also reenters the dark places both of her suicidal passion (1188-90) and his own still unsubdued violence.[29]

Instead of reconstituting an alternative image of a well-ordered house under firm and lucid male domination, Theseus, like Hippolytus before him, is drawn into the house as it exists for Phaedra, a dark, enclosing prison of self-destructive female desire, a place beyond their comprehension or control. Phaedra, appropriately, gave the first description of the house in the play: she envisaged it as "hated Penates" of a foreign household in which she is a prisoner (89-91). At the end she rejects the "chambers of a husband" for the "appeased hollows" of Hades (*coniugis thalamos*, 1185; *placatos sinus*, 1190); and she thus recasts her and Theseus' house as a place of death.

Even when Theseus returns with imperious commands to take possession and bring light, he remains surrounded by the circular rhythms of Phaedra's interior darkness (cf. 93f., 384, 863, 1275). His son's mangled corpse reminds him of the torments of sinners in Hades, "enclosed" by Phlegethon's "fiery stream girding them in" (*clausos . . . igneo cingens vado*, 1226f.). At the end images of enclosure, weight, and heaviness predom-

---

[29] Theseus' language in the last scene also recalls descriptions of his (desired) enclosure by Phaedra earlier: cf. *abditus*, "hidden," in 147 and 1203; *mersus*, "submerged," "sunken," in 220 and 1203; cf. also *clauserit*, "lock in," 222, and the *claustra* of Phaedra's Cretan and Athenian abode, 1171 and 863.

inate;[30] and these return us to the atmosphere of enclosure in passion, violence, and irrationality of the first act. By the end of the play ominous meanings cluster around the joyful images of enclosure and shadow in Hippolytus' opening cry to his hunting-companions, "Gird about the shady forests" (*ite, umbrosas cingite silvas*, 1).[31]

The atmosphere of imprisonment around Phaedra too is darker and deeper than at the beginning: it is literal rather than figurative. Yet it results from an act of moral choice and courage. Earlier her love-madness "compelled her to follow the worse" (*furor cogit sequi peiora*, 178f.); now she herself, not her *furor*, deliberately chooses what is ethically better.

IV

Phaedra presents her love as a tragedy of destiny (*fata*) that she has struggled in vain to resist.[32] In her first speech, when she was still battling against the love-madness (*furor*), she "recognized (*agnosco*) the doomed suffering (*fatale malum*) of an unhappy mother" and blamed her passion on the inherited curse of sinful love (113f.). She repeated her recognition of the curse of the *fata* in the central scene of her confession of love. Rejected once by Hippolytus, she prefaces her second offer and her second collapse at his knees with the lines, *et ipsa nostrae fata cognosco domus: / fugienda petimus: sed mei non sum potens* ("I myself recognize the destiny of the house: I seek what I should flee; but I have no control over myself," 698f.). Though she still invokes the *fata domus*, she makes no mention here of her mother but acknowledges her own emotional weakness, the loss of self-

---

[30] Cf. 1203, 1206, 1226, 1230, 1238f., 1247, 1280.

[31] E.g. Hippolytus' engulfment by the "hidden" enclosure of female lust in 778-80, *te nemore abdito / . . . cingent turba licens, Naiades improbae* ("Shameless Naiads, a licentious band, will gird you about in a hidden grove"). In 331f. the chorus uses another image of "enclosing" for the power of love: Amor rules "wherever the earth is girt around by the deep salt sea" (*qua terra salo / cingitur alto*). Cf. too the "shadows" that are now the "shades" of the Underworld in the last scene, e.g. *umbrae nocentes*, the "guilty shades" of the sinners, 1229. See above, chap. 3, ad init.

[32] On 1183f. and the *fata*, see Paratore (1952) 222f.; Lefèvre (1972) 367.

control (699). Finally, in her last speech, she accepts her *fata* as entirely her own (1184), says nothing of a curse on the house, and takes full responsibility for the wrong she has done. In joining destinies (*iunxisse fata*, 1184) with Hippolytus she now extends her sympathy and her vision of tragic doom (*fata*) to include him. Theseus too invokes the terrible destiny (*o dira fata*, 1271) that led him to kill his son, but his expression lacks the resonances of Phaedra's accursed past. He merely recognizes his crime (*crimen agnosco meum*, 1249); she recognizes that and something more: a long and helpless struggle against an inherited past.[33]

Phaedra's situation at the end contrasts with Theseus' in another way too. Through her perception of the common doom of *fata* in 1184, she sees herself as somehow joined with Hippolytus and separated from Theseus. This separation is made final in Theseus' last lines in the play, which juxtapose the two incomplete rites of burial (1277-80):

vos apparate regii flammam rogi;
et vos per agros corporis partes vagas
inquirite. istam terra defossam premat,
gravisque tellus impio capiti incubet.

Make ready the flames of the royal pyre; and search out the parts of the body scattered through the fields. As for her, let the earth press her down buried, and let the soil lie heavy on her unholy head.

The enormity of the father's violence unleashed on the son frustrates the first burial: the body is still scattered (1278). The un-

---

[33] It is also part of Phaedra's tragic *fata* that she can bring together moral "knowledge" and "will" only at her death. Earlier she "knew" but could not act: cf. 140f., 177-79, 249, 251 (also, of course, Eur., *Hipp.* 377ff.). For the Stoic dimension of the conflict, see Giomini (1955) 44-50 and Lefèvre (1972) 357, 361ff. The Nurse develops another, more immoral, facet of the Euripidean theme of knowledge in 724, *secreta cum sit culpa, quis testis sciet?* ("When the blame is hidden, what witness will know?"); cf. Eur. *Hipp.* 403ff., 462ff., 661ff. Theseus' "recognizing (his) crime" (*crimen agnosco meum*) is offset also by the chorus's "recognizing" the parts of the torn body (*laevi lateris agnosco notas*, 1260).

compassionate harshness of the husband's continuing need for vengeance turns the second burial into a curse. His last word, *incubet*, the last word of the play, echoes Phaedra's opening speech, with the weight of passion that "lies upon her in her grief" (*sed maior alius incubat maestae dolor*, 99).[34] This harsh word in Theseus' curse recalls a side of Phaedra that Theseus does not know, her struggle to resist a criminal passion and remain a chaste wife. His wish that the earth press heavy on her is a version of a traditional formula, but it also continues the motif of subterranean violence and suggests its continuing traces in himself.

Although Theseus speaks in the name of the Law and as the king and father who assesses guilt and punishment, he is still far from the compassionate father-figures who could perform the necessary rituals. He lacks the understanding that *both* the victims of his house deserve.[35] He has failed to grasp the full moral significance of Phaedra's last act. He pays as little attention to her in death as he did in life. In a curious way he responds to her last (true) speech to him in the same way as he responded to her first (false) speech. He fails to examine the details or the nuances of her (true) guilt, just as he failed to examine those of Hippolytus' false guilt. He invokes the Name of the Father as the one who sets the house in order and commands the burials (*genitor*, 1264; *parentem*, 1272; *dona genitoris*, 1273). But the still missing parts of the body recall the role of the violent and vengeful father that he has also played.

To Phaedra he is entirely fixed in this role. When she calls him

---

[34] See above, chap. 2, sec. VII.

[35] Herter (1971), 77, sees in Theseus' last words the definitive condemnation of Phaedra's guilt: "auch das letzte Wort des Philosophendichters, das in uns nachhalten soll." Leeman (1976), 209, seems to me on the right track in seeing in 1244f. "a bitter suggestion of (Theseus') lack of sincerity." Of 1279f. he says, "The man of Death will go on living, unredeemed and utterly despicable—a figure to be compared only with Atreus in the *Thyestes*" (209). This view, however, seems exaggerated in the direction just the opposite of Herter's (for some positive sides to Theseus, see Herrmann, 1924, 408), but it is closer to the mood of the final scene. For the grimness of mood here and the unsympathetic treatment of Theseus, see also Giomini (1955) 12f. and 107f., with note 3 on p. 107; Skovgaard-Hansen (1972) 123; Davis (1983) 125. Certainly by comparison to Phaedra, Theseus' role is weak, as Giomini points out.

"husband," it is only to mark the end of that relationship (1184f., cf. 1167). He remains for her, as he proved to Hippolytus, the punitive father (*pater, parens*, 1191, 1194, 1199). Her shift to "father" at the end marks the gap of sympathy and understanding between them as man and wife. The dissolution of the latter bond is made complete by his cruel closing command (1279f.). He is truly, as Phaedra had said (1164, 1167), "Theseus always harsh . . . , by love or hatred toward his wives harmful always" (*amore semper coniugum aut odio nocens*). She had meant that last phrase (1167) to refer to the equally disastrous effects of his excessive "love" for her and his "hatred" for Antiope; but Theseus at the end seems to have little room for *amor coniugum*. He treats Phaedra, after all, not so very differently from Antiope.[36]

Although the ending reaffirms Theseus' control, it does so in ambiguous terms. It questions his adequacy as a guardian of order, while Phaedra, through her final act and her last words, paradoxically, achieves a deeper moral authority than his and in some ways a stronger claim to be the guardian of the moral law. From subjection to isolating passion in the feminine space of the house, she moves to heroic and decisive action in the realm of law (cf. the legalistic language of her last speech, 1176ff., above). This, however, is a law more complex than merely punishing the "bad."

The play's closing movement questions Theseus' severe legality, with its absolute division between good and evil, innocent and guilty, victim and agent, judge and criminal. Theseus becomes aware of his own guilt; but Phaedra's tragedy, with its breakdown of the black-and-white distinctions of a simplistic legalism, is more involving emotionally and challenging intellectually. Theseus' behavior at the end suggests that he may not be entirely adequate to the moral and emotional complexities of which he has had to be the judge. Tragedy leaves us with something that the Law of the Father cannot fully resolve.

---

[36] The disastrously loved wives of 1167 could include also the abandoned Ariadne (cf. 245 and 665f.), even though her story eventually ended happily.

TEN

Seneca's Patricide and the Trace of Writing

I

As the secondary elaboration of a celebrated classic, Seneca's *Phaedra* is at nearly every point conscious of its literary ancestry and therefore of its literariness. The ghost of Euripides haunts every line. Seneca has his own message to convey; but, because that message is inextricable from his implicit commentary on the Euripidean play, his work calls attention to its textuality, that is, to its status as a work *written* in response to a pre-existent text that the author knows, presumably, through reading. It thus stands in a context of verbal artifice and artificiality; and its very existence implies and demands a hermeneutical orientation toward the literary past. The work itself has come about, in part, through the author's critical, interpretive stance toward a body of pre-existent literature.[1]

Such a text reveals the activity of its creation, the processes through which it produces meaning by asserting its relation (difference, sameness, agreement, hostility) to another text. It thus stands in relation not only to an "external" reality—a world of objects—but also to a world of literary discourse, a realm of texts.

This textuality involves a kind of double vision. In its bifocality Seneca's play takes a long, clear view of the mythical events which it dramatizes, but also looks down at the palimpsestic writings close at hand, the verses of Euripides (and also of

---

[1] For this notion of "text," see Barthes (1979). Barthes also stresses the continuation of this hermeneutic activity as the reader "produces" or "plays" the text (79ff.). For intertextuality and artifice, see also M. Riffaterre, "Intertextual Representation: On Mimesis as Interpretive Discourse," *Critical Inquiry* 11 (1984) 141-62, with further bibliography; also my essay, "Underreading and Intertexuality: Sappho, Simaetha, and Odysseus in Theocritus' Second *Idyll*," *Arethusa* 17 (1984) 201-9, with the literature there cited.

Ovid) half-visible and necessarily half-hidden by their present transformation. Interpreters of the play are inevitably involved in this double vision. To read the play in any depth is to recognize it as "the intertext of another text."[2]

This textuality, or intertextuality, surfaces most urgently in the motif of the sword. The sword not only takes the place of the dialogue that might have been spoken (and in the Euripidean *Hippolytus Crowned* is spoken) between father and son; it also takes the place of the letter, the written message, through which Phaedra in Euripides' extant play makes her accusation. In the lost *Hippolytus Veiled*, Phaedra probably made her accusation in person. She must have had some physical evidence to substantiate the charge, but we do not know what it was. In the second (extant) *Hippolytus*, Euripides softened the moral outrage of her face-to-face denunciation of Hippolytus to Theseus by having her commit suicide first and leave the incriminating letter.[3] Her suicide there was by hanging, not by the sword, as in Seneca's play.

The sword as proof of Hippolytus' guilt may well be original with Seneca. On present evidence we cannot be certain that Euripides did not use it in the lost *Hippolytus Veiled*.[4] Yet, as Hans Herter has argued, it is unlikely that Hippolytus, at the crucial moment, would complicate the dramatic gesture of covering himself up in shame (the gesture from which the *Hippolytos Kalyptomenos* took its name) with the very different action of drawing the sword.[5] Stage action aside, the two actions belong to very different moods, not easily reconcilable with one another. Also the violence of Hippolytus' gesture of twisting Phaedra's hair to pull back her head and expose her throat to his

[2] I take this phrase from Barthes (1979) 77.
[3] See Herter (1971) 52f., 57f.; also his "Theseus und Hippolytos," *RhM* 89 (1940) 288 with note 28.
[4] Friedrich (1953), 132, and Zintzen (1960), 88 and 103ff., argue that the sword motif derives from Euripides' lost play. For strong arguments in favor of Senecan originality here, see Herter (1971) 71-73, with the notes; Barrett (1964), p. 44 with note 2; Dingel (1970) 51ff., especially 54-56.
[5] Herter (1971) 71f.

blade seems more like Seneca than Euripides. Its closest model is Roman rather than Greek, Aeneas' slaughter of a helpless suppliant after the death of Pallas, a passage which in turn echoes Neoptolemus' killing of the helpless Priam.[6]

In the "speech" of the sword Seneca deliberately and unmistakably alludes to the device of the incriminating tablet of the surviving *Hippolytus*. There Theseus, reading the letter of his dead wife, exclaims, βοᾷ, βοᾷ δέλτος ἄλαστα, "The tablet shouts, it shouts things not to be forgotten" (877).[7] Here Phaedra says, *hic dicet ensis*, "The sword will tell" (896). In both cases the critical "speaking" is transferred to an inanimate object. The small signs on the hilt, furthermore, make the sword itself a form of writing, with a message that Theseus has to "read."

In Euripides, Phaedra appears, quite literally, as a trace in letters. In Seneca, Phaedra's presence with the sword, is the necessary complement to the absence of Hippolytus who has abandoned it and fled in horror. The Euripidean Phaedra's absence, in death, makes that silent speech of the letter more powerful than any living voice could be. In Seneca Phaedra's display of the sword in the private space of her chambers creates a symbolical reenactment of repressed fears and desires, all concerned with incest, among the three major characters.

The unspoken *monstrum* that Theseus reads on the hilt is only partially Hippolytus' terrible crime; it is also the monstrosity that Theseus calls up from the hidden part of himself. The replacement of the name of the son by the *monstrum* of the sword/phallus is parallel to the replacement of the Name of the Father (904f.) by the *monstrum* from the sea, with its overtly phallic shape (1015f., 1045-47). In both cases the "monster" is in effect the unspeakable form of Oedipal fears and desires: the son's sexual possession of the father's wife and the father's virtual castration of the son (1099).

Seneca precipitates the tragic crisis not through words (or through the traces of words on Phaedra's tablet) but through

---

[6] Virgil, *Aen.* 2.552f. and 10.534f.; see Grimal (1965) ad 707f.
[7] On this passage, see Segal (1982a) 148f.; also (1983c) 31f.

the very instrument of the unspeakable crime. His sword stands for a writing that speaks without words and replaces the verbal message of the Euripidean letter with a signifier of what may not be spoken. He probes the subsurface world of the unconscious through a rhetoric that is itself a special reading of Euripides, a reading that replaces explicit writing with emblematic image. Thus his play revolves around a knowledge that is present tangibly in the letters of the text but resists being spoken overtly onstage or written down on a tablet. Replacing tablet by sword is an index of this concern with what remains as image, just below the level of verbal articulation.

Without Euripides' plays, of course, Seneca's intertextual effect would not be possible. It results, at least in part, from the engagement of his imagination in reading and rewriting Euripides. The small figures on the hilt are not only a substitute for the letter of Euripides' Phaedra; they are also the mark of Seneca's substitution of his own play for that of Euripides. Thus they are a figure for the textuality of his work.[8] They point to the process by which writing generates meaning; and they indicate, at some level, the derivative work's consciousness of itself as a production of signs within a recessive series of highly coded systems, extending back from Ovid to Euripides and thence to the mythical corpus behind Greek drama.

---

[8] Recently Fantham (1982), whose book reached me only after I had written most of my study, has emphasized this textual aspect of Senecan drama, although in a perspective different from mine: "Ultimately the play would be known through written copies, and only the readers would experience the plays as complete works" (p. 48). "As a prose writer (Seneca) was used to achieving the effect of instruction through words alone, and I believe he was content to let the words serve as the unaided medium of his dramatic poetry" (p. 49). Even as early as the fourth century B.C. tragedians began to compose for readers: cf. Aristotle, *Rhet.* 3.12.1413b3-16; also *Poet.* 26.1462a11-17; see Albin Lesky, *Greek Tragedy*, trans. H. A. Frankfort (London and New York 1967) 204; G. F. Else, *Aristotle's Poetics: The Argument* (Cambridge, Mass. 1957) 635f., 640f. Silent reading is not as foreign to classical antiquity as is sometimes claimed: see Knox (1968). On the other hand, we should remember that in Seneca's day works were still "published" (at least in part) by being recited and that the practice of private readings in literary circles somewhat blurred the distinction between the written text as we book-readers think of it and a text intended for recitation or performance.

The "monster" that Theseus reads in these small signs, as in the miniature, symbolic form of the written text, expands to the overpowering reality of the *monstrum* soon to be described by the Messenger. The scale abruptly shifts from miniature and figural monstrosity on the one hand to the gigantesque, exaggerated shape in the narrative "event" on the other, from the symbolic mode to the representation of something massively corporeal. In this shift the text reveals its power to create images that we accept as living beings. Differently viewed, these small signs function as the letters of a writing that both requires and presupposes the supplement of imagination that makes words—whether written or spoken—into "reality."

The phantasmagoric quality of Seneca's plays is related to his self-conscious elaboration of a text that has been experienced through reading, for it is the texture and evocations of the words, rather than the action per se, that carry the meaning. Words fixed by a previous literary experience are elaborated to refract reality in the artificial light of rhetorical description. Language functions as the active medium of displacement, as the area where something analogous to the Freudian "transference" occurs.[9] Language here serves less as a transparent window to a signified than as a translucent screen behind which appears a chain of other signifiers.

II

Wilamowitz once observed that Seneca's Medea (the character) seemed to have read Euripides' play of that name.[10] The same could be said of the characters Phaedra and Hippolytus. Johannes Geffcken developed Wilamowitz's remark: "His [Seneca's] characters reflect not on their fate but on the known story (*Fabel*). Atreus has already a kind of tragic consciousness of his

[9] Freud's "transference," Shoshana Felman (1977), 137, remarks, could be defined as such a "movement of displacement through a chain of signifiers."
[10] U. von Wilamowitz-Moellendorff, *Griechische Tragödie* 10 (Berlin 1906) 4.

act; Deianeira rages in an already prescribed madness."[11] Seneca perceives his characters through the medium of a previous writing. The sword of the *Phaedra*, I would suggest, calls attention to this trace of a prior writing that is absorbed and then effaced by the play. Through such traces, Seneca marks both the origins of his work and also the effacement of those origins in the new work that results.

For Euripides, close to an oral culture in which writing still contains an element of novelty, intrusiveness, and power, the relation of the silent speech of writing and the discourse of oral speech has to do largely with the problem of knowledge and deception in a public world of evidence, proofs of guilt or innocence, juridical truth.[12] Seneca is fully immersed in a written culture and farther from the notion of the oral "truth" of myths, wise sayings, customs, and traditions that remain valid because they are alive on the lips of men. For him the relation of written to spoken discourse has more to do with the private, inner world, the gaps in consciousness that correspond to gaps created by the distancing process of writing itself, particularly in its attempt to record the hidden movements of the soul.[13]

The old debate about whether Seneca's plays were intended as stage performances or as closet dramas may perhaps be

[11] J. Geffcken, "Der Begriff des tragischen in der Antike," in *Bibliothek Warburg: Vorträge 1927-28*, ed. F. Saxl (Berlin 1930) 158.
[12] See Segal (1982a) 149 apropos of Euripides' *Hippolytus*. See especially *Hipp.* 921-31 and 1074-77.
[13] This issue has perhaps some applicability to Seneca's prose writings as well, especially to the *Epistles*. On the one hand these claim a spontaneity, openness, and frankness of tone (e.g., the opening of *Epist.* 17, 23, 26, 56, 57, 65), but on the other hand they self-consciously present a highly structured, rhetorically defined personality. They speak the voice of a cultural and moralistic, literary tradition as much as that of a particular individual; yet by their form and the occasional nature of some of their contents they also claim the freshness and casualness of the passing moment that communicates a transient individuality. Whatever Seneca's original intentions of self-revelation, he deliberately and artistically creates this quality of the occasional and the momentary as an act of conscious premeditation and contrivance. Ostensible self-revelation is in fact the artifice of self-(re-)presentation. The soul of Seneca the man, then, is enveloped and inevitably concealed by the authorial persona shaped by the opportunity of letters and conditioned by the very fact of writing. Much the same situation applies to the letters of the younger Pliny.

looked at afresh in this light: that is, their form does not betray a simple commitment to either mode of reception. They can be read satisfactorily both as staged dramas and as literary texts. Whatever the historical reality (and recent scholarship is no nearer a definitive solution), the very fact that the issue cannot be easily decided points to a special quality in the works themselves, a hesitation between public and private discourse, between the full "presence" of an enacted, orally created world realized three-dimensionally by actors onstage, and the studied absences of a writing that "speaks" in its paradoxical silent voice to a reader.[14]

From another perspective, the sword is the visible mark of Seneca's own "anxiety of influence."[15] It is the trace of the earlier writer's absence. In place of the letters (writing) of the absent poet (the tablet of Euripides' Phaedra), Seneca puts the sword. With the sword that replaces/effaces the Euripidean tablet, he has made his predecessor into a ghost, a trace of a trace of speech. That "writing" is also, to some extent, the letter of Ovid's Phaedra in *Heroides* 4, another work that calls attention to its textuality in letters.[16] Having symbolically usurped the creative power of the "father," Euripides and Ovid, Seneca leaves behind the sword—exactly as his character, Hippolytus, in another fiction about a son replacing a father (that is, in the lie of Phaedra), has left behind a sword. In both cases this substitution is the signifier of a crime against the father.[17]

[14] The fact that the ancient "reading" of a written text often (though not always) took place aloud does not change this relation. The reading, even *alta voce* and even by a servant/lector, still bears the self-conscious marks of the absent author and the sharp designation of the fact that the text, not the man himself, is "speaking." On the existence of silent reading, see Knox (1968) and above, note 6.

[15] Harold Bloom, *The Anxiety of Influence* (New York 1973), especially 6, 10, 30; see also Ferrucci (1980) 162, 166.

[16] Compare also Phaedra's writing in Ovid's *Heroides* 4.7-14, where the composing of the letter enables her to break her reserve of silence and "speak" to Hippolytus: see Paratore (1952) 224; Giomini (1955) 28; Jacobson (1974), p. 148 with note 16.

[17] See Felman (1977) 206f.: "There are letters from the moment there is no master to receive—or to read them: letters exist because a Master ceases to exist. We could indeed advance this statement as a definition of literature itself . . . :

Seneca's substitution of sword for letters thus partakes of what Derrida, commenting on the "fatherless word" of Plato's *Phaedrus* (275 d-e), calls the "patricidal subversion" of writing.[18] This is the process by which every writing kills its father and replaces the authority of the spoken word, the living Presence, with the trace, the sign of absence. The written word evokes the presence of that which it signifies, but under the sign of the letter, the symbol of a symbol, the mark of an absence. Writing is the signifier of a signifier, the graphic for the verbal sign (the sound of the voice), which in turn is the indication of the thing. The process of writing is a process of leaving traces, of making visible a distance between language and the solidity of presence that language attempts, and pretends, to close.[19] Seneca compounds the tracing of traces by using a double-edged symbol, a sword that annihilates a father's authority in his house, replaces the letters in the writing left by his own literary "father" (the tablets of Euripides' *Hippolytus*), and thereby inscribes his text into an infinite series of writings, words disseminated *in* the absence of fathers and *as* the absence of fathers. Possessing an ambiguous, asexual procreation of their own, however, these words about desire also claim the fertile power of the mother and break silence with their written "mark" (*nota*, 691) to create their own *ambiguus infans* (693).

The act of framing and distancing effected by letters and by literature always carries with it the possibility of subverting the ideology that it depicts. This potential subversion is probably inherent in the polyvalent meaning of complex literary works. Seneca's *Phaedra*, thanks in part to its Euripidean model and

---

literature (the very literality of letters) is nothing other than the Master's death, the Master's transformation into a ghost." Also p. 146, apropos of Henry James' *Turn of the Screw*: "How can one write *for* the very figure who signifies the suppression of what one has to say to him?"

[18] Jacques Derrida, "La pharmacie de Platon," in *La dissémination* (Paris 1972) 87: "Depuis la position de qui tient le sceptre, le désir de l'écriture est indiqué, désigné, dénoncé comme le désir de l'orphelinat et la subversion parricide. Ce *pharmakon* n'est-il pas criminel, n'est-ce pas un cadeau empoisonné?"

[19] For this view of writing, see Jacques Derrida, *La voix et le phénomène* (Paris 1972), especially chap. 6.

also to its own engrafting of the Roman concern with the *pater-familias* on the Greek material, is such a work. The re-assertion of the father's authority, after the disasters that result from his absence, is undercut by the violence that the father reintroduces into the sword as an emblem of that authority. The scene shown through the small signs on the sword's hilt is a microcosmic condensation of the role of the father. It presents the father as the center of order and continuity, assuring and safeguarding the succession of his property. But it also presents that paternal guardianship as a potential source of murderous jealousy and fearful monstrosity.

Through the literary echoes of the sword, the work reflects on itself as a constellation of multiple meanings, sometimes pulling in opposite directions. Thus the *Phaedra* (in this respect like the *Aeneid*) simultaneously asserts and questions, defends and violates, the patriarchal order. The hilt is both a symbolic microcosm of that order crystallized into art and an agent involved at an intense moment in the vicissitudes of that order. This ambiguity corresponds to the ambiguity of the father himself, who both banishes and enacts violence and monstrosity from/in his realm.

The sword and its hilt form the emblem of a realm whose inscribed story of a patriarchal order ("the glory of the race of Athens") is cancelled out by another story, a story told not *on* but *by means of* the sword. These small signs on the hilt thus lead us to a mirror-like regress of letters-within-letters and stories-within-stories. The shifting perspectives and interactions of truth and deception in the story told by the hilt reflect back to us the shifting perspectives and changing points of view contained in the story told by the play as a whole, by the "signs" that compose its text. Taken at the level of seriousness that the situation demands, the miniature plot embossed on the sword (a plot that is itself a palimpsestic tissue of intertexts: Euripides' *Aegeus* and Ovid's *Metamorphoses*) forces on us the awareness of all the fictional plottings that make up the work—those of the Nurse, of Phaedra, of Euripides, and of Seneca himself.

Desire arises in (and as) the absence of the father or master or model (Theseus, Euripides, Ovid), the desire to claim or possess the procreative power of the father. This power could be explained as desire for the phallus or for the scepter or for the kingdom or for the creative energy that belongs to the literary tradition, to the poetic "fathers" of Greece.[20] But to reduce the complex overlays of textual echoes to a simplistically Freudian phallic symbolism, rigid to the last, is to impoverish the suggestiveness of the work. As Theseus and Hippolytus meet only through the sword which emerges in the space created by the absence of the father, so too Euripides and Seneca meet most directly in the regression of signs, letters, and stories behind the sword. The sword fills the place left by the tablet, those written letters that Euripides' Phaedra, like Euripides himself, has left behind after his/her death.

The sword is, therefore, doubly the trace of a writing: it takes the place of a written tablet, which is in turn the trace of a voice—the voice of the dead Phaedra and of the dead Euripides. The sword is the mark of the newer author replacing the older, the son replacing the father. In these self-conscious literary echoes, the sword also signifies the displacement of a prior writing by a new creative thrust, a substitute mastery of the signifier of the phallus, which finally succeeds in driving that weapon home, incestuously, into the empty place where it has been so lacking and so desired.

The sword, as we have seen, is also the meeting place of Seneca with another father, Ovid.[21] We have noted how Seneca, "rewriting" *Metamorphoses* 7.422f. in *Phaedra* 899f., has put his own more elaborate sword in the place of his poetic father's. This replacement of an older sword by a newer also occurs in a context concerned with the succession of father and son, rightful succession in the case of Ovid's sword-bearer (Theseus to Aegeus), wrongful succession as we view Seneca's sword-bearer

---

[20] Compare Dionysus' "longing" (πόθος) for the "generative poet," the γόνι-μος ποιητής, in Aristophanes' *Frogs* (96).
[21] See above, chap. 8, sec. VII, pp. 170f.

in the terms of the fictions that Phaedra has so successfully spun around him.

III

As the sign of an absent writing, the sword is also, in another way, that which has made Seneca's tragedy possible. Phaedra's death by the sword is a condition of the play's existence, literally in that it constitutes the end of the story, and in a remoter sense in that it is the genesis of the story in the creative processes of the unconscious. By leaving Phaedra unsatisfied (or, more accurately, by recreating in his own words the myth of her hopeless desire), by having her penetrated by the sword of tragic love-in-death and not by a surrogate of his own phallus, Seneca makes the play, at some level, a substitute for his own fantasies and desires. The play protects him from the deadlock of Phaedra's tragic conflict between pleasure and duty and marks his successful passage along the path of socially acceptable sublimation, a path that his heroine refused to take. The sword, then, also marks the place where he has found a satisfactory substitute for Phaedra, resisting the temptations that she held out to Hippolytus. For the reader too, whether male or female, the pleasure in the play has some of its roots in the satisfaction of that substitution.

Viewed from the perspective of the audience, the sense of completeness and inevitability characteristic of classical tragedy has to do with the intense arousal of desire on the one hand and the acceptance of the absolute impossibility of fulfilling that desire on the other—the acceptance, in other words, of the necessity of sublimation without denying its problematical qualities. What Kenneth Burke remarked about audience involvement, though in a somewhat different context, is relevant here: "Form is the creation of an appetite in the mind of the auditor, and the adequate satisfying of that appetite. This satisfaction—so complicated in the human mechanism—at times involves a temporary set of frustrations, but in the end these frustrations prove to be simply a more involved kind of satisfaction, and furthermore serve to make the satisfaction of fulfilment more intense."[22]

The shift of the meaning of the sword in Phaedra's last scene, on a Freudian view, encourages reality over phantasy, ego over id or superego, and ego-integration over ego-dissolution. If the play gives pleasure by satisfying unconscious fantasies about incest and patricide and involves us by arousing our unconscious fears of monstrous maternal and paternal figures, it also allays our guilt about such pleasures and calms our anxieties about such terrors by showing us the punishment meted out to illicit desire. The process is analogous to the Freudian principle of negation (*Verneinung*): we can tolerate our repressed wishes by marking them with a negative sign. By disapproving of the repressed material, we protect ourselves from it, and also from the knowledge that this material is in fact part of ourselves. That is, we deny that it is really "ours." The tragic paradox—the contradiction between the pain of the contents and the pleasure of the literary form—is due in part to this interplay between elaboration on the one hand and denial (by punishing the "evil") on the other.

Luring us to take pleasure in the vicarious fulfilment of tabooed desires, the sword is the strongest signifier of our complicity in Phaedra's lie, our sympathy for her, our interest and participation in her desire. Like the servants and the chorus, we make the suppressions and suspensions that allow the sword to do its "speaking" for her. Imaginatively and emotionally, we join in their sympathetic silence so that the plot may go forward and the sword find its destined, inevitable goal, just where we want it to be.

In its ambiguous function as both a symbol of desire and a murderous weapon, the sword links the three main characters in their precarious interchange of the roles of agent and victim. The deaths of Phaedra and Hippolytus as agents of one another's destruction may satisfy some of our demand for moral and

[22] Kenneth Burke, *Counter-Statement* (New York 1931) 40.

psychological order; but their deaths as victims of one another point to something less easily reduced to moral or rational coherence: a blind force of desire for which no ultimate explanation is offered. It is in this elemental power of the irrational drive of desire, whether labelled a divine force as in Euripides or a failure of reason to overcome passion as in Seneca, that the tragic dimension of the story lies. Seneca ultimately follows Euripides in maintaining this interpretation of the myth.

For us, therefore, the sword cannot be the instrument of finality, as it is for Phaedra in her last gesture of the play. In our experience of the play we recreate the chain of signifiers behind the sword and undergo the deceptions and clarifications that they work on us. As a microcosm of the entire play, the sword is also a trap, luring us to violate its "reserve of silence," to speak about what it deliberately elides from speech, to articulate consciously what it leaves as suggestion or as intimation, to continue its plotting, and to fill with further writing and further speaking the silences of its own "small signs."

ELEVEN

Closure, Form, and the Father

I

The last scene of the *Phaedra* has a peculiarly complex form of literariness and textuality, for Seneca here "contaminates" Euripides' *Hippolytus* with the *Bacchae*. He suppresses the reconciliation between father and son that closes the extant *Hippolytus* and instead develops his own version of the aged, enfeebled father-figure, Cadmus, who pathetically recomposes the mutilated corpse of Pentheus.[1]

Just below the surface of Seneca's text, with the attempt to recompose mutilated fragments of a once beautiful form, lies Seneca's own authorial problem: recomposing into a beautiful unity the now scattered pieces of a past tradition: the two Hippolytus plays of Euripides, possibly his *Aegeus*, the finale of the *Bacchae*, Sophocles' *Phaedra*, even Ovid's Fourth *Heroides*, and the seventh book of the *Metamorphoses*. The self-conscious blending of two separate plays of Euripides at this point, *Hippolytus* and *Bacchae*, gives this issue an immediate grounding in the text.

Obviously a scene of such intense emotion should not be made over into a heavy-handed allegory of poetics, nor do I wish to diminish the powerful impact of the surface meaning. Two aspects of the scene, however, will bear further scrutiny: the ultimate failure of Theseus to "form" his son's body into the coherence necessary for burial, and the rapid shift from the more or less objective concern with form and beauty (*fingit, forma, decor, facies*) to bitter accusation of the fates and of the gods (1271f.; cf. also the self-accusation of 1249-52).

The burial of Hippolytus' scattered remains comes at the chorus's initiative, not Theseus'. While he laments, castigates his

---

[1] For Cadmus' role as a surrogate father in the *Bacchae*, see Segal (1982) 211f. and 323-27.

own severity, and talks of returning to Hades, the chorus inter-poses a practical note: "Theseus, for lamentation eternal time remains. Now pay what is just to your son and more quickly hide away the limbs foully scattered with savage rending" (1244-46). Theseus responds with two verses of instructions to carry in the remains (1247f.), but for seven lines cries out in lamentation and self-blame (1249-55). The chorus thereupon repeats its injunction, "Father, put the scattered limbs of the torn body into order and restore to their place the wandering parts . . ." (1256-58). Whereas Theseus is involved in the rec-ognition of his crime (*crimen agnosco meum*, 1249), the chorus's concern is with the recognition of the marks or signs that enable him to put the grisly pieces together (*laevi lateris agnosco notas*, "I recognize the marks of the left side," 1260). The word order of 1256 (spoken by the chorus) interlocks Theseus' role as fa-ther with the dismembered limbs of the son's torn body (*disiecta genitor membra laceri corporis*).[2] A few lines later Theseus even more pointedly combines the generative father who gives life and the wrathful father who caused death. Speaking of himself in the third person as *genitor*, "father," he describes his "count-ing up of the limbs" as "fashioning the body," as if he were again engaged in the creative act of giving life to his son (1264f.):

> dum membra nato genitor adnumerat suo
> corpusque fingit.

It is directly upon this statement that Theseus remarks on the horror of what is left of his son, something "lacking form and ugly, torn by many a wound on every side" (1265f.). The ugli-ness results from the absence of parts of the body itself, depriv-ing it of the wholeness of a human form (1265-68):

---

[2] With most editors, I keep E's attribution of 1256-61 to the chorus, with the change back to Theseus at the second-person plural, *durate*, in 1262. The A-mss. continue with Theseus as speaker, but the address to the father (*genitor*) in 1256 requires the change.

hoc quid est forma carens
et turpe, multo vulnere abruptum undique?
quae pars tui sit dubito; sed pars est tui:
hic, hic repone, non suo, at vacuo loco.

What is this thing lacking beauty and ugly, broken on every side with many a wound? What part of you it may be I am in doubt, but part of you it is. Here, here place it, not in its own but in an empty place.

At one level such a passage, like Manto's prophetic handling of entrails in the bloody depths of the sacrificed victim in the *Oedipus* (353-83), symbolically reveals the "autobiography of the work," the genesis of the play in the author's imagination.[3] The handling of wounds and recomposing the pieces of ancient pain into a new form generate a "fiction" (*corpusque fingit*, 1265) which has the paradoxical mixture of horror and beauty characteristic of the tragic paradox. The tragic work makes us share in Theseus' task of forming into a whole the pieces of past suffering, touching the places of old pain and guilt, and filling in the gaps in consciousness left by the traumas of the violence enacted in the play.

As Theseus recomposes the body, his creative shaping (*fingit*, 1265) of its form brings him full circle with his earlier murderous disjunction of the parts. He thereby recomposes his suffering in the distancing, objective frame of art. He speaks of himself and of his actions, momentarily, in the third person, in contrast to his first-person self-address of 1249ff., "*I* recognize *my* crime. *I* destroyed you . . ." (*crimen agnosco meum. / ego te peremi*, 1249f.).[4]

The brevity of Theseus' third-person address (1264f.) and his

---

[3] For the notion of the work's "autobiography" in the text (not necessarily the residue of events in the author's lived life but rather a symbolic reflection of the genesis of an idea and a style), see Ferrucci (1980) 30-33, 34-36, 78-84. See Segal (1983b) 241-44 and 249, with applications to Seneca's *Medea*, *Thyestes*, and *Oedipus*.

[4] Note too Theseus' first-person verbs, *fierem*, *advocavi*, *fruor*, in 1251f., and his second-person address to his "hands" and "cheeks" in 1262f.

lack of success in shaping the body into a form that can be so-
lemnized for a ritual of closure, both emotional and aesthetic,
also point to the fleeting and fragile quality of the moment in
which the poet can grasp and find metaphoric equivalents for
the mystery of his creative processes. The father's ultimate inability to fashion or form a complete image of his son's body is
also that absence of closure inherent in all tragedy: the residual
tensions, rifts, and contradictions between the order-imposing
coherence of the artistic form and the order-resisting chaos of
the experience that such art represents. Tragedy is about suffering whose parts refuse to be entirely accounted for, justified,
and laid to rest either by the social forms of ritual (burial) or the
rationalized logic of moral explanation (justice and law).[5]

The "absence" or "emptiness" that is part of Theseus' grief in
handling the body (*carens*, 1265; *vacuo loco*, 1268) has another
meaning too: each of those empty holes signifies the destructive
father-imago in himself, the tear in the fabric of his own conscious being through which the destructive side of the father
figure in himself becomes visible. That knowledge can exist only
after the catastrophe has breached some of the ego's defenses
against the unconscious.

The last words that Theseus speaks to Phaedra complement
those he spoke to Hippolytus; his contrasting reactions to the
two deaths explain one another. On the one hand there is the
emptiness of missing parts of a body that he desires to reconsti-
tute; on the other hand there is the hateful sight of a body that
he wants to crush into invisibility with the tangible solidity of
the "heavy earth" (1279f.). This curse on Phaedra's body would
remove from sight the object of the struggle between himself
and his son. Left above ground, that body accuses him implicitly, as her words accused him explicitly (1164ff., 1191-96f.) It
accuses him of complicity with her in his rivalry with Hippolytus. His intense, possessive engagement with her helped create
the discourse of the unconscious, the language of hidden fears

---

[5] For this aspect of tragic form, see Segal (1982), chap. 9, especially 342.

and desires in the "speaking" of the sword to which he was so ready to listen.

Theseus appears at the end to bury a son, but the troubling and troubled materiality of the body of the mother and wife remains a powerful entity on the stage. Though crushed beneath the counterweight of earth, it blocks by its recurrence any closure through the decree of the father, the word of Law. The very speech of that decree must contain, named within it, that which obstructs it, both its object and its obstacle. These last words of the father, and of the play, are pulled back into the orbit of Phaedra. They echo those conditions in the body of the mother/ wife that set into motion the catastrophic course of events whose outcome we now witness (cf. 1279f. and 99ff.).

II

The security of closure with the Word of the Father is, as Roland Barthes suggests, among the pleasures of literature, of stories:

> The death of the Father will remove from literature many of its pleasures. If there is no more Father, what good is it to tell stories? Does not every story lead back to Oedipus? To tell a story: is this not always to seek one's origin, one's entanglements with the Law, to enter into the dialectic of sadness and of hatred?[6]

The end of the *Phaedra* does not kill the Father, but leaves him problematically triumphant over the dead body of the son. He survives in order that the storytelling may go on, even after this story has reached its formal ending. But this story had its origins in the absence of the father, and specifically in absence concerning the generative realm of the father's power. This latter is also the subject of Theseus' concluding speech. The dead son, brought back to the origins of his life in the father, appears only as the negative aspect of the physicality that has been so

---

[6] Roland Barthes, *Le plaisir du texte* (Paris 1973) 75f. (my translation).

crucial in his and Phaedra's tragedy. As the mangled, lifeless corpse, he is a figure of absence, the negative side of the pro-creative potential of the father's sexual drive, the ambiguity of desire that both begets and destroys.

The mother/wife, Phaedra, is no less powerful by her ab-sence. Theseus would banish her from the scene, annihilate her presence. But the very terms of his decree, the play's ultimate language of Law, recreate that recalcitrance of the maternal, physical substance which the symbolic order of (his) language can never defeat. Her female desire serves as a symbol of what refuses ultimately to be confined and bounded as the unambig-uously possessed object of the father and as the secure posses-sion of a univocal language. This elusive element is variously de-fined as matter, the feminine, the sexual instinct, the life force, the irrational, the realm of the emotions. This desire beyond the control of the father destabilizes both his law and the symbolic order that constitutes his law in the register of language.

The weight of earth that Theseus would pile on Phaedra is another means by which this father would close the holes opened by the death of Hippolytus. The absences around the death of the son, however, are not simply the emptiness of loss. They point to that in Theseus the father, and in the reader who imaginatively reconstructs Theseus from Seneca's text, that can manifest itself only as the fugitive emptiness of the unconscious, to be filled in again and again as soon as opened. These gaps are the rents in the fabric of the symbolic order that the tragic ac-tion reveals and reopens perpetually as parts of us all.

TWELVE

Conclusion: Rhetoric and Reality

Following Freud, Lacan questions the Cartesian identification of our conscious mental processes with our identity as a "self" (*cogito ergo sum*). Going somewhat beyond Freud, he suggests too that the language in which we can express the existence of self is also the condition of our alienation from self. The processes of substitution implied in language make civilized life possible, but at the cost of our alienation from the primary "knowledge" of ourselves hidden in the unconscious.[1] Language is itself part of a series of absences through which the unconscious leaves its mark. For Lacan, as for Plato, the realm of desire (*eros* in Plato) appears as negative space, as a series of absences.[2] Such a signifier is analogous, Lacan suggests, to an imaginary number in mathematics, like the square root of -1.[3] Lacanian analysis is, in a sense, a retracking of the linguistic process by which the unconscious is hidden; it is an unconcealing (if one may borrow a term of Heidegger) of that of which the signifying process leaves only a trace.

Such a reflection on the relation between language and the unconscious in approaching literary discourse poses the question, how can language reveal that which uses language to conceal itself and masks what by its very nature refuses to be named and refuses "to know that it knows"? In other words, how can we read what is by definition unreadable?[4] If the unreadable,

[1] See Lacan in Felman (1977) 28: "The subject is deprived of something of himself, of his very life, which has assumed the value of that which binds him to the signifier." See also Jameson (1977) 363, citing A. Rifflet-Lemaire, *Jacques Lacan* (Brussels 1970) 129: "The subject mediated by language is irremediably divided because it has been excluded from the symbolic chain at the very moment at which it became 'represented' in it."

[2] John Brenkman, "The Other and the One: Psychoanalysis, Reading, the *Symposium*," in Felman (1977) 451. See also Lacan/Wilden (1968) 163: "For the object to be discovered by the child it must be absent."

[3] See Lacan/Sheridan (1977) 318.

[4] See Orlando (1973) 16ff. = (1978) 129ff.; also Felman (1977) 142.

the unconscious, is made readable, it ceases to be unconscious knowledge, or knowledge of the unconscious. One solution, as Shoshana Felman suggests, is "to rethink the readable itself, and hence to attempt to read it as a variant of the unreadable."[5] In other words, our reading will point to that in the story which refuses to tell, which masks its knowing with the signifier of its absence. The linguistic distortions and transformations of Seneca's rhetoric, I have suggested, calls attention to the deliberate substitution of verbal forms for what can be known only as an absence, as something namable only indirectly at the end of a chain of signifiers.

Seneca's rhetorical figures also convey a vision of the transformative processes of psychic life. Hence the applicability to his work of a psychoanalytic approach, for here (as Freud and after him Lacan theorized) the processes of the unconscious mind parallel the figures of language, particularly metonymy and metaphor, substitution and symbolic transformation.[6] In Seneca the distortions that the passions work upon language take the form of those displacements, metaphors, and exaggerations that we pejoratively label rhetoric. These figures give a kind of animate life to the emotions. Phaedra's love-madness (*furor*) compels, conquers, rules (178, 184f.). Elsewhere it grows or burns or seethes like volcanic smoke (101-3), or is a fire that "glows hot submerged in inmost vitals" (641f.). In one sense such expressions are ornaments, mere figures of speech; in another, profounder sense they are the substance of the soul's transformations and hidden movements, a tissue rendered into language, bearing the traces of the invisible and mysterious feelings that help make us what we "are." In life it may be that we are what we do; in literature we are what we say.

Both the psychoanalyst and the dramatist searching for equivalents that visualize and concretize the unknown, probe language as the trace of the shadow-side of our existence. Both

---

[5] Ibid. 143.
[6] See Lacan/Wilden (1968) 31 and 51; Orlando (1973) 56ff. (= 1978, 161ff.); Jameson in Felman (1977) 367f. See above, chap. 1, sec. I, ad fin.

seek a mode of speech that can hold in the momentary clarity of verbal expression that which eludes words and folds back, inevitably, into the reserve of silence that surrounds speech.

Seneca's concentration on the verbal surface implies a deeper perception of tragic alienation built into human life, though this is never fully articulated in the plays. The increasing elaboration of the symbolic order in the manifestations of culture goes hand in hand with increasing alienation from the irrational, destructive and self-destructive violence contained in the unconscious, in the hidden, archaic strata of our emotional lives. The consequence of this schizoid situation is domination by our primal but still uncontrolled aggressions.

This elaboration of the symbolic order through verbal, visual, and the other signifying languages of conscious life is, as we see today, carried on above the abyss of universal destruction and alongside the impulses toward unlimited and ever more meticulously rationalized violence. These forces seem to be somehow beyond the reach of our communicating discourse. Like Phaedra, we know, rationally, the good, but lack the power to stem the dizzy plunge toward evil. In this condition of alienation from the unconscious through the opacity of language, modern man, like Senecan man, is tragically deaf to what his own words are telling him, could he but listen to their silences as well as to their signifying sounds. The signifying languages of conscious life allow us to rationalize the madness that we (like many of Seneca's contemporaries in the age of Nero) are in fact living in the world.

In the rhetorical exaggerations of Senecan tragedy speech ceases to dissemble irrationality. The monstrosity that bursts into language in the exaggerations and distortions of the rhetorical figures enables us to discern the corresponding monstrosity in the signified, in the reality that we accept as sane and reasonable, merely because we can speak it. When the signifier points us to what we cannot speak, our eyes are opened to a different order of reality, and this vision is far less reassuring.

The intensely inward focus of both Seneca and modern psychoanalysis develops at a time when belief in a larger cosmic or supernatural order is problematical and when individual action seems insignificant against huge national and supranational organizations. For Seneca too the authority-figure who stands in the place of the Father—a Caligula or a Nero—appears remote, capricious, unstable, possibly insane, and all-powerful. In the massive bureaucracy and complicated conglomerates of vast empires or computerized superpowers, the irrational and arbitrary take the polarized forms of terrifying outbursts of unpredictable violence from the surface order on the one hand and a rationalized regularity of day-to-day insanity that itself becomes "reality" on the other. In such a world the gaze turns inward; and the Stoic sage, like his modern counterpart, seeks to gain rational comprehension of what of the self is left in his control.

For Freud, God is of interest solely as part of the patient's defense-mechanism against painful emotions or as a residue of infantile yearnings for "oceanic" safety in total benignity and generosity. As a Stoic philosopher, Seneca believes in a divinely governed world-order; but in his tragedies the gods, despite all the invocations, are distant, mysterious, unhelpful. They may cause sudden madness, as in the *Hercules Furens*, but in fact have little major impact on the human action. They are essentially metaphors for the passions or a screen on which the characters, left to the isolation of their own devouring emotions, can project their anxieties about the meaninglessness and uncertainty of life.[7]

Senecan drama comes as close to depicting a godless world— or at least a world where the controlling hand of divinity is far from the center of action—as is permitted by the conventions of his inherited literary form, once part of a religious celebration at the festival of Dionysus. Seneca's elimination of Euripides' divine framework in the *Phaedra* is a striking example. For all the appeals to Jupiter, Neptune, Diana, Apollo, what is essential in the play happens exclusively in the realm of human emo-

---

[7] See Paratore (1957) 72 on this "assenza paurosamente desolata dell' umana individualità lasciata in balia a sè stessa."

tions.[8] Even Neptune's answer to Theseus' curse is more important for its psychological than for its religious meaning. This is not to deny the deep psychological truth of the curses and what they evoke in Euripides' play.[9] But the theological elements—the question of the gods' existence, their intervention in human life, the mystical otherness, and the religious symbolism—are far more alive for the Euripidean than for the Senecan work. Violence, impetuosity, anger, jealousy, vengefulness, sexual tension, rather than devotion or longing for a purer world, dominate the mental life of the Senecan character.

Were one to look through the other end of the psychoanalytic telescope, perhaps one would see not the unspeakable miniaturized shadows of the unconscious but the blinding luminosity of the ineffable God, transformed into the unknown secret of man. The concern with that which can only leave a trace in language also characterizes the language of religious mystics. But for Freud and Lacan, as for Seneca, the ultimate secrets of existence lie not in some vast exterior world, some luminous universe to which language opens a wide portal, as in the visions of Lucretius or Parmenides,[10] but in the dark human interior into which language channels a narrow labyrinthine path. What is found at the end is not the ineffable radiance of divine Being, but the unspeakable of the unconscious where chaos and order are in precarious balance.

When a Senecan protagonist emerges into the luminous spaces of the divine aether, it is to banish divinity from those celestial realms. Jason sees Medea soaring in her serpent-drawn car above the bloodstained house in which his children and new bride lie dead and exclaims,

---

[8] Giomini (1955), 39, seems to me to overstate the religious element in Hippolytus' opening prayer; for a more balanced assessment, see Herrmann (1924) 441; Tschiedel (1969) 56; Heldmann (1974) 85.

[9] On the tension between theology and psychology in the Euripidean Theseus' curses, see Segal, "Curse and Oath in Euripides' *Hippolytus*," *Ramus* 1 (1972) 165-80, especially 173ff.

[10] Lucretius 1.69ff.; Parmenides 28 B1 Diels-Kranz.

per alta vade spatia sublimi aethere;
testare nullos esse, qua veheris, deos.

Pass through the high reaches in the lofty air;
Bear witness that where you drive there are no gods.[11]

In a not entirely unrelated mood, the chorus of the *Phaedra* puzzles over the moral disorder in human affairs as it contemplates Nature's regularity in the remote heavens (964f.):

cur tanta tibi cura perennes
agitare vias aetheris alti?

Why so much care
To keep eternal motion
In the sky's steep paths?

[11] *Medea* 1026f. On the possible interpretations of this passage, see Eliot (1927, 1961), p. 59 with note 3; Dingel (1974) 190; Liebermann (1974), p. 195 with note 145; C.D.N. Costa, *Medea* (Oxford 1973) ad loc. Liebermann cites the translation by J. Studley (1566): "Go through the ample spaces wyde, / infecte the poysoned ayre, / Beare witnesse grace of God is none / in place of thy repayre."

Selected Bibliography

Adams, J. N. (1982). *The Latin Sexual Vocabulary*, Baltimore.

Barrett, W. S., ed. (1964). *Euripides, Hippolytos*, Oxford.

Barthes, Roland (1979). "From Work to Text" (1971), in Josué V. Harari, ed., *Textual Strategies: Perspectives in Post-Structuralist Criticism*, Ithaca, N. Y.: 73-81.

Boyle, A. J., ed. (1983). *Seneca Tragicus. Ramus Essays on Senecan Drama*, Berwick, Australia.

——— (1985). "In Nature's Bonds: A Study of Seneca's 'Phaedra,' " in *Aufstieg und Niedergang der römischen Welt*, 2.32.2:1284-1347.

Braden, Gordon (1970). "The Rhetoric and Psychology of Power in the Dramas of Seneca," *Arion* 9: 5-41.

Brooks, Peter (1977). "Freud's Masterplot: Questions of Narrative," in Felman: 280-300.

Brower, Reuben A. (1971). *Hero and Saint: Shakespeare and the Graeco-Roman Heroic Tradition*, Oxford.

Calder, William M., III (1976/77). "Seneca, Tragedian of Imperial Rome," *Classical Journal* 72: 1-11.

Campos, José António Segurado (1972). "O Simbolismo do fogo nas tragèdias de Sèneca," *Euphrosyne* NS 5: 185-247.

Cattin, A. (1963). "La géographie dans les tragédies de Sénèque," *Latomus* 22: 685-703.

Coffey, Michael (1957). "Seneca: Tragedies 1922-1955," *Lustrum* 2: 113-186.

Croisille, J. M. (1964). "Lieux communs, *sententiae* et intentions philosophiques dans la *Phèdre* de Sénèque," *Revue d'Etudes Latines* 42: 276-301.

Curran, L. (1972). "Transformation and Anti-Augustanism in Ovid's *Metamorphoses,*" *Arethusa* 5: 71-91.

Davis, Peter J. (1983). "Vindicat Omnes Natura Sibi: A Reading of Seneca's Phaedra," in Boyle (1983): 114-27.

——— (1984). "The First Chorus of Seneca's *Phaedra*," *Latomus* 43: 396-401.

Dingel, Joachim (1970). "*Hippolytos Xiphoulkos*. Zu Senecas Phaedra und dem ersten Hippolytus des Euripides," *Hermes* 98: 44-56.

——— (1974). *Seneca und die Dichtung*, Heidelberg.

Durand, Gilbert (1976). *Les structures anthropologiques de l'imaginaire*, Paris.

Eliot, T. S. (1961). "Seneca in Elizabethan Translation" (1927) and

"Shakespeare and the Stoicism of Seneca" (1927), in *Selected Essays*, 2nd ed., London: 65-105 and 126-40.

Enk, P. J. (1957). "Roman Tragedy," *Neophilologus* 41: 282-307.

Fantham, Elaine (1975). "Virgil's Dido and Seneca's Tragic Heroines," *Greece and Rome*, 2nd series, vol. 22: 1-10.

————— (1982). *Seneca's Troades: A Literary Introduction*, Princeton.

Fauth, W. (1958). "Hippolytos und Phaidra: Bemerkungen zum religiösen Hintergrund eines tragischen Konflikts I," *Abhandlungen der Akademie der Wissenschaften und der Litteratur*, Geistes- und sozialwiss. Klasse, Mainz. Heft 9: 517-588.

Felman, Shoshana (1977). "Turning the Screw of Interpretation," in *Literature and Psychoanalysis: The Question of Reading: Otherwise*, ed. S. Felman, *Yale French Studies*, 55/56: 94-207.

Ferrucci, Franco (1980). *The Poetics of Disguise: The Autobiography of the Work in Homer, Dante and Shakespeare*, trans. Ann Dunnigan, Ithaca, N.Y.

Flygt, Steng (1933-34). "Treatment of Character in Euripides and Seneca: The Hippolytus," *Classical Journal* 29: 507-16.

Friedrich, Wolf H. (1933). *Untersuchungen zu Senecas dramatischer Technik*, Diss. Freiburg, Borna-Leipzig.

————— (1953). *Euripides und Diphilos, Zetemata* 5, Munich: 110-49.

Fortey, Stuart and John Glucker (1975). "Actus Tragicus: Seneca on the Stage," *Latomus* 34: 699-715.

Frischer, Bernard (1970). "*Concordia Discors* and Characterization in Euripides' *Hippolytos*," *Greek, Roman and Byzantine Studies* 11: 85-100.

Gallardo, M. D. (1973). "Análisis mitográfico y estético de la *Fedra* de Séneca," *Cuadernos de Filología Clásica* 5: 63-105.

Gallop, Jane (1982). *The Daughter's Seduction: Feminism and Psychoanalysis*, Ithaca, N.Y.

Garton, Charles (1972). *Personal Aspects of the Roman Theatre*, Toronto.

Gatz, Bodo (1967). *Weltalter, goldene Zeit und sinnverwandte Vorstellungen, Spudasmata* 17, Hildesheim.

Giardina, Ioannes Carolus (1966). *L. Annaei Senecae Tragoediae*, 2 volumes, Bologna.

Giomini, Remo (1955). *Saggio sulla "Fedra" di Seneca*, Rome.

Glenn, Justin (1975-76). "The Phantasies of Phaedra: A Psychoanalytic Reading," *Classical World* 69: 435-42.

Green, André (1977). "Thésée et Oedipe: Une interprétation psychoanalytique de la Théséide," in B. Gentili and G. Paioni, eds., *Il mito greco*, Rome: 137-89.

Grimal, Pierre (1963). "L'originalité de Sénèque dans la tragédie de *Phèdre*," *Revue d'Etudes Latines* 41: 297-312.

———, ed. (1965). *L. Annaei Senecae "Phaedra," Paris.*

Hadot, Ilsetraut (1969). *Seneca und die griechische-römische Tradition der Seelenleitung*, Berlin.

Heldmann, Konrad (1968). "Senecas Phaedra und ihre griechischen Vorbilder," *Hermes* 96: 88-117.

——— (1974). *Untersuchungen zu den Tragödien Senecas, Hermes Einzelschriften* 31, Weisbaden.

Henry, D., and Walker, B. (1965). "The Futility of Action: A Study of Seneca's 'Hercules Furens,' " *Classical Philology* 60: 11-22.

——— (1966). "Phantasmagoria and Idyll: An Element of Seneca's *Phaedra*," *Greece and Rome*, 2nd series, vol. 13: 223-39.

Henry, Elizabeth (1982). "Seneca the Younger," *Scribner's Ancient Writers: Greece and Rome*, ed. T. J. Luce, New York: 2.807-832.

Herington, C. J. (1966). "Senecan Tragedy," *Arion* 5: 422-71.

——— (1982). "The Younger Seneca," *Cambridge History of Classical Literature*, vol. 2, eds. E. J. Kenney and W. V. Clausen, Cambridge: 511-32.

Herrmann, Léon (1924). *Théâtre de Sénèque*, Paris.

———, ed. (1925). *Sénèque, Tragédies,* Société d' Edition "Les Belles Lettres," vol. 1, Paris.

Herter, Hans (1971). "Phaidra in griechischer und römischer Gestalt," *Rheinisches Museum für Philologie* 114: 14-77.

Holland, Norman (1975, 1980). "Unity Identity Text Self," in Tompkins (1980): 118-33. Reprinted from *PMLA* 90: 813-22.

Jacobson, Howard (1974). *Ovid's Heroides*, Princeton.

Jameson, Frederic (1977). "Imaginary and Symbolic in Lacan: Marxism, Psychoanalytic Criticism and the Problem of the Subject," in Felman: 338-395.

Knox, B.M.W. (1952). "*The Hippolytus* of Euripides," *Yale Classical Studies* 13: 3-31; Reprinted in Knox (1979): 205-30.

——— (1968). "Silent Reading in Antiquity," *Greek, Roman and Byzantine Studies* 9: 421-435.

——— (1979). *Word and Action: Essays on the Ancient Theatre*, Baltimore and London.

Lacan, Jacques (1977). "Desire and the Interpretation of Desire in *Hamlet*," in Felman: 11-52.

——— (1977). *Ecrits: A Selection*, trans. A. Sheridan, New York and London.

——— (1968). *The Function of Language in Psychoanalysis*, trans. with notes and commentary by A. Wilden, Baltimore and London.

Lattimore, Richmond (1962). "Phaedra and Hippolytus," *Arion*, vol. 1, no. 3: 5-18.

Lawall, G. (1979). "Seneca's *Medea*: The Elusive Triumph of Civilization," in *Arktouros: Hellenic Studies presented to B.M.W. Knox*, ed. G. Bowersock, W. Burkert, M.C.J. Putnam, Berlin and New York: 419-26.

Lawall, Gilbert and Sarah, and Gerda Kunkel, eds. (1982). *The Phaedra of Seneca*, 2nd ed., Chicago.

Leach, Eleanor Winsor (1975). "Roman Pastoral and the World of Power," *Ramus* 4: 204-30.

Leeman, A. D. (1976). "Seneca's *Phaedra* as a Stoic Tragedy," *Miscellanea Tragica in honorem J. C. Kamerbeek*, Amsterdam: 199-212.

Lefèvre, Eckard (1972). "*Quid ratio possit*: Senecas *Phaedra* als stoisches Drama," in E. Lefèvre, ed., *Senecas Tragödien, Wege der Forschung* 310, Darmstadt: 343-75. Reprinted from *Wiener Studien* NF 3 (1969): 131-60.

Leo, Friedrich, ed. (1878). *L. Annaei Senecae Tragoediae*, 2 volumes, Berlin.

Lewis, Bradford (1974). "The Rape of Troy: Infantile Perspective in Book II of *The Aeneid*," *Arethusa* 7: 103-13.

Liebermann, Wolf-Lüder (1974). *Studien zu Senecas Tragödien, Beiträge zur Klassische Philologie* 39, Meisenheim/Glan.

MacCary, W. Thomas (1982). *Childlike Achilles: Ontogeny and Phylogeny in the Iliad*, New York.

Marti, Berthe (1945). "Seneca's Tragedies: A New Interpretation," *Transactions of the American Philological Association* 76: 216-45.

Mastronarde, Donald J. (1970). "Seneca's *Oedipus*: The Drama in the Word," *Transactions of the American Philological Association* 101: 291-315.

Méridier, Louis (n.d.; ca. 1931). *Hippolyte d'Euripide: Etude et analyse*, Paris.

Mette, H. J. (1964). "Die römische Tragödie und die Neufunde zur griechischen Tragödie für die Jahre 1945-64," *Lustrum* 9: 5-211.

Miller, F. J., ed. and trans. (1917). *Seneca's Tragedies*, Loeb Classical Library, 2 volumes, London and Cambridge, Mass.

Motto, Anna L., and J. R. Clark (1982). "Art and Ethics in the Drama: Seneca's 'Pseudotragedy' Reconsidered," *Illinois Classical Studies* 7: 125-40.

Mueller, Martin (1980). *Children of Oedipus and Other Essays on the Imitation of Greek Tragedy 1550-1800*, Toronto.

Mugellesi, Rossana (1973). "Il senso della natura in Seneca tragico,"

Argentea Aetas: In memoriam E. V. Marmorale. Pubbl. dell' Istituto di Filologia Classica di Genova 37: 29-66.

Neumann, Erich (1954). *The Origins and History of Consciousness,* trans. R.F.C. Hull, Princeton.

Newbold, R. F. (1979). "Boundaries and Bodies in Late Antiquity," *Arethusa* 12: 93-114.

Opelt, Ilona (1972). "Senecas Konzeption des Tragischen," in Lefèvre (1972): 92-128.

Orlando, Francesco (1973). *Per una teoria freudiana della letteratura,* Torino.

——— (1978). *Toward a Freudian Theory of Literature, with an Analysis of Racine's Phèdre,* trans. Charmaine Lee, Baltimore.

Owen, William H. (1968). "Commonplace and Dramatic Symbol in Seneca's Tragedies," *Transactions of the American Philological Association* 99: 291-313.

Paratore, Ettore (1952). "Sulla 'Phaedra' di Seneca," *Dioniso* 15: 199-234.

——— (1957). "Originalità del teatro di Seneca," *Dioniso* 20: 53-74.

Petrone, Gianna (1984). *La scrittura tragica dell' irrazionale. Note di lettura al teatro di Seneca,* Palermo.

Pratt, Norman T. (1948). "The Stoic Base of Senecan Drama," *Transactions of the American Philological Association* 79: 1-11.

——— (1963). "Major Systems of Figurative Language in Senecan Melodrama," *Transactions of the American Philological Association* 94: 199-234.

——— (1983). *Seneca's Drama,* Chapel Hill, N.C.

Primmer, Adolf (1976). "Die Vergleiche in Senecas Dramen," *Grazer Beiträge* 5: 211-32.

Rankin, Anne V. (1974). "Euripides' Hippolytus: A Psychopathological Hero," *Arethusa* 7: 71-94.

Reckford, K. J. (1972). "Phaethon, Hippolytus and Aphrodite," *Transactions of the American Philological Association* 103: 405-32.

Regenbogen, Otto (1930). "Schmerz und Tod in den Tragödien Senecas," *Vorträge der Bibliothek Warburg, Vorträge 1927-1928,* ed. Fritz Saxl, Leipzig and Berlin: 167-218.

Rozelaar, Marc (1976). *Seneca, Eine Gesamtdarstellung* Amsterdam.

Ruch, M. (1964). "La langue de la psychologie amoureuse dans 'la Phèdre' de Sénèque," *Les Etudes Classiques* 32: 356-63.

Runchina, Giovanni (1966). "Sulla *Phaedra* di Seneca," *Rivista di Cultura Classica e Medioevale* 8: 12-37.

Segal, Charles [P.] (1965). "The Tragedy of the *Hippolytus*: The

Waters of Ocean and the Untouched Meadow," *Harvard Studies in Classical Philology* 70: 117-69.

—— (1969). *Landscape in Ovid's Metamorphoses, Hermes Einzelschriften*, 23, Wiesbaden.

—— (1970). "Shame and Purity in Euripides' Hippolytus," *Hermes* 98: 278-99.

—— (1978/9). "Pentheus and Hippolytus on the Couch and on the Grid: Psychoanalytic and Structuralist Readings of Greek Tragedy," *Classical World* 72: 129-48.

—— (1979). "Solar Imagery and Tragic Heroism in Euripides' Hippolytus," in *Arktouros: Hellenic Studies Presented to B.M.W. Knox*, ed. G. Bowersock, W. Burkert, M.C.J. Putnam, Berlin and New York: 151-61.

—— (1979a). "The Myth of Bacchylides 17: Heroic Quest and Heroic Identity," *Eranos* 77: 23-37.

—— (1981). *Tragedy and Civilization: An Interpretation of Sophocles*, Martin Classical Lectures 26, Cambridge, Mass.

—— (1982). *Dionysiac Poetics and Euripides' Bacchae*, Princeton.

—— (1982a). "Tragédie, oralité, écriture," *Poétique* 50: 131-54.

—— (1982b). "*Nomen Sacrum*: Medea and Other Names in Senecan Tragedy," *Maia* 34: 241-46.

—— (1983a). "Boundary Violation and the Landscape of the Self in Senecan Tragedy," *Antike und Abendland* 29: 172-87.

—— (1983b). "Dissonant Sympathy: Song, Orpheus and the Golden Age in Seneca's Tragedies," in Boyle (1983): 229-51.

—— (1983c). "*Mythos* and *Logos*: Language, Reality and Appearance in Greek Tragedy and Plato," in *Tragique et tragédie dans la tradition occidentale*, ed. T. J. Reiss and Pierre Gravel, Montreal: 25-41.

—— (1984). "Senecan Baroque: The Death of Hippolytus in Seneca, Ovid, and Euripides," *Transactions of the American Philological Association* 114: 311-26.

—— (198–). "Image and Action in Seneca's *Phaedra*: Five Motifs," forthcoming.

Seidensticker, Bernd (1969). *Die Gesprächsverdichtung in den Tragödien Senecas*, Heidelberg.

Shelton, Jo-Ann (1978). *Seneca's Hercules Furens: Theme, Structure and Style, Hypomnemata* 50, Göttingen.

Sibony, Daniel (1977). "*Hamlet*: A Writing-Effect," in Felman: 53-93.

Skovgaard-Hansen, M. (1972). "The Fall of Phaethon: Meaning in Seneca's 'Hippolytus,' " *Classica et Mediaevalia* 29: 92-123.

Smoot, Jeanne J. (1976). "Hippolytus as Narcissus: An Amplification," *Arethusa* 9: 37-51.

Snell, Bruno (1964). *Scenes from Greek Drama*, Sather Classical Lectures 34, Berkeley and Los Angeles.

Solimano, Giannina (1980). "Il mito di Orfeo-Ippolito in Seneca," *Sandalion* 3: 151-74.

Stähli-Peter, Monika Maria (1974). *Die Arie des Hippolytus. Kommentar zu Eingangsmonodie in der Phaedra des Seneca.* Diss. Zurich.

Starobinski, Jean (1970). *L'oeil vivant II. La relation critique*, Paris.

Tarrant, R. J. (1972). "Senecan Drama and its Antecedents," *Harvard Studies in Classical Philology* 82: 213-63.

Tompkins, Jane P., ed. (1980). *Reader-Response Criticism*, Baltimore and London.

Traina, Alfonso (1979). "Due note a Seneca tragico," *Maia* 31: 273-76.

Tschiedel, Hans-Jürgen (1969). *Phaedra und Hippolytus: Variation eines tragischen Konfliktes*, Diss. Erlangen-Nürnberg: Warnsdorf/Sudetenland.

Turkle, Sherry (1978). *Psychoanalytic Politics* New York.

Vretska, Helmut (1968). "Zwei Interpretationsprobleme in Senecas Phaedra," *Wiener Studien* 81: 153-70.

Williams, Gordon (1978). *Change and Decline: Roman Literature in the Early Empire*, Sather Classical Lectures 45, Berkeley and Los Angeles.

Zintzen, Clemens (1960). *Analytisches Hypomnema zu Senecas Phaedra, Beiträge zur Klassische Philologie* 1, Meisenheim/Glan.

Zwierlein, Otto (1966). *Die Rezitationsdramen Senecas, Beiträge zur Klassische Philologie* 20, Meisenheim/Glan.

Index

Actaeon, 106
Admetus, 66
Adonis, 106
Aegeus, 130f., 170f., 211. *See also*
Euripides, hilt, Ovid, sword
Aeneas, 180, 204. *See also* Virgil
Aeschylus, *Oresteia*, 3
Aethra, 130
Aetna, 36
Ajax, 78
Allecto, in *Aeneid*, 180
Amazon, 15, 64f., 94-96, 104, 116,
121-25, 131, 152, 195. *See also*
Antiope, mother-figure, purity
Amor, 42, 57, 66, 118-21, 135
Antiope, 123-25, 135, 201. *See also*
Amazon, mother-figure
anxiety of influence, in Seneca, 208ff.
Aphrodite, 63, 71. *See also* Venus
Apollo, 66, 109, 224
Apollodorus, Pseudo-, 165
Ara Pacis, 62
Argo, 88
Ariadne, 39, 51, 80, 112, 120, 152,
159f. *See also* labyrinth, Minos,
Minotaur
Aristophanes, *Lysistrata*, 165
Artemis, 71. *See also* Diana
Assyria, 34
Athena, 130; in Homer's *Odyssey*,
180
Athens, 79f. *See also* city

Bacchus, 55, 109. *See also* Dionysus;
Euripides, *Bacchae*
Bacchylides, 106
baroque style, of Seneca, 152
Barthes, R., 16, 150, 219
beatitude, figure of, 108
Bellerophon, 106
Blake, W., 127
Bloom, H., 27
Boyle, A., 13
Brooks, P., 37
Brower, R., 11

bull, 74f., 111, 113f., 177, 183. *See
also* heredity, labyrinth, Minotaur,
monstrosity, Pasiphae
burial, of Hippolytus, 193f., 199f.,
215f., 218f.
Burke, K., 212

Caligula, 224
Calypso, 180
Castor, 109
castration, of Hippolytus, 124,
127f., 177, 204
catabasis, 187
Catullus, 77, 78, 105
Ceres, 101
character, in drama, 20ff., 115f.; in
Seneca, 14-17. *See also* Hippolytus,
Phaedra, tragedy
chastity. See *pudor*
childhood, 95, 106, 125f.; and
Golden Age, 77-80, 83-97
city, 176; and language, 155f. *See
also* Athens
coincidentia oppositorum, 74f., 99
corporeality, 29-39
Crete, 34, 39, 42, 51, 81. *See also* labyrinth, Minos, Minotaur, Pasi-
phae, sea
Cyparissus, 106

Daedalus, 6, 35, 114. *See also* labyrinth, Minotaur
Deianeira, 78
deinon, to, 6
Derrida, J., 16
Descartes, R., 221
desire, 150-56, 211, 213f.; imagery
of, 29-56; and language, 220. *See
also* fire, Phaedra, torch, sky
Diana, 15, 61f., 64, 66, 70-72, 85,
116, 131f., 136, 152, 224. *See also*
hunt
Dido, 31, 34. *See also* Virgil
Dingel, J., 11
Dionysus, 20, 150. *See also* Bacchus;

LIBRARY OF CONGRESS CATALOGING-IN-PUBLICATION DATA

Segal, Charles, 1936-
Language and desire in Seneca's Phaedra.

Bibliography: p.
Includes index.
1. Seneca, Lucius Annaeus, ca. 4 B.C.-65 A.D. Phaedra. 2. Phaedra (Greek
mythology) in literature. 3. Psychoanalysis and literature. I. Title.

PA6664.P53S44 1986   872'.01   85-43311
ISBN 0-691-05472-X (alk. paper)